FOR BETTER OR FOR WORSE

A MEMOIR OF SOUTH AFRICA - DURING AND
AFTER APARTHEID

BERNHARD R. TEICHER

BIOCOMM

It always seems impossible, until it is done.

— NELSON MANDELA

CONTENTS

EDITOR'S NOTE

The Germanic linguistic subject-object-verb (SOV) typology of the Author has deliberately been retained, to authentically reflect the "voice" of the Author.

AUTHORS NOTE

In this book about South Africa, you will notice that I have used the terms 'European' and 'White' interchangeably.

Similarly, the terms 'Non-European' and 'Non-White' have been utilized to describe the two categories of human beings, as recognized by the Apartheid regime.

PROLOGUE

For most of my life I have been a stamp collector. When all my material had finally been disposed of, I started compiling *Timeline of Geophysical/Paleontological Parallel Developments*, which was finally published in 2016.

After that, a collection of rocks and minerals was started. But after a few years this also came to an end, because we were now living in a retirement village, and there was just not enough space to extend the collections any further and, therefore, interest waned. A compilation titled *Rock Identification* rounded up this endeavor, and will be published in 2018.

What now? Sitting idly around was simply not an option for me. Talking to an old friend about my dilemma of how to spend my time, he suggested that I write something, just to keep busy, as he himself had done quite successfully. I laughingly dismissed the idea, because I knew I could never write the novel of the century, not even a halfway decent story. All I had ever written were reports. Accordingly, that is what this story ended as, when I eventually followed his advice.

I soon understood that an entire post-war generation - and in particular my family - might be interested in what went on and what went wrong in Nazi Germany, since they had no personal experience of these dramatic and traumatic years.

Events following this period give an insight into the troubled world of post-war Germany and Apartheid South Africa, and once I had started with this, memories and impressions simply continued to pour out.

I

In March 2015, I started to jot down reminiscences and ideas as they popped up in my mind. Soon I realized that this would be a *curriculum vitae* or, even more likely, resemble a report like those I used to write as a management consultant in the dim past. After I had painfully filled six pages, I thought: that's it, there is nothing else to report.

It was amazing for me to experience how much I remembered from these long-past years. But it was equally amazing to realize, in how many instances my memory failed me.

An interesting observation I made, in the process of clicking on the computer keyboard, was the fact that the more I wrung out of what went for my brains, the more reminiscences and forgotten snippets of information popped up in my mind. This will probably mean, that this opus never gets completed. Unfortunately, I am of a competitive nature, so I will pressure myself to finish the job as quickly as possible. Which counteracts the reason for doing this, namely to have something to do!

I have tried to record, to the best of my knowledge and of what I remember, what has happened. But I also have recorded, as honestly as possible, my emotions and my thoughts at the relevant times. This has had several unintended consequences. Memories have floated up, obviously from my sub-conscious, which I had thought were lost or suppressed a long time ago.

In addition, I had to face some questions which I had never asked myself before. It was a cathartic process in many ways. I had to abandon, at least to a large extent, my ingrained refusal of showing emotion, to record a true and complete picture.

In the unlikely event that you find any mistakes or inconsistencies in these pages, I must plead utter innocence, as usual, since any such accidents are clearly the proof-reader's fault, in the person of my wife.

She has helped me very much by her proof-reading efforts to avoid the most stupid typing mistakes. It is quite unbelievable, what silly mistakes I made in the excitement of digging up one more morsel of memory. She spotted most of these (each incident did cost me dearly!), but despite her heroic efforts, the odd mistake may have escaped her eagle eye. In which case it is, of course, my fault.

———

FOREWORD

This is the sequel to my first book, '**For All it was Worth**', which covered my time in Germany: the Nazi period and my military service during World War II, my time as a Prisoner of War as well as the aftermath of these periods from 1947 until 1965, when we emigrated to South Africa.

A short explanation of what had happened before we emigrated:

Both my wife and I were born in Eastern Germany in what after the last war became the Russian Zone and later the GDR, the German Democratic Republic. We both had, at different times, left the communist state and moved to Frankfurt/Main in what later became the German Federal Republic of West Germany.

I had been working as a management consultant for the US Army in Europe, but we both felt the urge to leave behind the somewhat restrictive German society and its miserable weather and to emigrate to a distant, sunny country.

PART I

SOUTH AFRICA

A NEW BEGINNING (1965 TO 2014)

1

ARRIVAL IN JOHANNESBURG

These were our first impressions after we had landed on 29 October 1965 at Jan Smuts airport in Johannesburg:

- a modern airport, not unlike any medium-sized one in Europe,
- the vast majority of people visible were Europeans, with a few African and Asiatic workers moving luggage and the like.
- all customs and police personnel were Whites, as were most of the other passengers in sight.
- the temperature was in the high twenties (Celsius), in stark contrast to the freezing weather we had just escaped from in Germany.

It took a while to sink in that we were now in the southern hemisphere. We knew that we had to expect many changes in relation to Germany, but South Africa had already in 1961 (in expectation of our arrival?) decimalized their currency and measurements. At least we were spared this otherwise traumatic change.

After leaving the airport we found a taxi to take us to the hotel which my employer had arranged for us. There we met the first of many culture shocks. Three African ladies were walking in front of us, and our eyes were in danger of popping out of their sockets, when we contemplated their ample back-sides. Thus, the first photo on African soil was taken. We had never before seen a sight like this.

Sure, there are plenty of obese people in Europe, too but these African ladies were in a league of their own! They must have been something special, because during our following fifty years in South Africa we never saw such an impressive assembly again, but later we definitely encountered plenty of similar individual sights.

Our transit hotel was situated in Hillbrow, an inner-city quarter of Johannesburg. As the name implies, it rises on a hill crest above the city center. The hotel was a bit basic, just a typical transit place. When we opened the cold water tap to get some cool water to mix a fruit juice, the water temperature was between warm and hot. We soon found out the reason: In South Africa in most places the main water pipes run on the outside walls of the buildings, and this fact, combined with the sub-tropical sunshine, explains this solar-heating effect.

About two weeks after our arrival my colleague from the US Army unit in Frankfurt which I had just left had also arrived here with his wife. His documentation had hit a snag somewhere. It was nice to have some company, after arriving 'cold' in a foreign country and continent. Unfortunately, his marriage was not as it should have been, so we did not have much social contact with them.

He had previously been working for the US Air Force at the Adana Air Force base in Turkey, before he had joined our Frankfurt US Army unit. His wife had stayed behind in Germany during his absence, a recipe for threatening disaster, as I would find out soon myself.

We went early on to an estate agent to find permanent accommodation for our family. No scarcity of housing here, like we had experienced it in Frankfurt. The whole city was full of tower apartment blocks. We found what we needed almost immediately, on the top floor of one of those high-rises, and started to unpack our container, which had just arrived. If I remember correctly, nothing, or at least nothing important, was broken. Quite remarkable, considering the distance covered by the poor container. If I could only have done the same with our car! With the benefit of hindsight, it became clear that we should have shipped our Karman Ghia as well.

On this day we experienced a typical Johannesburg introduction: an earth tremor or an earthquake. One could never be sure here, whether one of the underground tunnels of one of the gold mines had collapsed, or whether we had actually experienced a light earthquake. Our just-arrived cutlery and crockery had its first wake-up call in our 12th floor apartment, but without casualties.

By now we had got used to a typical weather phenomenon of

this city: every day at about 5 o'clock in the afternoon, a gutsy thundershower for ten minutes or so would soak everybody in the open, and thereafter the sun would shine again for another hour from a blue sky, as if nothing had happened, before dusk would settle-in quickly.

We had to get used to the fact that we were now much closer to the equator, with the result that throughout the year, day and night were almost of even length here, and the difference in the number of daylight hours between summer and winter, which were so drastic in Germany, appeared very muted here.

Shopping for provisions was a bit more adventurous as it had been in Germany. When my wife wanted to buy at the local supermarket some flour to bake a cake, she was probably thinking of the German word *Mehl*. When she saw a packet of *'Meal'* she grabbed it, only to discover at home that this was the Afrikaans word for maize flour. Not serious, there were always uses for this one, too. The close relationship between German and Afrikaans, the language of the ancestors of Dutch, French and most German immigrants in this country, sometimes became a bit problematic.

Then I went to town and bought at the Central News Agency some British English-language books to study accounting and economics. Because up to now I had used German and US English almost exclusively for these purposes. The differences between the two English languages were not too serious, but the British bookkeeping and their accountancy systems were very different from the German ones.

In those days, this city quarter was almost exclusively home to Europeans; most of them recent immigrants. As a matter of fact, the whole of this suburb was one large immigration transit camp. Most of the continuous arrivals dispersed soon enough into this vast country, but even more newcomers constantly ensured a high-density living style there. It was quite safe to walk around at night, to have a late dinner in one of the numerous diversified ethnic restaurants, or to browse late at night in a large polyglot bookstore. All the shops and restaurants were then managed by Whites, and the serving staff were mostly Indians.

You could hear in those days many European languages spoken in this place, but surprisingly little Afrikaans, the Dutch dialect spoken by the Afrikaners. They were the dominant group of Whites in the country, who ruled the State and much of the economy. The relatively small number of Africans living in this area managed to speak enough

English to survive in this strange European island on a Black continent.

Shortly after our arrival, when I had some spare time, I wrote to our US Army colonel in Frankfurt about the safe arrival of both of his former team members, and some weeks later I received a very nice reply, updating me on happenings in our unit in the now very distant Germany.

Unfortunately, some subsequent rather hectic developments caused me to lose contact with him. Apart from my wife's family, we did not keep up any contacts in Germany. The distances were just too large, and the mail took two weeks as airmail, and four weeks as surface mail. Mind you, airmail to South Africa requires now four to six weeks! If we would have had e-mail already, things might have developed differently.

2

A GYPSY LIFE WITH INEFEN

Now it was time to start working in my new job at INEFEN, the management consultancy company. We had modern offices in a commercial high-rise block near the center of the city. Three sections, apart from the administration and finance set-up, made up the consultancy operation: sales, analysis and implementation or installation.

Businesses in South Africa were generally somewhat behind modern developments in Europe and the US, even though all the managers and most of the office personnel were Europeans. This applied particularly to the family-owned-and-operated medium-sized operations. But these firms usually were quite profitable, so it was not too difficult to get a sales and analysis contract signed.

The salespeople (they hated to be called that, they preferred 'Business Advisors') had to convince the owners or managers of the enterprises that they needed management consultancy services:

- to spruce up performance,
- to introduce new systems or, quite often,
- to solve a personnel problem, which the people in charge were unwilling or unable to tackle themselves.

One or more analysts then started their work. They had to determine what the problems were, what actions were needed to correct them, and how many man hours would be required for the installation team to solve all the problems the analysis had unearthed. Translating this sales talk into English, the analyst had to tell the prospective clients how long this would take and what all this would cost them. At this stage a few sales fell through, but in most cases the analysts were competent enough to convince the clients to sign on the dotted line of the follow-up contract for the implementation phase.

Now our management had to select either the correct team of people from the installation section to tackle the various identified problems; or occasionally, to select a 'solo-flyer'. This was my section, where I was working.

This company had some peculiarities I was not used to. They did not pay monthly by check or bank transfer, as was the custom in Germany, but they paid weekly in cash, like it was usual in England and the States. My weekly wage was 110 Rand. The Rand was then worth DM5,60. This wage translated therefore to about DM2 650 per month, almost double my last salary in Frankfurt.

But my *sang-froid* was badly shaken, when in the first week I was given an old £5 note, instead of the expected R10 note. Nobody had explained to us that the old Sterling notes were still valid tender, in the relation of £1 equals R2, even though the currency had already been decimalized back in 1961.

INEFEN, or Industrial Efficiency Engineering, maintained offices not only in Johannesburg, but also in the city centers of Cape Town and Durban. Each of these three branches had a full complement of the three functions explained above. Each of the branches had installed telex machines in their offices, which seemed to rattle along all day. These offices were needed there, because the company worked all over the large country.

We even operated in the neighboring British colonies and protectorates within Southern Africa:

- Southern Rhodesia (now Zimbabwe)
- Northern Rhodesia (now Zambia)
- Nyasaland (now Malawi)
- Bechuanaland (now Botswana)
- Basutoland (now Lesotho)
- Swaziland (then still named so, now Eswatini)
- South West Africa (now Namibia)

The last one was the South African *de-facto* protectorate over the former German colony of German-Southwest-Africa, even though the United Nations had rescinded this mandate some years earlier. Over the following decades all these territories were in the process of obtaining their independence, usually painless, but sometimes with violent birth complications.

Shortly after our arrival in South Africa, one of these colonies, Southern Rhodesia, announced her UDI, the Unilateral Declaration of Independence from Great Britain. This created a political fallout for South Africa, when the newly created State of Rhodesia needed assistance from South Africa to survive. Very soon South African troops were helping to fight the 'terrorists', or the 'freedom fighters', depending on where one was standing.

Because of the British naval blockade to prevent any fuel supplies reaching Rhodesia, the supply from South Africa was also vital for the survival of this country. My guess would be that some people made a lot of money out of this dilemma! But we were not in Italy, and I had nothing to do with this! (*vide* my first book "For All it Was Worth" at Amazon for details, how something like that is done properly).

My literary and internet agent, also known as our son, will probably scold me over my repeated self-advertising of my books, as being contrary to established norms and conventions of the book-publishing world. I have always more or less done as I wanted, as long as I did not harm others in so doing. And I am too old to change now. Anyway, to hell with awkward conventions!

I had forgotten to record that we had already bought a red secondhand Volkswagen Beetle for 550 Rand. In order to safeguard our meagre cash reserves, we were looking for a way to avoid having to pay cash for this purchase, or for a deposit. The dealer organized the purchase in the same way this was done here when a Black wanted to buy a secondhand car but did not have the legally required deposit of twenty-five percent: the purchase price was increased by fifty percent, and the dealer gave a receipt for twenty-five percent of the 'adjusted' (inflated) price. The extra cost was worth for us the saved cash. After just a few months our car was paid in full.

In the real world this fictitious transaction looked like this: if the list price was 500 Rand, the inflated one became 750 Rand. The legally required deposit on this was twenty-five percent, equal to 187,50 Rand. The African now had to repay 750 Rand, minus the fictitious deposit of 187,50 Rand, and the dealer had an extra 62,50 Rand tax-free in his back pocket.

My first work assignment saw all three of us drive to Kimberley, to help reorganize the largest car dealership in town. Here I met for the first time the Afrikaans language barrier. Only the owner spoke

English, so at least I could write my reports in this language. Otherwise I would have been stuck, with my lack of Afrikaans.

Another first for us was the Afrikaner 'braai' when we had been invited one evening to a party. This was similar to an American barbecue, but more rustic. The *Boerewors* was as delicious as the now unfortunately disappeared *Grobe Bratwurst* in Germany. *Mealy pap* was another novelty for us: a hot maize-flour porridge, indispensable at any Afrikaner *braai*. I seem vaguely to remember that there also was the odd alcoholic brew on offer. They had quite a decent assortment of beers.

This dealership made a surprisingly large percentage of their secondhand car sales to Africans on credit. This was surprising, because the wages for the unskilled and semi-skilled laborers were low; and practically all employed Africans at this time were such low paid workers. It appears that they must have managed to earn some money on the side!

With some astonishment I realized how this firm granted credit to the African secondhand car buyers: they demanded a deposit large enough to virtually rule out default. If the African did not have the deposit, then they followed exactly the same route as the car dealer who had sold us our VW. And both sides, they claimed, were happy. This shows that this trick was in general use in the country, and that the banks must have been aware of and condoned this practice.

Kimberley was of course the home of the famous 'Big Hole', dug towards the end of the nineteenth century by thousands of diamond diggers from all over the world. Cecil Rhodes made here his fortune. It is now a round deep and big water hole with vertical rock walls. The local diamond mining museum was another priceless experience for us.

Just as priceless was our experience on one early Saturday evening, when we were perambulating through town. The impressive sandstone buildings in a pseudo-classical style were still radiating the day's heat, when dozens of White ladies in evening dresses, with their partners in tails (tuxedos), were marching in a festive tempo in the direction of an imposing building: the local cinema palace.

This peculiar performance had become rather less astonishing after we realized that the country did not have television yet. This weekend spectacle could only be observed on a Saturday, because on Sundays the cinema, or as it usually was called here, the "bioscope", was of course closed.

The Minister of Posts had declared that this was the devil's way of subverting the minds of the god-fearing and morally upright Afrikaners. Maybe he also feared that TV could subvert the 'simple-minded Blacks' to reject Apartheid, which was claimed to be sooo beneficial to them. I do not remember when we eventually started to have TV in South Africa, probably in the 1970s.

The Afrikaners were not only obsessed with their racist attitudes, but also with their ultra-conservative views regarding public morals (the personal morals of many of them were much more relaxed!). A very strict publications and film censorship was in place, dominated by the dictates of the Afrikaans churches.

Sunday was a day when absolutely everything was boarded up and nailed down. No gambling was allowed, and pornography was unheard of (but see the following comments referring to the Homelands!). Hotly debated amongst the Afrikaners was the all-important question whether fishing or angling should be allowed or forbidden on this day.

Liquor was only allowed to be sold in Bottle Stores, which should be owned and operated by a hotel. One of the ideas behind this was the intention to control and minimize the sale of liquor, particularly to Coloreds and Africans. The other aspect was, to allow hotels the monopoly of selling liquor, and thereby to preserve their financial viability. In the case of many country inns this was probably a valid point, but very quickly some companies owned a chain of such stores, defeating this latter purpose.

When after World War 2 global attitudes towards racism began to subtly but progressively change, the cabinet minister Verwoerd came up with the 'ingenious' idea of hiding the racist attitude of the Afrikaners behind the semi-convincing slogan of "Separate but Equal Development".

This was a reasonable description in so far as all the various Non-European peoples were now equally discriminated against. But then as now, some were more equal than others. The Japanese, for instance, were made 'Honorable Whites', because Japan had invested millions of dollars in the huge Toyota car factory outside Durban.

In fairness it must be noted here that the Afrikaners were, however, also quite serious about the aspect of their obligations to look after the Africans. They really believed that they were doing the right thing in their God-given mission to uplift them.

It is interesting to remember that in the Great War thousands of African laborers were serving the Allies loyally and courageously in France, and hundreds of them lost their lives, including all or most passengers on a troop ship which sank in the Channel after a collision. These facts were rigorously suppressed, by the government. The school children did not hear about this facet of the war, because this would have sat poorly with the prevailing Apartheid fantasy.

My next assignment was to implement our analyst's re-commendations for the reorganization of a long-established firm of plumber's suppliers in Port Elizabeth. This job turned out to be a very mixed bag for myself. The long-retired, but still powerful and meddling owner, was a member of the English-speaking Whites and resented to have to deal with a 'bloody German'.

Apparently, he had only agreed to our involvement in the hope for a painless way to get rid of his manager. The fact that his also English-speaking manager got on with me splendidly, having fought as a soldier in Italy like me, did not help. After work we swopped many a tale and reminisced for hours. I found myself stuck in between these two chaps. My implementation report, quite correctly, supported the manager, and the owner asked our company to replace me, which our management categorically refused to do.

At this client I encountered another peculiarity of the colonial British Empire, the profession of the Quantity Surveyor or QS, which was new to me. This existed in all successor states of the Empire, but not in the USA (developed only after their independence). It emanated from the British Army's role in erecting barracks all over the Empire for the troops, but also buildings for district commissioners, schools, magistrate courts, hospitals, etc.

The army had to simplify this work, since they did not always have the necessary experts locally available. They standardized the designs and the lists of materials to be used for each type and size of building, by way of a 'Bill of Quantities'. This was created by the QS and administered by him during the building phase. In the end, he prepared the 'Final Account' for each building operation.

While on this job, the family stayed in a hutted holiday camp on the extremely wide beach. Our son had a whale of a time in this huge sand box and in the warm waters of the Indian Ocean. Who would have thought that we would ever see this? My wife was kept busy: washing, cooking and whatever a housewife does all day long, while I was at work.

She was vaguely aware of friends of her parents from her home-town of Rosslau in Germany, who had emigrated to this area after the last war. The families had been close friends, and the husbands often 'painted the town red', as the saying goes. She remembered the surname and eventually we found a telephone number and contacted them.

Towards the end of the war this friend had been the production manager at the Volkswagen factory in Kassel, with company car and chauffeur! He had now become the manager of Ferodo, one of the numerous automotive firms which were supplying brake assemblies and similar parts to Volkswagen, General Motors and Ford, all of them having their factories in this town.

The family had a 'smallholding', or small farm, just outside of Port Elizabeth. As a sideline they kept some pigs and a few cows to supplement their income. One of their calves became tame enough to follow our friend around the yard, just like a dog.

One day he took us in his 'bakkie', a Ford pick-up truck, to the drive-in cinema. Maybe you remember what I said in the first book "For All it was Worth" about my father's dentures, the two halves of which were connected by some kind of a hinge, similar to a pair of scissors or pliers. When one of the laborers there was looking for some pliers, he offered the man his dentures. The poor chap almost died laughing. Yes, our friend was not exactly of a melancholic disposition.

Their married son was of my own age group and was also employed in the same firm as his father. One evening we were all six playing cards, and I had a full glass of beer sitting next to my elbow. Numerous admonishes by his wife to be careful and not to knock it over were registered only sub-consciously. Something like that does not happen to me, surely. It is not necessary to dwell on the subject any further!

Further assignments followed (still with the Army?), mostly of short duration, at various places in the country. From now on my wife stayed at home with our son. But then I had to travel to Cape Town for a longish job, and my wife felt understandably unhappy about being left alone in Johannesburg, because she knew almost nobody in this foreign city, and she was still battling somewhat with her English.

The Cape Town job was simple enough, but it was very time-consuming. The surroundings of this city were exceptional. Table Mountain was a 'must see', of course, even when the gondola of the cable car was frighteningly swaying precariously in a strong and gusty wind.

Cape Point, where the waters of the Atlantic and Indian Oceans meet, was another unforgettable impression. At this point the Atlantic Ocean's northwards flowing cold Benguela Stream, straight from Antarctica and on its way up the west coast of Africa, over a short distance rubbed shoulders, so to speak, with the southwards moving warm Agulhas Stream of the Indian Ocean, coming from East Africa. Both, due to their different water temperatures, were visibly kept separated from each other, streaming for some distance side-by-side, but in opposite directions.

When we visited this place with friends many years later, this phenomenon could, to my huge disappointment, not be observed by us. Apparently, it only manifests itself under certain given conditions.

Amazing was also the huge difference in water temperatures between the Western and the Eastern beaches of the Cape peninsula, which was caused by these currents. Muizenberg in the 'False Bay' and Clifton beaches in the 'Good Hope Bay' were like different worlds.

Then in 1966 the next even longer-lasting implementation job came up for me; this time in the Durban area, about six hundred kilometers from our home. This time I insisted that the company footed the bill for my wife and son staying with me, which they accepted.

The Durban INEFEN office was located in one of the less than half a dozen high-rises in the center of the city. Today there exist probably about a hundred of these tall structures. Durban harbor was the largest and most important in Africa, serving the industrialized South African hinterland up to Johannesburg and Pretoria, as well as the inland mining districts.

We stayed for one or two nights next to the Durban City Hall at the Central Hotel, long gone by now, where we for the first time encountered an air conditioning unit. This one was mounted in the window of our hotel room; it was noisy and not very effective. Later we were accommodated by the company in a large block of holiday apartments next to the beach. This position was ideal, because my family could spend most of their time on the sandy beach. In the evenings we often went for a stroll along the beach promenade.

Still later, the family relocated to another block of holiday apartments, or holiday flats, as they are called here, this time in Umhlanga Rocks, fifteen kilometers north of Durban.

Then I set out for the 'short' round trip of rather more than one thousand kilometers to Johannesburg, to bring some of our movable belongings to Natal. While I was gone, my wife one night entered the kitchen of the apartment and was confronted by an army of cockroaches. With the help of a neighbor they were able to defeat this invasion with two spray cans of insecticides.

On my return trip I encountered for the first time the type of natural phenomenon one only finds in the tropics and subtropics. A thunderstorm lasting for almost five hundred kilometers, virtually all the way from Johannesburg to Durban, with frightening lightning strikes and terrible thunder claps every few seconds.

The new job was in Pinetown, a small country town some thirty kilometers inland from Durban. The land was rising a few hundred meters over this distance, which created a rather different climate zone, from a most of the time muggy coastal area to an elevated dryer inland region.

A group of large building and construction companies needed reorganization and had to be sorted out. The duration of this assignment was scheduled for a few months and this job was considered of great importance to INEFEN (no wonder with this kind of cash flow). As the leader of our group I got stuck in with the systems and organizational side of things. A German accountant was to reorganize the bookkeeping and accounting aspects, and a local engineer was to deal with the equipment and vehicles.

However, both the client and I could soon see that the accountancy consultant was out of his depth. He could not handle the traditional British way of unstructured alphabetical lists of accounts, which inevitably led to many mis-postings. I had to take over this side of the assignment as well and introduced properly structured accounts schedules for all sixteen companies of the group.

In addition, I introduced the German *BAB*, the *Betriebs-Abrechnungs-Bogen*. Unfortunately, I cannot furnish a proper translation for this typical German tapeworm-word, but this document provided certain structured accounting controls.

Here I found again what I had learned already at the Griesheim depot in Frankfurt: the problems which, for unknown reasons, most of the Anglo-American bookkeepers had with the percentage calculations and the international decimal system.

Despite my best efforts, the group's owner, who also acted as hard-nosed chief executive, commented on my final eighty-odd pages report as being full of mistakes. It turned out that he had found a typing mistake on one of the pages. A man quite to my liking! But he was not quite as tough when it came to himself.

I had to use my considerable abilities to read between the lines (my wife hotly disputes that I can do this) to catch-on that he was, amongst other things, looking for a (for him) painless way to get rid of his Finance and Administration Manager. During my work I had found proof that this chap had falsified the annual audit documents by inflating stock figures, to cover-up the fact that he had a holiday cottage built for himself with the company's materials and labor. This provided the solution to the owner's problem, to (almost) everybody's satisfaction.

During my work at this site a major set-back happened to the South African subsidiary of INEFEN. The Dutch owner had made a cash withdrawal of thirty thousand Rand out of the company's bank account, at this time about forty thousand US dollars. And when he was returning to the Netherlands, he was caught with the cash at the airport (a tip-off?).

This incident made the local widely read financial press, and the company was considered untouchable from then on. The South Africans, particularly the white Afrikaners, were extremely conservative people and refused to have anything to do with such unpatriotic skullduggery, particularly when commit-ted by a foreigner. The immediate results: no more contracts, soon followed by the bankruptcy of the local company, and unemployment for all our staff.

When I discussed this development with the client, we resolved that I would carry on with the assignment, but from now on for my own account. This worked out very well for me, because the INEFEN charges to the clients were almost ten times the salary they paid their consultants, to cover all their overheads and profit margin. I took a day off, flew (for about thirty-five Rand both ways!) to Pretoria, the capital of the country, and registered my newly formed company Management Efficiency (Pty) Ltd.

Earlier, I had discussed this move with the group's auditors and lawyers. They explained to me that this was theoretically possible, but it was practically never done in this country, because it was too involved and should therefore better be left to the experts (the auditors and lawyers!).

When I had finalized my work at the building companies, I decided to give this management consultancy business a try. Then I hired a sales executive and an analyst, who had both previously worked for INEFEN. We tried to find work for my company, but I had underestimated the conservative attitude of the largely Jewish and British businesspeople of Durban. They were still fighting the last war against the Nazis, and my 'wrong' nationality sunk us.

We could have gone back to Johannesburg, where I am convinced, we would have made a go of it. But we liked the climate and the ambience of the coastal regions here. Thus, I was forced to pay off my employees, which I had fortunately only engaged subject to a successful start, and who had, just as myself, lost their jobs with INEFEN to start with.

The family now decided (the opinion of our three-year old son was not researched) to stay in Pinetown, near Durban and the Natal coast, and to look for a house there. And my wife found a suitable one, which she fell in love with immediately. The asking price of eight thousand Rand appeared to be reasonable.

A deposit of twenty-five percent was required, in order to obtain a building society bond, or real estate loan for the balance of the purchase price. In addition, the agent wanted four hundred Rand (under the table?). Unfortunately, we simply did not have available an amount like this in ready cash to spend. As newly arrived immigrants we had to preserve our cash as far as possible. We also did not want to borrow over and above the bond on the property.

Shortly after this disappointment my wife found another suitable property in Kloof, a suburb of Pinetown, elevated a further one-hundred meters. This was a new house which the landowner, an estate agent, had built himself and which was reasonably priced. I suspect he had miscalculated somewhere, because he was keen to sell, even without a deposit.

We signed the purchase agreement and he then applied success-fully on our behalf for a bond which covered the full purchase price, presumably because the building society valuation exceeded the amount of the bond.

This property had originally been used for a nursery and was completely overgrown. For two weeks I had to work very hard to clear the land from a botanical explosion. At the bottom of our property a little stream was gurgling along, with some fern trees alongside (or should that read tree ferns?), which I had assumed to be extinct for millennia, based on what we had learned at High School. We also had a magnificent tree full of avocado pears, another novelty for us.

A further new, exciting and unusual discovery was a Black Mamba, a very poisonous African snake, which I had found amongst the overgrowth. Very stupidly, I grabbed this snake behind the head and placed it into an old sack. It could easily have bitten me, despite the fact that it was winter, when they were supposed to be not as aggressive as normally. I knew that, but did the snake know it?

Here I better explain the pricing of residential proper-ties in our area at that time, and why they were here so much cheaper than in Germany, particularly if the property was not yet connected to the municipal sewage system and used a 'soak-pit' instead. That was a covered pit the builder had dug in the garden, and which had a lump of rotting meat thrown in to start the necessary natural processes. Efficient and cheap!

Due to the huge land area of this country and the generally low population density, the land prices were very low, except in the so-called 'posh areas', where they easily could reach European levels.

Local houses generally had neither cellars nor central heating, neither double-glazing nor lofts and no insulated roofs. The outside walls were universally double-brick cavity walls without any insulation between. The pipes for electricity and water supplies were installed on one of the outside walls. The explanation for these cost savings was, of course, the local subtropical climate.

The standard procedure for buying such a property followed an established course:

- signing of the purchase contract,
- paying a deposit of twenty-five percent to the estate agent,
- he approached a building society and applied for a bond,
- the society sent an appraiser to check the valuation,
- if approved, the buyer signed a contract detailing the monthly payment of interest and initially a very small amount for the redemption of the bond (loan) capital.

These bonds for the balance of the purchase price were at this time provided over a repayment period of twenty-five years at a fixed rate of interest, because there existed virtually no inflation in South Africa at the time. In lieu of the deposit, handing over the title deeds of the fully paid land could generally serve the same purpose.

In later years the fixed rate of interest was scrapped by the societies, after inflation started to increase substantially. The building societies were specialized in awarding bonds on real estate. In those days they were the only suppliers of this type of finance. Some years later they had all been taken over by the commercial banks of the country.

By then, we must have received our furniture from Johannesburg, but I do not remember anything about that. According to South African customs (very low wages for servants!), the purchase of a house required, at the very least, the hiring of one servant 'girl', if not a 'garden boy' as well.

She was an unmarried English-speaking Zulu woman with a daughter of our son's age. Mother and daughter were living in a room in our house, called here the 'servant quarters'. The two kids got along fine, but later she decided to send her daughter home to her family in Zululand, because she felt that it was not right that the kid should grow up in a White household. I thought she had a point, particularly during the Apartheid period. Later we learned that she had another two children, who lived with the family in Zululand, one-hundred and fifty kilometers north of us.

This situation of an unmarried mother with three children was not at all unusual amongst the South African Blacks. While many of the men were quick to produce progeny, they were often reluctant to shoulder the responsibilities and they simply abandoned the pregnant mothers.

Because of the huge area of the country and the fact that this was a developing country, with all the negative adjectives (and without a system of registration by the police), it was in most cases impossible to locate the fathers (sometimes more than one) of a mother's children, or to force them to pay for their offspring.

When my last consultancy client offered me the job of the ousted Administration and Finance Manager for the group, I gladly accepted, after some arm-wrestling about my remuneration. Since I knew all the salaries of the managers, I could demand a sum which established me as the number two in the group, after the boss and owner himself.

However, I organized things in such a way that I did not become an employee. Instead, his group hired my management consultancy company, which in turn undertook to provide (by me) the management services required. This saved him the employer contributions to both the company's pension fund and the medical aid, and it spared me the PAYE tax deductions. This arrangement made it possible for me to place certain private expenses, as for instance the interest on our property bond and those relating to my car, as well as my medical aid and pension plan payments, on the accounts of my company. All of that was perfectly legal!

Because of the isolated position of our house I decided, on the advice of friends to buy a gun. As far as I remember the gun license was only a minor chore for the gun dealer and materialized *pronto*. The shop also sported a shooting range to try out the gun. Now I possessed again a 9mm automatic. Luckily, I never had to fire the pistol in earnest.

We had now also for the first time a dog: Bully, a Rhodesian Ridgeback of slightly dubious parentage, which we had bought as a puppy from my sales executive at the time. One night, when I had let the dog out to attend to his business, I observed the lights of a high-flying plane. But it turned out to be the Russian Sputnik, the first satellite. In those days, the times of the night-time passes of this new 'star' were widely publicized in the local papers.

In October of 1968, after living for two years in Kloof, we decided to sell, at a nice profit, because we suffered all three from permanent colds. In winter we had at night minimum temperatures close to freezing. Most mornings there was a thin crust of ice on the grass next to our little stream. This up-market suburb boasted a typical English climate: cold, rainy and foggy, and was for this reason popular with English people and their descendants - and was therefore an up-market sought-after suburb.

Again, my wife went house hunting, until she found some-thing outside Pinetown that we, and in particular my wife, liked very much: A pretty split-level house with sea view, unfortunately at a twenty to twenty-five kilometers distance. The climate here was far more subtropical and pleasant for our taste: a compromise between the Atlantic English one of our previous area and the soggy heat of subtropical Durban.

In the meantime, the property prices had shot up und we signed the purchase contract for eleven thousand six-hundred Rand. After we had paid the customary twenty-five percent deposit, financed by the profit we had made on the sale of our Kloof house, I was off to the building society for a bond for the balance of the purchase price. Which was refused, because the property was deemed by the manager to be too isolated and too far from town.

Luckily, I was able to persuade another society that this justification was not realistic and for them to grant the bond, and we were finally settled. While we were living there, the whole area has been developed and carpeted with middle-income housing. So much for the understanding of a bank manager!

In the same month we had to deal with another shock. We learned that the parents of my wife had both died within a week of each other, her father of stomach cancer and her mother of lung cancer, even so neither of them had ever been smoking.

We were not able to fly to Germany for the funerals, since we had received the notification very late. No e-mail yet! Also, airfares were then relatively very much higher than now, and we had a bit over-reached ourselves financially with the purchase of the house. Plus, I had no choice but to try to get established in my new job.

My wife was bequeathed a helpful sum of money, as well as a heavy Persian bracelet of gold links with Carnelian stones which showed Arabic etchings of a *surah* of the Quran, so we were told. For myself there was a heavy golden signet ring with a similarly engraved stone. In addition, she inherited a number of Persian carpets which her parents had bought in Tabriz and Esfahan. These were shipped to us by her eldest sister, who acted as the administrator of the estates of her parents.

As one of my first decisions after starting my work in the new company, early in December of 1966, I had scrapped the Christmas "bribes" list, which this firm, like most others as well, used to dispatch "presents" to the recipients early in December. Soon afterwards I received a furious call: "Where is my bloody case of Whiskey?" This was the chief of the Quantity Surveying division of the City of Durban, responsible for the monthly progress payments to the building firms working on contracts for the city, like we were.

Somehow, somewhere, there was a jinx in our plans. In April of 1967, five months after joining the holding company of this group of about fifteen companies, a dispute arose about our largest building contract (about eighty percent of our monthly turnover). This was the contract to build a hospital for the Indian community of Durban for the Natal provincial administration, which was administered by the City of Durban.

The architects had overlooked to provide access to the X-ray section, and they wanted to amend their plans. Fine, not a problem! But when we demanded payment, not only for the extra work, but also for the disruption of our scheduled workflow, they refused both and demanded (!) that we condone the variation without compensation, which we in turn were unable to accede to.

These same architects were the authority to certify every month how much work we had completed, und how much money we were entitled to receive as progress payments. This was done via the Quantity Surveyors, as this was the usual practice in this country. They, in turn, passed on the documentation to the Chief Quantity Surveyor of the Durban Corporation. The office of the City Treasurer of the City of Durban then handed over a check which I collected and deposited into our bank account.

Because of this dispute the Chief Quantity Surveyor stopped certifying the large monthly progress payments (spot the connection!), which appeared to us to be a clear case of revenge. We simply could not survive this loss of our cash flow, and as a consequence our group of companies ran out of cash and we were forced to apply for Judicial Management.

In the past, the group's owner had been forced to give his personal guarantees for the bank overdrafts of the group companies, and he was declared insolvent when he was unable to meet these guarantees when his group of companies went down. Which also meant, that he could no longer be a "director of companies". He asked me to become the sole director of all the companies of the group, in order to protect his personal interests.

3

NORMAL LIFE WITH ILCO HOMES

In the beginning the Judicial Manager was kept extremely busy, trying to get the 'foundered ship' back on an even keel. First, he had to get the blocked bank accounts replaced by new ones, the most pressing and the most important of all his tasks. The accounts for electricity and water had also to be replaced, and many other arrangements had to be made by him and his CAs, the Chartered Accountant partners of his firm.

We now carried on under 'new management', and battled along with our contracts, including the big hospital one. The owner of the group continued as CEO, the Chief Executive Officer. For most of the employees nothing much changed in the daily routine. Only the boss and I were intricately involved with the new regime. We had to report to the Judicial Manager monthly, and sometimes more often, about the progress on the various contracts, and how I managed with cash flow and the accounts. One of his auditors was now permanently in our office, dealing with our pre-judicial debts, especially the claims by the aggrieved creditors.

For many months during this miserable period we battled to stay afloat. There was always the danger that the Judicial Manager would 'pull the plug' and close down the place, to ensure that the bank, on whose benevolence his career depended, would not lose money on their post-judicial over-draft.

Additionally, I was constantly involved in heavy 'defensive battles' (still in the army!) with the pre-judicial creditors of the company, who kept angling for preferential treatment. The Durban Receiver of

Revenue also kept trying his luck, until I asked him eventually, what he intended to find in the pockets of a naked man.

In 1969 South Africa suffered a rare natural event: an earthquake of a respectable 6.9 on the Richter scale. The epicenter was near Tulbagh in the Cape Province. This quaint little country town was largely destroyed, and several human lives were lost.

This tremor was a strong reminder to me that Southern Africa was sitting astride a huge geological *Graben*, which will probably sometime in the future split the African continent from top to bottom. The famous East-African Rift Valley is just the beginning of this tectonic process. However, this is unlikely to happen before this important manuscript will be completed.

Our group of companies was at this stage building apartment blocks, schools and hospitals for the State, the province of Natal and the city of Durban, but our specialty was the construction of complete housing schemes. Amongst others, we have built the Durban suburbs of Chatsworth and Phoenix, two completely new residential areas for the Indian community of Durban. These contracts were awarded by the Department of Community Development and financed and coordinated by them. Several thousand one- and two-story houses have been built by us over the years to their complete satisfaction.

Eventually, the group was released from judicial management. This was achieved by way of a compromise with the creditors, which was financed by the Jewish wholesaler, who at the time had refused to deal with my management consultancy company, because of my objectionable German nationality.

All companies of the group, with the exception of the holding company and one of our building companies, were liquidated at this stage. This remaining construction company we now renamed "Ilco Homes". Since my boss was still not rehabilitated, which only became possible many years later, I remained the sole director of both companies.

Sometime in the early 1970s things finally started to look up for us. The original weak spots in the group had been corrected by now. Good contracts allowed good profits. The executives were now given company cars, which provided welcome tax relief for our managers. Originally, they were just the ubiquitous VW Beetles. And our offices were now getting too small for the additional staff we needed to employ.

We were offered a high-rise office building in downtown Durban. This went cheaply, because the Security Police of the Apartheid government, as the main tenant, had a long lease at a low rental. This tenant created a high probability of a bomb attack by the Anti-Apartheid freedom fighters. This explained why the building was half empty, because prospective tenants feared for their lives. And this in turn was responsible for the low valuation and selling price.

As soon as I began checking the documentation, I noticed that the rental contract of the Security Police had only one more month to go before expiry. They had, however, as was usual in this country, a renewal option for another five years, but no pre-determined rental amount was quoted.

As an 'unqualified lawyer' I knew that in South African law such an option, without the stated rental amounts for the option period, was unenforceable. Sometimes the small print in the law gets over-looked or is forgotten, even by lawyers. After the remaining one month of the lease had passed, we were able to get rid of the Security Police and their concomitant risk. This resulted in more than doubling of the market value of this property.

Later we sold this asset at a hefty profit and bought instead some large vacant real estate in Queensburgh, outside Durban. There we built an office tower for the group, work-shops and warehouses for the storage of our building materials, a concrete batching plant for our concrete truck-mixers and a yard for the production of our concrete building blocks.

As mentioned already, South African small and medium-sized businesses were often somewhat lagging behind their European coun-terparts, especially regarding their accounting and office systems. I had just managed to remedy that for this group, when the first pieces of modern office equipment became available in this country.

We started this revolution in our work by leasing a small Olivetti bookkeeping machine, which basically was hard-wired similar to the previously mentioned IBM tabulators. Next came an ICL (proto-)com-puter, which already had a sort of built-in program and did already quite a decent job for the accounts department.

And then the proper computer age was upon us. We had just moved our operations from Durban and had provided in our new office building in Queensburgh a large computer room with a double-floor for the miles of hidden cables. We were able to purchase a main-frame computer. Our little new baby was a second-hand Burroughs machine, costing us about a million dollars. It required, in addition to its own large special room, additional air conditioning equipment and a UPS, the Uninterruptable Power Supply.

We also now had to set up a computer section within my Finance and Administration Division, and we had to hire a computer manager, three computer analysts, eight programmers and two dozen Indian clerks, mainly for data capture. I was conscious of the fact that this looked suspiciously like 'empire building' on my part, but I had checked with two similar large installations in town and had made sure that our staffing was adequate and not excessive.

In those long-ago days you could not just contact a computer dealer or search the internet and order a dozen application programs for your new toy. To start with, there were neither of these things in existence, yet. Each computer manufacturer did his own marketing. IBM and Apple had their own offices in Durban. Even proper Operating Systems did not yet exist. Microsoft and Windows had not appeared on the 'screen'. All programs had to be written by the user or by some computer consultant. The programmers used different languages. Basic, Fortran and Cobol come to mind.

The first suite of programs our computer section had produced was for wages and salaries. For the processing of the wages we acquired a further piece of equipment, the name of which I forgot. C-something, I think. This system provided for the information from the timecards to be entered twice, by different clerks, and the system compared the two inputs and highlighted any discrepancies. This virtually fool-proof part I liked best of all of the, for me, rather confusing many new gadgets and concepts.

The technical specifications of our equipment were really laughable, when compared with present-day computers. We had to use a cumbersome *fixed - removable – disk* system, because there were no hard-drives available yet. We had about three dozen of these nifty large removable disks, each with a diameter of about thirty centimeters, and a thickness of about ten centimeters, which were stored on large wall-shelves. A clerk was busy full time to move the disks, hopefully the correct ones, from the shelf onto the computer, then back to the shelf, all manually of course.

Computer memory was an even worse joke. I remember that we were able to lend one megabyte of memory to the City of Durban, because we had two megabytes available, which we did not need just then. I suspect that my memory may be again playing a trick on me here, because these numbers look simply ridiculous. On the other hand, I am sure that I did not know the term 'gigabyte' in those days, even if it existed then already.

Back-up was naturally also required, and was provided by a

magnetic tape system, which ran for hours every night. And not to forget a printer (or two?). Over time many more application programs were added by our computer section: stock control, bookkeeping, asset control, supply chain management, building progress, etc.

When I was offered a medium-sized property development site in Queensburgh, just outside Pinetown, I decided to take the plunge to become a small investor and property developer, and my Management Efficiency company bought the land. This had provisionally been subdivided into four individual plots. Then I asked our building company for a quote to develop these four properties. Our people built there four individual small houses for me. This all took many months, to finalize all the permits and particularly the subdivisions at the Deeds Office. Bureaucracy seems to be more or less the same everywhere!

These houses we rented out, which gave my company a welcome monthly cash income, but also created a lot of hassles over the years. The properties served two main purposes: to protect us against the effects of the high local inflation rate of usually up to fifteen percent, and peaking at twenty-five percent annually, and they allowed us to actually profit from this climate of high inflation.

My company had raised large bonds of almost ninety percent of their value on these properties. The interest payable to the bank was to a large extend offsetting the rental revenue, thus together with other costs obviating any income tax liability for the company. Additionally, the bonds represented a slowly reducing proportion of the gross valuation of the properties. And since the currency lost much value every year due to the high inflation rate, with time the bonds became cheaper in real terms. Eventually, we were able to pay back the balances 'out of our back pocket'.

The Electronic Era now started to slowly invade the private space as well. Early in the 1970s we had bought an eight-millimeter video camera, but the results of my cinematographic efforts were rather disappointing. Most of the recordings were 'nervous', and the usually strong wind produced unwelcome background noises. However, my wife has nevertheless salvaged a few cassettes, avoiding the fall-out of a full-blown waste of money.

But something else had almost become a serious matter! One Sunday morning we all drove to the Durban beach and I went for a swim. On this morning there was a strong riptide in the surf. Either no warning was sounded, or I had missed it. I rather suspect that there was no warning, because the surf was packed with bathers. Therefore, the following happenings were not restricted only to me, but a large number of fellow-sufferers were involved as well.

All of a sudden, a large wave keeled me over and tumbled me about in the surf. My head paid a number of unpleasant visits to the bottom of the sea, which luckily consisted just of sand. But it is amazing, how hard such a sandy bottom has become after it has been pounded long enough by angry waves. The current pulled me out to sea for about a hundred meters and against this strong tide I was not able to swim back to the beach.

The only possibility for me was to play 'dead man', floating on my back and keeping my face above water. I let myself drift and saw the beach und the beach guards getting more and more distant, but again and again the waves broke over my face and I swallowed water like crazy.

My thoughts concentrated around a simple set of alter-natives: either the lifeguards will see me, or they will not see me. I mentally transported myself into an equivalent life-threatening position during the war and resigned myself to wait and see what will happen. Provisionally, I had shut down all further thought and realized, that this could easily be the end of this story.

Obviously, the beach guards had seen me before I arrived in Australia, at the other end of our not so little Indian Ocean. They delivered me to the Provincial Hospital, propitiously just across the beach road. After I had regurgitated oodles of saltwater my wife took me back home. I lay in bed for a few hours, sporting a bright-red tongue and I was ready for use again.

In the 1970s our construction group had tendered for the largest housing contract ever awarded in South Africa, and well over a thousand kilometers from Durban. This was intended for the design and the building of the completely new town of Mitchells Plain, thirty-two kilometers outside of Cape Town. More than four thousand houses were intended for the Capetonian Colored community, which the Apartheid regime planned to uproot from District Six, their ancestral home for centuries. Included in this contract was the planning and the construction of all the roads and services as well as the schools and community buildings required for this new town.

Our tender for more than forty-two million Rand was successful. One of our tender conditions had been that we would require a lump sum pre-payment of seven million Rand, to enable us to establish our builder's yard, including a concrete block factory, a concrete batching plant imported from Germany, storage sheds and our Cape Town branch offices. The fact that we had already successfully built thousands of such houses to the satisfaction of the municipality in Durban provided enough performance security for the municipality of Cape Town to accept such an unusual tender condition.

Now I have to apologize and digress for a moment. Wearing my hat as Financial Director of the group, I had attended a few taxation seminars given by the then doyen and authority regarding the South African Income Tax, Professor Silke. He had also published and regularly updated the standard reference book on the subject.

In each one of these seminars he recited the story of the Rhodesian farmer who had in June booked and paid in advance his room in a Durban hotel. His holiday stay was to start in July. The financial year of the hotel company ran from 1 July to 30 June. The hotel, therefore, had received the money in the financial year prior to the guest's arrival. This transaction had increased the hotel's revenue, and therefore their taxable profit for that prior year, in the full amount of the guest's pre-payment, since they had not incurred any costs to reduce this 'windfall'.

The reason for this abnormal situation could be found in the history of the English Income Tax. In the Middle Ages (I know, I know, but we are dealing with England here!), this tax originated as a means to collect money from individuals and small private undertakings, such as farmers, artisans, artists and small commerce (except the Church, *bene nota*). The construct of companies, as we have them today, did not exist yet in England.

When these appeared much later, no proper laws to deal with the taxation of their profits were ever promulgated there. Therefore, the companies had also to be taxed on their income (revenue) rather than on their profits, but logically the Income Tax laws had to allow them to deduct their costs from their income, in order to arrive in a circuitous way at taxing them on their profits.

This illogical situation required the logical proviso that they could only deduct from their revenue the 'costs expanded in the production of income'. This construct necessitated much mental acrobatics, if one thinks for instance of depreciation of machinery or of the treatment of immaterial assets. At the end of the seminars the esteemed lecturer and the assembled financial experts of the province joined Professor Silke's sarcasm about some silly tax laws and laughed about this ridiculous situation, but neither he nor any of the hundreds of chartered accountants ever did anything to correct this anomaly. In his case maybe understandable!

Now we can carry on with our story. Just before the end of our financial year we had invoiced the City of Cape Town for the above-mentioned pre-payment of seven million Rand for our yard and offices, and the taxman wanted to tax us on this revenue as a profit, because we had not yet been able to spend a penny on our preparatory construction work. According to the tax law the Receiver of Revenue was correct. But we simply did not have that sort of money he wanted from us, because this was not a profit, but merely a pre-payment. After the tax assessor had threatened with liquidation of the company if we did not pay, I had to do something rather drastic.

When I appealed to the Secretary of the South African Department of Finance, he refused to talk to me, because I was neither a South African citizen, nor was I a Chartered Accountant, and I was therefore deemed to be unqualified to question a complicated and sensitive subject like the Income Tax Act of this country.

My boss had become a member of the National Party and had established good connections, because he had supported, in a modest way, the ruling party financially (he also contributed something to the United Party, the Official Opposition!). I had earlier met the financial secretary of the National Party in Natal, the blind Senator Hendrik Klopper, and in my desperation, I asked Oom (uncle) Hendrik for his help. Even though I was not a member of his party, he arranged a meeting with the then Minister of Finance Senator Horwood, for myself as well as the Chartered Accountant running the administration division of our newly established Cape Town branch.

Mr. Fourie, the Secretary of Finance also attended this meeting. He strongly objected to even talking about any change to the Income Tax Act. He was clearly very upset about the whole meeting and its subject, and particularly with me. These Afrikaners could be very aggressive and direct, if their interests were threatened by outsiders!

The Minister had previously been a professor of economics at the University of Natal, and he was the only English speaker in the South African cabinet. After I had quoted him actual sample experiences of this illogical situation from the income tax practice, he agreed that this looked wrong. He said he would investigate this, "but what can be done about it, without upsetting the whole income tax system?"

The contribution of our chartered accountant to the discussions had been nil. But I was prepared for this objection and handed the Minister a suggested draft for a new sub-section to section twenty-four of the Income Tax Act, if I remember this number correctly.

It took about half a year, but then it was reported that Parliament had passed an amendment to the income tax legislation. This took the form of section 24a, if I remember correctly. This addition to the legislation authorized companies to create a provision in their accounts, neutralizing the revenue received prior to having incurred the relevant expenditure.

In effect, they now were allowed to capitalize pre-payments as liabilities, offsetting the relevant amount in the debtor accounts. Such a provision had to be reversed automatically in the following tax year. This amendment, naturally slightly changed into official and barely understandable legalese, appeared finally in the Government Gazette, and the company was saved. Give the man a cigar!

Something else just popped-up in my memory. For decades the international gold price had been fixed at thirty-five US Dollar per ounce, until America had been persuaded to break the connection of their currency to the gold price. Shortly after, the price of gold had risen to 80 Rand. The course of the South African Rand in those far-off days had been close to the US dollar, occasionally it hovered even above the green-back.

Because I was convinced that the gold price would soon increase further, I had recommended to the Boss that the company make a short-term investment (speculation) of some of our surplus cash into Kruger Rand gold coins. They afforded a straight, simple and cost-effective entry into the gold price movement.

For eighty thousand Rand we bought one thousand Kruger Rand coins, each containing one ounce of 99.99 percent pure gold. I collected them in two sexy steel cash boxes, very cool. After a few weeks the gold price had doubled again, and we sold the coins back to the bank. Our bank manager kept mentioning this transaction for a long time, marveling at our financial astuteness, but more correctly he should have referred to our luck!

Because of the huge amount of this new Cape Town contract and the concomitant large risks, and probably thinking of his earlier insolvency experience, my boss decided to sell fifty percent of our group to the local construction group of Murray & Steward Ltd., which later merged with Roberts Construction Ltd. of Johannesburg, to ultimately become Murray & Roberts Ltd.

Our Ilco Homes company undertook the establishment of the builder's yard and the construction of the houses and other buildings, while Murray & Steward as sub-contractors performed the civil engineering part of the contract, because we did not have the necessary competences in our group for this type of work.

For all of our work for the government we had to submit tenders, which were adjudicated at the State Tender Board in Pretoria. The procedure was that the sealed tender documents had to be submitted to this office by a fixed time and date, when they would be opened, and all the tender amounts and the names of the companies would be read out in public. I always flew up to Pretoria and hand-carried our tenders, to make sure we did not miss any deadline. The extra expense was easily justified, in view of the usually large amounts of these contracts.

On one such opening of tenders the individual documents had already been read out to the waiting crowd, with our tender amount being the lowest. Then a representative of one of the largest construction companies in the country entered the room, mumbling some excuse for being 'a bit' late, and submitted his document, which had the tender amount inserted in handwriting. The official in charge accepted this late and therefore irregular document and - surprise, surprise, - that late tender, the lowest by a small margin, was declared the winner.

On procedural grounds I protested strongly against this irregular action by the official in charge. When my protest was brushed aside, with the justification, that this tender was only 'a bit' late, and when no mention was made of the hand-written tender amount, I walked immediately to the nearby headquarters of the South African Police, the SAP. There I requested to see a senior officer of the CID, the Criminal Investigation Department.

A Major came to attend to me. First, I reported the handwritten tender amount and the official's attitude and comment regarding the late submission of this tender, which strongly suggested corruption. Then I explained to him, how one man could have listened to the reading-out of the tender amounts, and he could then have passed on the lowest price to another representative outside the room, who could then have filled in a lower amount into his tender document.

The officer took me right away to the office of the Commanding General of the CID. Five minutes later, the General walked with me back to the Tender Board, where he confiscated the suspect document. A week later, we were awarded the contract and I was asked by the General to prepare a report on how collusion like this could best be prevented in future. This was done *post-haste* and we never had a tender problem like this again. On the other hand, we were forthwith and for unknown reasons not exactly the blue-eyed members of the South African building industry.

We were now finally able to set up the group properly. The executives were now driving Mercedes-Benz cars and had decent offices. Bankers, auditors, lawyers and others were now treating us as equals and were angling for our business. Suppliers were now constantly on the phone and their representatives were courting our Supply Manager.

Now we started also to submit our tender documents for work in Johannesburg. A year or so later we had opened our branch office and our builder's yard outside Johannesburg. Once a month I flew now for two or three days to Cape Town and once a month for two days to Johannesburg. It was a busy life, additional to my work in Durban. But I enjoyed every moment of it (well, maybe not every single one!)

When I flew to our Cape Town and Johannesburg offices, I enjoyed the challenges; to hire and to guide the administration manager of the branch, to control the setup of their internal systems and to check their administrative performances once a month *in loco*.

The flights to Johannesburg were uneventful, but some of the flights to Cape Town were rather nerve-wrecking, due to the fact that the air over the lower South African east coast was often quite turbulent. This area was not called the 'Wild Coast' for nothing! Sometimes we rattled along, with not only the wing tips, but with the entire wing rather frighteningly flapping up and down.

But well-deserved compensation was provided for that. Meals on this route of the SAA, the South African Airways, at the time the only airline in the country, were the best I ever experienced on any plane. This is where I encountered for the first time the famous "LM Prawns", named after Lourenco Marques, the capital of Mozambique, and the present-day Maputo. By the way, the big Durban cockroaches mentioned ear-lier were only half-jokingly called "Durban Prawns".

In addition to Bully, our faithful dog, we also had at different times a number of cats. One of these, a tomcat, had established himself single-mindedly in our house. We asked our 'girl' (our domestic worker) to find out where the animal was domiciled. She reported that he belonged to somebody living several houses down the road from us. She returned the cat to his owners, but the animal decided otherwise and came back to live with us.

Bully and the cat existed in a state of 'armed neutrality'. This tomcat was a funny chap, with his own mind, and he gave us much pleasure. When I was reading in my easy chair, he would jump on my lap, and when I leaned back, he stretched out and pummeled my chest and belly into the (by him) desired form. Unfortunately, we lost a few of our cats to road traffic, despite the usually quiet street. This included a Siamese with blue eyes, which was the most demanding of the lot. She pummeled my wife's legs if she wanted her attention, but left me in peace, probably after I had given her one of my alleged dirty looks.

However, we were not restricted to just pets. A number of the members of the local wildlife population were also quite interesting. Lions we did not have in our garden, and tigers neither (they do not live in Africa). But we had many different species of birds and, amongst others, we also had 'golden moles' in our garden. They were comparable to the European moles, but they dug their tunnels immediately below the turf, with the roofs raised above the ground. It is easy to see what keen gardeners and the staff at the numerous golf courses thought about the lovely but busy little critters.

One year these chaps had excavated in our front garden a big underground cavity for themselves, without us noticing anything. After several cloudbursts had soaked the ground and softened it, the ceiling of their bunker collapsed. The resulting hole in the ground was almost large enough to accommodate a Volkswagen 'Beetle'. Unbelievable! The downpours had been so excessive that a large old tree next to their 'palace' also toppled over when a strong wind had come up. Its roots had lost their grip in this soggy ground. For months our front garden looked like a battlefield!

Our son grew up fast and joined Pinetown primary school in the early 1970s. Actually, he did not grow up any faster than all the other kids, but time was simply flying for us. He was a late starter, like his father, because we were both the youngest in our respective classes when we started with school.

I will keep his involvement, same as his mother's, to a minimum in this recital, "because I don't want them to steal my lime-light". No, it is no good to be too honest, so I correct this latter statement to read "because this story is about my life". Let me therefore just summarize that he fast improved as he went along through primary and high schools in Pinetown.

My wife's involvement is interwoven with my own story and does therefore not require any lengthy extrapolation. Suffice to say, that at one stage she grew tired of sitting at home all by herself. She had bought a knitting machine and we looked for a cost-efficient way to buy her wool. A lady at my office mentioned that her parents wanted to sell their local little wool shop.

We bought 'Busy Bees', and her supply problem was solved. Now she was running this small shop and expanded its scope by additionally stocking uniforms for a few nearby schools. This went quite well, but when I later prepared to open our stamp auction business, I needed her help and in 1982 this micro-enterprise had to be sold.

Shortly after we asked our building company to give us a quotation to add to our house a second garage. Its roof to be utilized as a patio, with direct access from our lounge. When this was built, my wife planted next to this new addition several Pawpaw or papaya trees, which could reach a height of almost four meters. When they started to fruit, she was able to harvest them manually in comfort from this patio. A very efficient lady, my wife!

Sometime in the early 1970s the son of my father-in-law's old friend in Port Elizabeth visited us with his family. Their son was about our son's age, their girl was slightly younger. We were driving at the time a Volkswagen Beetle and went with them to the nearby Lion Park. It had been raining all day. Yes, occasionally this happens in South Africa, too. When we found a lioness with her cubs, we stopped to watch them play. The kids (ours) were sitting in the back under the large rear window, where they could watch the proceedings in safety.

After a while the lioness got up onto her hind legs behind the Beetle, with her front paws on the roof, and started to lick the rain drops off the back window. The shrieks of the three kids and the screams of the women (there was no chance of calling them 'ladies' at that moment) would have done a pop concert proud. Us men, naturally, did not show any reaction, but I managed to start the car in record time and to get us to safety. A grown-up lioness looks surprisingly big and menacing when seen from underneath her.

In the middle of the 1970s we had to have our faithful Bully put to sleep, because his urinary troubles as an 'old man' made life miserable for him. We now bought Vashti, a multiple-crowned German Shepherd lady. If I remember correctly, she was named after a Persian princess. She had a pedigree I could only ogle with envy. I was ashamed to have such an illustrious animal; champion of this and champion of that, with nobility ancestors going back to Adam. And everything properly documented, of course. We should by rights have addressed her as Lady Vashti.

After we had arranged the services of an equally distinguished German Shepard gentleman for her, we could expect a brood of the purest of the pure German Shepherd dogs. But we had reckoned without our servant 'girl', who had for a moment let our doggy out of her sight.

As a result, we landed up with exactly a dozen little mongrel doggies, half of them black, half of them brown. We kept one each and I called the brown boy 'Bruno' and the black girl 'Nera'. Not very original, I know, but I had been in Italy for quite a while and had very much liked this episode of my life, and I still remembered what brown and black were in Italian.

In 1977 my wife had arranged for our son to start horse riding, and she joined in as well. To keep them company I also started with this perceived nonsense, at age fifty-three. This turned out, maybe for the first time, to be a proper family experience. We had wonderful days with the three horses we had bought; Man of War, Buttercup and Vicenza. Together, we took part in the usual low-level local horse shows, with mixed results. Our son was more successful than we were, but the results were unimportant for us, anyway (so we claimed).

In one such show my wife had a terrible-looking fall. She landed on her head and I had immediate visions of a catastrophe. But she survived this fall better than I did shortly after, after I in turn hit the dust. When I got up, I did not know where I was, nor what had happened. But after ten minutes I was back to my usual cantankerous self. This was not the first time in my life that I suffered a mild concussion. At age ten or so, somebody had organized a boxing contest, with a proper ring and with proper gloves, and I had then the same kind of experience.

We also had proper riding lessons in a paddock, but that was more or less boring, so I will skip this part. Galloping along a narrow muddy footpath in the African veld (grass-lands), with a sharp bend looming in front of the noses of our horses, accelerated the adrenalin flow markedly and was much more exciting. We undertook many such exhilarating outrides with plenty of thrills (and spills).

On one of these occasions my wife decided to swerve to the right to avoid a bush in her way, but 'Buttercup' thought it would be better to pass on the left. The horse won, as usual in such situations, and my wife tasted the African soil. I also had my fair share of sampling the same dirt on several occasions.

Our most memorable outrides were in 'Pretty Valley', which we had so christened. At that time, we decided that we wanted our eventual ashes scattered there. Fat chance; twenty years later this beautiful valley had become a housing development. This is one of the reasons why I am still around, because I just cannot make up my mind, how I want my ashes disposed of.

Sometimes our horses got spooked by something or other, such as the wind rustling in a bush or the man-high grass, and they attempted to run quickly home to their stables, which they were very much inclined to do, and at the slightest excuse. But we always managed to reign them in and to stop such nonsense 'desertion of the flag'.

On one of our outrides our 'Vashti' got lost. Without us noticing it, she had decided to chase a monkey up a high tree, and then waited underneath, maybe hoping the branch with the monkey would break off. We were quite a few kilometers from the stables at that moment. A week later we were informed by our 'girl', through the African bush telegraph, that the dog had been 'found' at a certain African hut. A moderate tip secured her safe return to us.

Our son had one day a scary experience, probably frightening us even more. While he was in the company of some girls of his age, someone spotted a snake. Our son tried to grab the snake behind the head, naturally without giving any thought of trying to impress the young ladies, and for his heroic effort he was promptly bitten by the disturbed animal.

We found out later that the culprit was a vine snake, one of the most poisonous snakes we have in South Africa. It twists its body into a few ninety-degree angles, looking just like some old and shriveled vines in a vineyard, showing the identical brown color and surface markings. Then the snake remains motionless and waits for a bird, for instance, to come close enough for her to strike.

We rushed him to the provincial hospital in Durban, and the doctor in the emergency room told us, that no antidote existed for the poison of this particular species, and there was nothing he could do to help him.

Luckily, I remembered the just retired Dr. White, the outstanding expert in Natal on snake bites, and the doyen of the snake-poison experts of South Africa. I obtained his phone number and explained to him the situation. He remembered our previous encounter at one or another cocktail party and rushed to the hospital and ordered a number of blood transfusions and a series of 'blood washings', which after a few days had removed almost all traces of the venom from our son's blood. It was a close call for him and a frightening period for all of us.

A few years later the birds in our garden in Pinetown made one day a terrible noise and commotion, and I found an identical specimen of this snake (but surely not the same individual!) in our hedge. It appeared that it had just swallowed a small bird or an egg, because that was what its swelled body looked like. When it had slithered onto our verandah, we quickly called the Durban Snake Park. By the time an expert came to collect this dangerous beast, it had moved into our Bougainvillea. He was able to save us from a scary fate, and to add a rare species to the Snake Park's collection.

At another occasion we observed in our front garden about a dozen yellow-billed kites, gobbling-up flying termites, which in our parts are called 'flying ants'. Thousands of them left the holes in the earth where they had developed, then rising into the air in a large cloud. These large birds performed an amazing orchestrated ballet close to the ground, as they swallowed the termites which were appearing like on a production line. The survivors were hunted by other birds, such as our ubiquitous Indian Mynahs. By then, still surviving in large numbers, the termites were already beginning to shed their plastic-like wings.

In the second half of the 1970s my wife had established contact with a sugar-cane farmer's family, who took in young boys to give them a farm experience. This turned out to be a godsend for our son, who looked up to the farmer as a role model, which probably created an early interest in farming and, by implication, in biology. The farmer had been trained at Weston Agricultural College outside Mooi River, in the foothills of the Drakensberg, and had later managed a number of different types of farms.

In 1979 our son joined the same college, a boarding-school, about one hundred-fifty kilometers from our home in Pinetown. Here again he was the youngest in his class and he successfully completed there his Matric. During his time at Weston we visited him once a month. That was mandatory, since otherwise he would have starved to death, as he assured us earnestly and repeatedly.

During our visits we stayed at the Sierra Ranch, a nearby Western-style resort. We even had bought two Stetson hats, to fit in with the theme and, unusually for us, spent a little time in the bar, which I had not done for at least twenty years. The 'number two' of the hotel management, who was looking after the money printing press, also known as the bar, we met again thirty years later in Margate, as a partner in a dealership, when we bought a new car.

The managers were real 'sharpies', who had a border-line scheme going, selling shares to the public. But since I know nothing about such things, I just played along. If one bought just one share, one could stay there, but if one owned ten, one received preferential booking service and a rebate. Additional shares were offered cheaper to existing share-holders. *Ergo*, I first bought one share, and then I bought another nine at the reduced price.

The resort had a number of horses, and often all three of us went on outrides. My favorite was Dallas, a smallish horse similar to an Iceland Pony, with a remarkably fast trot. This was strictly speaking not really a trot, but an extremely quick walk, like a power-walk. This horse could traverse a field of small boulders at full speed. I was often worried that he might break a leg, and that I would break my neck, but nothing ever happened while I was riding him. But one day, when we were not there, he did break a leg and he had to be put down. What a pity!

The most memorable of these outrides had led all three of us down to the Mooi River, when a thunderstorm broke: fast, furious and unexpected, as so often happens in the foothills of the mountains. The lightning was frightening, as we were standing with our horses next to the river. Surely, not the safest place to be!

I ordered the squadron to conduct an accelerated withdrawal and to race back to the ranch, because I was worried about the river attracting the lightning. Because of the rain the ground was muddy, and my wife and my son were covered in mud, thrown up by the hooves of the galloping horses. They were forced to have their bath, but as the first in line, I was spared this ordeal. Goody!

After his matriculation our son studied for a few years at Cedara Agricultural College near Pietermaritzburg. We had bought him a motorcycle, so he could come home as often as possible. As soon as he had concluded his education the realistic danger came up that he would be drafted into the South African Army, battling against the infiltrating Freedom Fighters in Namibia and on the northern boarders of South Africa.

As a Permanent Resident, and therefore not being a citizen, he should have been exempt from military service. But the Apartheid government had by now become desperate to find soldiers for their wars, first in Rhodesia and now in South-West-Africa. We therefore decided that our son should better go oversees for some months or years, and he would look around Europe to widen his horizon. Just as expected, shortly after he had left us, two young civilians (most likely lieutenants) turned up on our doorstep and wanted to know where the son of the house was. They looked rather unhappy, but not at all surprised, when we enlightened them. Obviously, this had not been their first disappointment of the day.

After extensive travels all over Europe, and all at minimum

expense, he decided to go to Israel for a stint in a kibbutz. He worked there for a while and visited many interesting places, in Israel and in Egypt.

After his time as a *Kibbutznik* he returned to Germany and stayed with the family of my wife's younger brother near Frankfurt. There he immediately started two jobs, as a dish-washer and as a landscape gardener, to find his feet. Then he started to work, as a civilian employee, for the US Army, Europe as a train attendant on the Staff Train of USAREUR, the organization which I had left not that long ago. Many trips brought him to Berlin, and he was even able to visit my aunt in Quohren outside of Dresden.

He then went back to Israel for a second period as a *Kibbutznik*. After this second stint in Israel he returned with the girlfriend he had met there, to settle with her family in Denmark. There he started working for a firm of garden architects, which sent him all over the country and even to England.

These were hard times for him. We intentionally had not supported him financially, because I believed that such a harsh and difficult time would form him for life. At the time we could only hope we did the right thing. With the benefit of hindsight, we can now safely say that things had worked out more than all right, but I'm not going to say anything more. No use to spoil him!

Luckily, his girlfriend persuaded (pushed?) him to apply for a place at the Agricultural School of the University of Copenhagen. He was forced to quickly learn the language to be able to study there. His time at Weston and Cedara greatly helped him in his studies in Copenhagen, where he left with first a Master's degree and then his PhD. Well done, son!

At Ilco Homes we were not only constructing housing contracts for public authorities like central government, the provinces and municipalities, but we built also individual houses for private clients. Our boss had developed a system to construct both types of dwellings in four stages and using four specialized gangs:

- foundations and connections to services,
- external and internal walls,
- roofs,
- painting and finishes.

For individual buildings the four small gangs worked under a foreman each. They were organized in such a way that each of these gangs was able to complete their stage for one building in one day. Theoretically, we were building a house in four workdays. But for a number of practical reasons there had to be gaps between the four stages. If any of these gangs were progressing faster than this program, we reduced the number of workers, or on the other hand, we increased them if this became necessary.

In the case of housing contracts, the labor force for each of these four stages was obviously much greater. The gangs were subdivided, each of the sub-gangs worked under a foreman, and the four basic structures operated each under a specialized site agent.

On one of our contracts for individual houses outside of Pietermaritzburg, probably in 1971, a few of us were sitting in a caravan on site, because it was raining 'cats and dogs'. We were listening to a radio broadcast, there was no TV yet in South Africa, of one of the later moon landings. When one of our young drafts-ladies looked out of the window at the terrible rain, she pronounced amidst the general excitement a really profound statement of human compassion: "These poor chaps, what a lousy weather they are having!" It took a moment for us to explode laughing. Her comment, I thought, was much more meaningful than Shepard's golf stroke, surely the most expensive one ever.

Every year our large external auditing firm invaded our offices like a swarm of locusts. A group of about ten accountants, under the leadership of one of the partners, took apart my carefully crafted annual accounts. Needless to say, I had to watch them like a hawk, to prevent them from wrecking my skillful constructions to avoid paying unnecessary company taxes.

One year the agent-in-charge, sorry, the partner-in-charge reported to his boss, that during this year's audit I had behaved almost humanly. Nice, feeling to be appreciated! Like when the family doctor came for a house-visit when I had the flu. Yes, that actually was possible in those days, and you did not even have to rob a bank to pay him.

During my time with this group of companies I flew every year during my annual leave for a month to Germany, mainly to buy stamps and covers of the Southern African colonies and protectorates of the British Empire. These were very much cheaper in continental Europe than in Britain or in South Africa. This was normal for the global stamp market. Stamps were always most expensive in their country of origin, provided this had a developed and prosperous stamp market.

The differences in prices covered my air tickets and the costs of staying in Europe, and then some. The thus accumulated hoard of philatelic material enabled me later to start my auction business with a useful opening stock. Already at this time I regularly had placed 'smalls' advertisements to buy and to sell philatelic material in the German and the South African stamp trade papers.

One of my local customers was a German gentleman who was living with his wife no more than a hundred kilometers from us (this terminology means here the same as 'nearby'). He had built up a prosperous medium-sized business in Germany, despite his serious disability caused by having suffered from polio-myelitis in his youth.

When emigrating with his wife to South Africa, they had travelled in their camping car, a modified Volkswagen bus, all the way from Germany and through the Sahara. We had to admire their adventurous spirit. Several times they came to our house in Pinetown, and we visited him and his wife a few times in Shelly Beach, quite close to our later retirement home, and in walking distance of our regional shopping mall which we now visit every week.

Every Thursday evening, I drove to the Durban Chess Club, reported to be the largest in the southern hemisphere. This was the time of Bobby Fisher, and chess was immensely popular then. At the time we had almost two hundred chess-playing members, and the weekly attendance figure was usually above eighty players. We played, I think, in eight groups, based on our respective rankings. I managed to win a few cups in the lower groups, but I never proceeded much above the average club player's level of fourteen-hundred points.

On one of these evenings one of the younger (naturally) members brought a 'portable' computer to the meeting. This was a box the size of a small car, sorry, of about one meter by one meter, and almost half a meter high, according to my recollection.

This piece of electronic 'miracle weapon' was able to sort out the pairings in a seven-round Swiss tournament almost as fast as our Captain-of-Play managed to do it on the back of his pack of cigarettes. These calculations were straight-forward but voluminous. Therefore, they were ideal for these new gadgets. Still, it was impressive and showed what to expect in the near future in this field. The next stage in this development was reached, when I had won in one of our club competitions one of the new small chess computers.

Once a year, the club organized the Natal Open Championship. Every year I took part because it was exciting to play against top players from all over the country, and occasionally even from abroad. In one of these tournaments I won my game against the champion of the Free State province, which earned me a rating price of several hundred Rand, when this was still good money.

In another such tournament, which was split in two groups, one of about forty players with a ranking above fifteen-hundred points, and a second one for players ranked below this. Since my ranking was only around fourteen-hundred, it was a nice result for me when I won this lower group. The prize money of four-hundred Rand also did not go amiss. Coming home, my car radio was blaring out of the open car windows the 'Eroica', Beethoven's tribute to Napoleon. That was maybe slightly 'over the top'.

Some evening in the 1970s or early 80s the former chess world champion and president of the World Chess Federation FIDE appeared in Durban. He had probably been invited by the South African Chess Federation to play in a few larger cities. Our club organized a tournament with him, with about fifteen to twenty club members playing simultaneously against the ex-world champion.

To nobody's surprise he won all games, except for one draw, if I remember correctly. The list of losers, also not surprisingly, included me. But it has been a very special feeling to have played against a former world champion. I still have a cut-out of a local newspaper picture, which shows my deep concentration during this game.

This was also the time, when the Apartheid National Party became rather aggressive. First of all, they insisted that, because of the many government housing contracts we had won, it was now high time for me as the sole director of the group to learn to speak Afrikaans. When I pointed out that I already had a few languages, they were not amused. After I had reluctantly, in the interests of our companies, attended a few language sessions, I soon abandoned any pretense of a follow-up.

They also pointed out, rather insistently, that the fact that I was still not a South African citizen would in future prevent the State to award any new housing contracts to our companies, even though we were the cheapest and delivered good quality and on time, because we would be deemed to be a foreign organization. This one I deflected by informing them that no German citizen was allowed dual citizenship. Later I learned that they actually had verified this correct statement with the German embassy.

Early in 1983, after some disastrous losses on a large contract, my boss was forced to sell his fifty percent share in our holding company to Murray & Roberts, the other share-holder, and to leave the group he had created. Surprisingly, at this stage I was still the sole director of all companies in the group.

Since my style of management, which was similar to that of my boss, but was vastly different from that of M&R, I decided to resign as well, after fifteen years of ups and downs with this group. A further reason for this decision was the fact that one could clearly see in which direction the political development, and therefore the labor situation, was headed in this country.

After having successfully negotiated a 'golden hand-shake', I was finally able to fulfill my decades' long dream to start my own stamp auction business.

4

DREAM LIFE WITH DURBAN STAMP AUCTIONS

Even before I left Ilco Homes in 1983, and right from the start of Durban Stamp Auctions, my wife was participating in all basic decisions regarding this exciting but risky and worrisome undertaking. We had decided that we would run the auctions from our home, to save the costs of office premises and the times, hassles and costs of commuting.

Before we could start with any auction preparations, we decided to have a strongroom added to our house. This was to be linked to the small bedroom, which was converted into my study and the office for the auctions. At the same time, I had to begin with converting all the items of my accumulated stamp stock into about ten thousand auction lots. For this task we ordered from our local printer a large supply of small, medium and large auction lot cards, into which we pasted glassine pockets as envelopes for the philatelic material.

This took many months, financed by my generous 'Golden Handshake', which I collected for two full years on the last Friday afternoon of every month at Ilco Homes, joining-in with the managers and the foremen for the usual hour of having a drop to drink, some cheese or sausages and the camaraderie in a building company.

Simultaneously, I started to look into the possibility of using a small computer instead of employing a clerk, also because of the cost savings, but mainly because I was well aware of the dangers of employing staff in this type of business, because of the almost impossible to control risk of pilferage.

The first PCs, the Personal Computers, had just started to make their appearances. The IBM 360 had just recently been introduced to South Africa, but it was rather expensive. I decided therefore on the only other suitable piece of equipment, an Apple IIE, with 64kB RAM, 16kB ROM, two 3.5-inch floppy drives A and B using the 5.25-inch flexible disks, each with 113.5kB data storage capacity (Wikipedia).

For the younger generation, if you have ever wondered why your hard drive is called the C:\ drive: the two floppy drives A and B were the reason for that. The just quoted data capacities were no jokes, but the bitter reality of computing then!

The two disk drives had become necessary because the Apple dealer had not been able to get the originally intended 5MB hard-drive to work properly. We also bought two Epson dot-matrix printers, because of the possibility of a break-down and the probability that in this country no immediate replacement would be available when needed.

These choices were simple, since there were virtually no alternatives available. The standard configuration of our typewriter-sized Personal Computer was archaic, as illustrated above. But the move from our Burroughs main frame dinosaur at Ilco Homes to this nifty little chap was exhilarating, nevertheless, illustrating the vast progress being made by the computer industry. This reminded us how fast the 'electronic age' was rushing forward.

In 1983 existed no proper computer operating systems, yet. Microsoft's Windows 1.0 appeared in the United States only in 1985 (Wikipedia), in South Africa probably around the middle of 1986. Also, there were no off-the-shelf computer programs available. There was only the machine software. Everybody had to write their own applications or had them written by some computer programmer.

A young collaborator of the computer shop wrote the first programs for our auctions, based on my analysis und sizing exercises for the required and anticipated data. These things I had learned at the Burroughs machine. The sizing was now even more critical than at Ilco, because of the tiny size of our installation.

One of the programs he wrote in Basic was quite fast. It only took twenty-four hours to sort our small customer database. After my pleading with him for mercy, he shortened that to about two hours. An amazing technological advance on something our modern computers do in seconds.

My wife and I, we both tried to find our way through this for us impossible to understand labyrinth. Swopping floppies like mad, we somehow managed our first halting steps into this new electronic world. In 1984 we conducted our first public auction, utilizing our computer and programs.

In 1984 we had in Pinetown the most unusual weather of all our time in Africa. The tropical storm Domoina, a northeasterly gale force cyclone, was an extension of the Indian monsoon downpours, with winds and rains as one encounters them normally only in the tropics, and which caused severe flooding in Mozambique and here in Natal.

This catastrophic flooding laid waste to parts of both countries. Roads were submerged, and bridges had disappeared. Near our home a bridge over a brook was washed away, and this disrupted traffic badly. A nearby house on a steep slope slid down into the valley, because the builders obviously had not anchored the foundations properly into the base rock, but only into the soil cover.

All of a sudden, the roof of our house began leaking like a sieve, because the hurricane drove the rainwater underneath the roof tiles. The water was dripping into the study, exactly onto the top of my desk. At the time I was preparing the photo-plates for the next catalogue, which naturally were going to show the most important and the most valuable stamps and covers of this auction. Many of these lots were mint stamps, and their original gum was ruined by the moisture. This resulted in them losing most of their value.

The financial damage was substantial, and the insurance company paid up. But shortly afterwards they cancelled the policy and we had to continue thereafter without any insurance cover. But luck was on our side: no more serious losses of this kind to our auctions. Subsequently I was crawling for many days all over our roof, to press bitumen underneath the roof tiles to fix the leaks.

There was one further insurance problem shortly after this, when a seller's consignment parcel was stolen on the railways before it reached us. But this was covered by the post office's or the railway's insurance and had really nothing to do with us.

Our neighbor had a dog which had the nasty habit of barking repeatedly at night. When we complained, the neighbors claimed not to know what we were talking about. When it happened again, I phoned them in the middle of the night, and the nightly barking mysteriously stopped. Presumably, their dog resented to be woken like that.

Once a week we went together to town: to the post office, to the supermarket and for any other chore to attend to. As soon as my wife started to prepare for our 'outing', the dogs knew immediately what was going on. They were sitting on the balcony and they rendered their most convincing and accusing faces: "How can you do this to us?!"

Vashti, our Alsatian dog, was by now very old and became sick, suffering from cancer, as the vet told us later. She was a very clever dog, right to the end. We took her, as we had done with all our dogs, regularly on extended hikes. In the end, when it became difficult for her to walk, she would position herself in front of my legs, to indicate that she wanted to stop walking.

When we eventually brought her to the veterinarian to have her put to sleep, and when we were sitting in the waiting room, she stuck her head between my knees, something she had never done before. Did she know, or sense, what was going to happen? I had no idea, but tears started to run down my cheeks, for the first time since boyhood. And while I am typing this, I start feeling constricted again.

It must have been around this time that my wife discovered that her trusted AEG washing machine had all of a sudden given up its ghost. Panic stations! Luckily, we (my wife, of course) still had the address of the German mechanic who had connected the machine to the water in- and outlets. He eventually arrived and solved the problem within minutes. He showed us that we had become victims of a ferocious African wildlife attack!

He had discovered that a tiny mouse had made a nest for herself and her brood within the innards of this complex machine. A wire had been in her way, so she bit through it, to create more space and to be more comfortable. A perfectly efficient way for her to achieve these goals. We apologized to our sub-tenant for having disturbed her maternal bliss.

After some time it had become clear to me that a larger computer would allow us to computerize all of the auction activities by using a consolidated suite of integrated pro-grams:

- placing the stock of all of my auction lots on the computer,
- creating new auction lots,
- administration of buyers and sellers,
- assembly of lots for any one auction,
- printing the text of the auction catalogue for the printer,
- printing the address labels,
- printing invoices for the buyers,
- printing payment vouchers for the sellers,
- preparation of specialized price lists.

In 1984 or 1985 I developed a terrible lower back pain, possibly caused, or at least aggravated, by the sitting trot at which we had often exercised our horses in the arena. The surgeon fused two vertebrae together, and no more pain or trouble. But it took me two months, before I was able to continue working at full speed again, but the operation was successful to the present day.

During this time the taxman challenged our firm. He would not allow us to deduct the cost of building our strong room, claiming this was an addition to our house and increased its value. Naturally, I had to object strongly, arguing that this addition actually represented a decrease of the value, because the house looked now somewhat asymmetric and unbalanced. Furthermore, we had now lost the use of the drying and games room.

The Receiver of Revenue scoffed at such a flimsy reasoning and refused to budge. When I indicated that I would approach the Income Tax Court in this matter, the taxman withdrew his ruling. Another first in the history of the South African income tax regime, as I was later informed by Ilco Homes' lawyer, who was sitting as an assessor at the Natal provincial Income Tax Court.

We soon realized that our Apple IIE simply did not have the necessary capacities to operate an integrated suite of programs, which I considered necessary to run larger and more frequent auctions efficiently and without employees. A larger computer would allow us to combine and consolidate all of the stamp auction activities.

In 1985 or '86 our existing computer had to be replaced by one of the early towers now becoming available. Make and model are forgotten, but it had already a phenomenally improved hard drive of 35MB. I do not remember what the operating system was, but I suspect it was probably dBase IV, which was then popular.

The computer manager of Ilco Homes had now started to write a proper suite of really useful programs for us, based on my sizing exercises (still vitally important!) and my program analyses. He used COBOL as a programming language. These programs were, naturally enough, full of bugs, which we had to sort out over time. In the end, after a few years and very high costs, we had a suite of programs for stamp auctions which was excellent, in my humble opinion.

Humble? What the heck! I was really proud of having been able to provide the analyses and sizing exercises for these programs, even though I had not been able to write the programs themselves.

My main job was to describe and to value the auction lots, to select them for the catalogue of the next auction and to prepare the lay-out of the photo plates for the more important items in this auction. These, the commercial printer later photographed (or scanned?) and incorporated into the catalogue printing. I insisted that they would fit the standard letter-size oblong envelops, which saved us oodles of money on postage.

My wife had to type the about forty text pages of the auction catalogue on her old portable typewriter which she had brought with us from Germany. This was a back-breaking kind of job for her every month. Eventually, we bought an IBM electric typewriter, which made life a little easier for her. Surprisingly, in those days one could still sell a second-hand German portable typewriter in South Africa for a decent price.

Finally, it was the printer's job to scan (or photograph?) the typed catalogue pages and the photo plates. In the mean-time we had bought the stamps for posting the finished catalogues, printed the address labels and pasted them and the stamps onto the envelopes. As soon as the printers were finished with the printing, we collected the catalogues and filled the several thousand prepared envelopes and brought them to the post office.

This reminds me: one day, when I went to buy the stamps for a catalogue run, I had 600 Rand on me. When it was time to pay, the money was gone! I was alone on this occasion, and a young African girl had stood behind me in the queue. She had been the only one who could have stolen the money out of my banana-bag. This was a lot of money in those days. I still cannot figure out how she managed to do it. And why did she do this to such a nice man!

With all this going on we still found the time to go one or two times a week horse-riding. On one of these outrides I had a bad fall, when my horse Man of War stumbled over Nera, one of our dogs. While everybody else would have broken his collar bone, I had to experience something more complicated: the tendons connecting the clavicle to the shoulder bones snapped! Not too serious, but a stark warning. I was at this stage totally dependent on my ability to write the auction lot descriptions onto the lot cards, to enable my wife to type the catalogues. So, I did the sensible but sad thing and stopped riding.

Our little auctions rolled along nicely, but it was all a bit too much for the two of us, since we also wanted to have some time off from the business. We decided therefore to have the auctions from now on only every three months, but with more lots per auction instead.

Harassing all the stamp dealers which I knew in the country for auction material, we could now start the business properly, particularly since we also received more and more auction material from our buyers inside and outside the country. Even a few overseas dealers had now started to submit their material.

After a few years we progressed to the final computer of the stamp auction business. The name of the manufacturer is forgotten, and the agents went bankrupt shortly after our purchase. This was our first desktop computer, which provided further improvements in speed, applications and capacities. It was probably running now on Windows 3.1. We were still using our trusted original Epson dot-matrix printer of the Apple IIE installation.

We were finally able to print the catalogue text, ready for the commercial printers, instead of my wife having to type it. Now she was finally relieved of this Sisyphus work and we could also sell the electrical IBM typewriter, because we could now utilize the WordPerfect computer program and our printer. We now held auctions every three months, the turnover had multiplied, and the firm was finally properly established. But preparing the catalogues for mailing and dispatching the lot to the Post Office still took us more than a night and a day.

The fact that the catalogue text was now computer-created, enabled us during the following years to fly for some short holidays to the Indian Ocean islands of Mauritius and Réunion. A pleasant side-effect was that these flights on their way from Johannesburg made a stop-over at the Durban, obviating the otherwise necessary hop to Johannesburg airport, if one wanted to fly anywhere outside the country.

Particularly the Réunion stay was very interesting for us. We had hired a car through the travel agent and were able to really explore this island thoroughly, with its peculiar mixture of French, Indian and, to a lesser extent, African people and cultures. The original name of the island, as part of the colonial empire of the French kings, was Île Bourbon. Later, at the time of Napoleon, it was occupied by the British. The present name was reinstated when French rule was restituted in the 1830s.

The scenery was breathtaking, but the local French-speaking people gave us the impression of being aloof. When we had enquired, in English, about something from a bank teller in the capital St. Denis, we were rudely asked: "Why did you come here if you cannot speak French?". A symptom of an inferiority complex, maybe? The white population was very proud of the fact that the island was an Overseas

Department of France, even though it was in Africa. We found out later that France was heavily subsidizing the island's population, a mixture of Whites, *Creoles* (of mixed blood) and Africans, descendants of former slaves.

Mauritius was less controversial for us, since we could speak English to the people. The official language here was English, and everybody understood us, even though the majority of the mixed-race inhabitants spoke *Creole*, just as the people on Réunion. This language is a variety of French, which was spoken by the indigenous people of the French colonies, similarly to the Pidgin English of the British Empire.

Sitting at the breakfast table on the open-air veranda of the hotel, we were entertained by a flock of sparrows. They were not tame, of course, but they were so used to people that they joined us at our meal, sitting patiently on our table. I do not think they were trained and provided by the hotel management for the entertainment of the guests, but it is more likely that they were self-employed, only interested to fill their stomachs. But they were much fun to watch, and to feed a little on the side. Another species of birds we were interested to watch were the local bulbuls with their red vents. The same species in South Africa had yellow ones.

After we had explored the capital Port Louis, the hotel recommended an Indian taxi driver to us, whom we hired for a few days. He took us to all the must-see places on the island. This was more comfortable, and only slightly more expensive, than hiring a car and doing all the hauling and exploring ourselves.

The history of this island is also interesting. Originally it was occupied, but not properly settled and colonized, by the Dutch, as a stopover for their ships sailing from Holland to Batavia, the present-day Indonesia. They called the island Mauritius, after their Prince Maurice van Nassau. After the French had later occupied and settled this island, it was called the Isle de France. They left their *Creole* language as an inheritance to the present day, spoken by the majority of the mixed-race inhabitants.

At the end of the Napoleonic rule the British added the island to their motley collection of colonies in the Indian Ocean, and English became the official language, used mostly by the officials and businesspeople. The new rulers changed the name back to Mauritius, to wipe out the detested French heritage.

The European inhabitants were mostly descendants of the French occupation period, whereas only very few from the Dutch period were still to be found, and the British were mostly involved in finance, commerce and administration, and had either no time or not enough interest to think about progeny. After all: "We are British". Instead, their ancestors imported hundreds of Indian 'coolies' to work the sugar cane plantations. The offspring of these semi-slaves represented now the vast majority of the island's population. They were speaking *Creole*, the French-based vernacular, as did most of the numerous mixed-blood people.

Why *Isle de France*, but *Île Bourbon* at *Réunion*? My guess is that the 's' in '*Isle*' was dropped because it was or became mute. The *accent circonflexe* of *Île* seems to point in the same direction.

Also at about this time we were invited by friends to stay with them for a few days at their holiday home just outside the Kruger National Park. It was a long trip in their Volkswagen minibus, via Northern Natal and Swaziland, with the usual border hassles to break the numbing long hours of driving.

Our stay was highly interesting for us, because we saw many plants and animals we did not experience in southern Natal. The nature at this National Park is really something to remember. We saw all the famous and important inhabitants of the 'Kruger', including lion, rhino, elephant, leopard, crocodile, hippo, giraffe, etc., but also some seldom-seen birds and some of those we do not have near home.

The Kruger National Park is not a place to travers in an hour or so. It is approximately the size of Switzerland, with a number of distinct climate zones, and consequently with a much-varied plant and animal life.

On our way back the fertilizer hit the fan. I fell ill all of a sudden, presumably from travel sickness, and all I could manage was to open the window, and my last meal went the way of all things. Unfortunately, all was splashed alongside their beautiful bus. Come to think of it, for unknown reasons they never invited us again. Maybe my wife must have done or said something unbecoming, to have upset them.

At the end of the 80s the Soviet Empire had collapsed. Since I had nothing to do with that, this should not be mentioned in this book, but it influenced the situation in South Africa. The Soviets had supported the ANC heavily for decades. This collapse had therefore severe repercussions for the political developments in this country. This did not concern us directly, but we realized what this would mean for my wife's family.

During the late 1980s we sometimes went to the Wild Coast casino complex in the Transkei, about one-hundred forty kilometers from our home. This was part of the Apartheid government's grandiose and infamous Homelands scheme, which is further explained in the next Part of this book. Our government even had built a semi-highway from Margate to the casino, which daily carried hundreds of mostly Indian gamblers from Durban to the casino.

But the casino was not the only draw card. There was also a huge hotel, an eighteen-hole golf course designed by the famous golfer Gary Player, as well as water sports and horse-riding facilities, which we also used several times. The huge grounds also offered us interesting hiking trails.

In 1990 my wife's widowed oldest sister visited us. Her husband had been about twenty years older and had passed away recently. She now proudly paraded her toy-boy companion who was about twenty years younger than her. Unfortunately, she now had a chip on her shoulder, assuming that the family resented her choice. Maybe some did, but we were quite happy for them. All the luck of the Irish to her!

Her partner was, unfortunately, a type of person, who had managed to alienate every member of my wife's family. When the three went to Durban without me, he shouted at my wife and threw a tantrum like a spoilt brat (which is exactly what he was). Back at home I had to threaten to throw him out, if he ever did anything like that again. He didn't.

As Permanent Residents we did not have the right to vote in this country, but in 1992 we were given the opportunity to vote for the first time in the coming referendum about the acceptance of the new non-racial constitution by the South Africans. In Germany, as explained in my earlier book "For All it was Worth", we never voted in any election, but this new beginning was deemed appropriate for a new start in this regard as well. We now did something very satisfying: we went to cast our vote in Pinetown in the referendum to introduce real democracy in South Africa. It was the only time, un-fortunately, when we were allowed to do so.

In 1993 we decided that it was finally getting time for us to retire, also because of the political developments in South Africa. We sold the auction business for a nice sum. After helping the new owner for a few months to learn the ropes, particularly how to use our self-made computer programs, we started looking for a place to retire to, and we also started thinking of what we would do with our oodles of free time as pensioners.

We realized also that we would be on our own as we became older, without the benefit of having any family members nearby to rely on for help. Considering all the implications, we finally settled for a retirement village complex on the Natal South Coast, the Village of Happiness, which is now called Margate Retirement Village. It was located just outside Margate, but in walking distance.

This institution had proper security, with guards and electric fencing, things which were for us of particular importance, due to the pending take-over of the country by the African majority. Nobody could predict how events would eventually develop.

A further reason for this choice was the fact that this complex had a frail-care department, with a doctor visiting daily, a matron and a number of nurses and nursing assistants. They also had all the facilities one would need as pensioners: a large library, several sports and hobby facilities, even a small chess club. And, on top of all this, a local climate which we considered ideal for us.

A nearby satellite of this organization, the Ramsgate Retirement Village, was our final choice. This smaller village was actually still under further development to double its size, with many trees, an abundance of bird life and with the beaches of the Indian Ocean in walking distance. Maybe the for us most important plus for this satellite was the fact that our investment would be safe, because of the financial guarantees which had been given this development by the prosperous local municipality of Ramsgate.

The Retirement Village concept was based on the principle of selling 'living rights' to retirees, instead of cottages. These rights guaranteed that we could remain in our cottage as long as we were screaming and kicking. A welcome side-effect of this arrangement was the fact that for tax purposes the cottages would not be assets in the hands of the residents, because legally they remained in the possession of the Retirement Village.

After some tricky negotiations with the developers of the Ramsgate Village we signed the contract to buy the 'living rights' to our cottage of two bedrooms, one with a walk-in cupboard, lounge, kitchen, two bathrooms, an integrated garage with direct access from the kitchen and an open drying yard.

Since our future cottage had been used by the developers as the show house, I argued that this was now actually a second-hand property, which naturally required a substantial discount. We also needed, without extra charges, a transparent roof over the drying yard and the installation of our air conditioning unit in what we had decided would be the stamps room and our study, to persuade us to be interested in this 'used' property.

This room we knew we needed to house the large quantity of auction lots, left over from our stamp auctions. They agreed to all that, since times were difficult for selling any real estate, because the looming takeover of the country by the Black majority had unsettled the property market of the Europeans. They also seemed a bit desperate to get out of this development, probably for the same reason.

At this time a monumental shift was taking place in this country. South Africa would soon emerge from the Apartheid past into a democratic presence, and hopefully an alike future. This was keenly looked forward to by the Non-White majority, but it was awaited with much trepidation by the White minority, particularly the Afrikaners, but partially also by the Colored and the Asian sectors of the population. New laws were passed now, to give in future the voting rights to the former Non-Europeans.

Before the coming elections in June of 1994, the law was changed and the Permanent Residents were stripped of their (passive) voting rights, which they had enjoyed only during the constitutional referendum of 1992. Instead, these rights were given to all imprisoned criminals. Ah, well, so it goes.

Everybody, but particularly the White population of South Africa, was worried about what would happen during the build-up to the first democratic elections, and if the results were not accepted by one of the parties. There were many African parties, and the African voters had had no experience with democratic election processes.

We had arranged to lease our Pinetown house to an engineer working for ESKOM, our state-owned electricity generating and distributing company. We could not sell at this time, for the same reasons as explained earlier, regarding the situation of the property market of the Europeans. We were now ready to jump into the deep water and leave Pinetown and our friends, after many happy years in our 'second homeland'.

Arranging the removal of all our belongings was another challenge, but by now we were seasoned movers. We had to dispose of much of our furniture, since our future cottage in Margate was quite a bit smaller than our Pinetown house.

We said good-bye to friends and acquaintances, particularly on the horsey side of my wife's circle. Luckily, the distance of our moving, of one hundred and thirty kilometers, was no serious problem in a country like South Africa, where farmers were used to drive this distance to see a movie at the 'local' cinema.

While on my Europe trip in the previous year, I had bought in Frankfurt a second-hand Peugeot camping car. This we were lucky to be able to leave at my brother-in-law's workshop in Neu-Isenburg near Frankfurt, while we were back in South Africa. He also kindly agreed to license and insure the vehicle for us (being reimbursed, obviously), since one could not do this without having a residence in Germany.

To try out this new acquisition, I drove to several places in Germany and to visit our son in Copenhagen in Denmark, before returning to South Africa. I was very happy with my purchase. Over the years this camper, and later a brand-new successor to it, became our home-from-home, with most of the implements of a second household hidden in its storage cabinets.

PART II

MARGATE AND OUR GYPSY HOLIDAYS IN EUROPE

1994 TO 2014

5

MARGATE AND THE PEUGEOT

In April of 1994 we arrived at our new home in Margate. It did not take us long to settle in, because our cottage was small, but big enough for the two of us. The main bedroom, with attached bathroom and dressing alcove, was usurped as our study and for the substantial stock of stamp and coin auction lots which I still had. In this room we had installed our two desks and our new air-conditioning unit, to protect the stamps from the high humidity of this area near the sea.

When I left Ilco Homes and that company was forced to downsize their operations, I had bought five large shelving units from them. These were filled with boxes full of my prepared auction lots. The computer, printer, filing cabinet and dehumidifier had also found a home in this room. Only the dressing room, more like an open walk-in wardrobe, was available for the household.

In our retirement village we only had to take care of ourselves, our car and my wife's horse, which the SPCA had given her to look after (and to ride). We did not have to worry about anything in connection with our cottage. All repairs, and even the replacement of a burnt-out bulb, were taken care of by our village free of charge.

These expenses were covered by the monthly levy, which also took care of the security and partially of the health service. The latter included the private General Practitioner, who visited the frail care section at the Village of Happiness every morning. The charges for accommodation and care in hospital and for the terminal-ill at the Frail Care facility were levied separately.

We received a monthly newsletter with all the parochial news from all of our retirement villages. There were three of these by now. Every month we enjoyed a nice selection of sometimes quite juicy jokes. The fact that we were all fossils and that many of the inmates were more or less religious did not interfere with this publication.

We did not want to take a chance before and during the elections and decided to go overseas for a while. As it turned out, our fears were unfounded, and the whole process went exceptionally well. The outcome was considered a miracle by most people, and rightly so, because political violence was prevalent before the elections, particularly in our province of Natal, where the South African majority party, the ANC, the African National Congress, was opposed by the IFP, the Inkhata Freedom Party, a traditionalist Zulu party supported by their king.

Here we did not experience a huge difference, unlike in Germany and in Johannesburg, between summer and winter temperatures. The reason for this was that we were at sea level on the coast of the Indian Ocean, which acted as a temperature buffer and balance.

In summer we could have a maximum of about thirty degrees Celsius and in winter, early in the morning, a minimum of about thirteen. As soon as the sun came out, the thermometer shot up and often we found ourselves overdressed when on the road, going for a walk or when we went shopping.

There was, however, a fly in the ointment of this perfect picture. In summer the humidity level went through the roof. We sometimes got readings of up to almost one-hundred percent saturation. This high level lasted from about the middle of January to the middle of March. But we suffered silently, and I changed my shirt for the third time today. No, just kidding! I must check with my wife whether I still have that many shirts. This question was justified in so far as I did not own a single suit anymore, because I did not need them. We had given them away to one of the Africans working in the village.

As mentioned earlier, I had bought in 1993 in Frankfurt a camping car, in anticipation of our plans as pensioners. From 1994 onwards for the next twenty years we went every year for three or four months to Europe during our winter, the European summer.

My wife's diaries over these years enabled me to write this part of my book. All details relating to these overseas stays are gleaned from calendars and diary notes made by my ever efficient and reliable wife (remember my earlier remark regarding her proofreading?). But, honestly, this was a perfectly correct and fair statement, made without fear or favor!

We were now ready to start the first of our annual European voyages, using our newly acquired but pre-owned Peugeot camping car. Utilizing the camper was not only cost-effective but allowed us total freedom of traveling and staying in any places of our choice, and for as long as we wanted. In many cases we decided at the last moment to change our itinerary or the duration of our *sojourn* at a particular place. Something we could never have done so easily with hotel bookings and most types of public transport.

Almost all our overnight stays during our European travels were at caravan or caravan parks. We used these because of the relative security and the availability of decent ablution facilities, as opposed to the dangers of 'wild camping' and the lack of such opportunities. There my wife was also able to find washing machines and small shops for basic necessities. A further important point was that most private and municipal camping grounds had a convenient nearby bus stop.

Over the years we accumulated in our camper so many items of clothing, household implements, tools and even spare parts that we in fact now had a second household. After all, over the next almost twenty years we lived in our camper for three or four months of every year, so we wanted to be comfortable and not to miss anything away from home.

We even had there a large selection of books; something like half a dozen botanical ones for my wife, and double that as suspense paperbacks for myself. Added to this were a number of French dictionaries. And, of course, I always took my laptop with me to Europe as well.

During all those years my wife's younger brother and his partner, and later his wife, collected us at the Frankfurt airport. For the first few years our camper was stationed at his workshop in Neu-Isenburg, just outside Frankfurt, during the eight or nine months when we had returned to South Africa.

Unfortunately, his first marriage had fallen apart shortly before the beginning of this arrangement. He then had met his partner. She had been an airline stewardess and she told us that she loved any excuse to visit the Frankfurt airport and its ambiance. They lived in Frankfurt in an apartment building owned by his partner's parents. Since they had enough space, they kindly invited us to stay with them for a few days, until we set sail with our chariot to venture into the unknown. In later years they moved into a beautiful home they had designed themselves and built in the Spessart mountains, about forty kilometers away. There our camper found its new temporary parking place during our time back home in Margate.

Every year we flew from South Africa to Frankfurt. But often we did not fly direct, because we wanted to use stopovers to visit as many different countries and cities as possible on our way. Particularly since this generally did not cost extra, except if we stayed overnight at the stopover city. In this way we were able to visit many places which we would have missed otherwise, because they were too far out of the way for our 'home on wheels'.

In June of 1994, in the first year of our European travels, *en-route* to Frankfurt we stopped over at Sofia, the capital of Bulgaria. More correctly, we stopped over at the airport of Sofia! Instead of being allowed to visit this beautiful old city, we were marooned in this shabby concourse.

No service personnel to be seen, but police everywhere, both uniformed and in mufti. With nothing to buy or to enjoy, except for offers to convert our foreign currency into Bulgarian *Lewa*. The paranoia of the local rulers was pathetic. And this so many years after the collapse of the Soviet Empire!

After our arrival in Frankfurt we first drove to Dresden, to check on some property which I had inherited from my paternal grandfather, and which had been inaccessible to me during the communist era. All we could achieve there for the moment was the filing of an application for information. Then we were on our way to Denmark to visit with our son and his partner.

We had driven all the way to Putgarden, on the coast of the Baltic Sea opposite Denmark, when I realized that I had left the cap of the fuel tank at our last filling station near Berlin, 324km back. Grim-faced we saddled our horses again and rushed back. The cap was still at the pump and 648km later we found ourselves back at Putgarden again, waiting for the ferry to Denmark. On this day I drove for well over 1 100km, which felt less strenuous than driving such a distance by car instead of the camper.

In this first year my wife complained in her diary that everybody was driving on the right (we are driving on the left in South Africa, a legacy of the British Empire!), how scary the dense German traffic was, and about the frightening width of our camper. By the way, the fact that we drove back home on the left never presented a problem for me in Europe, probably due to the many years of driving on the right side (sic) of the road before our emigration to South Africa.

We arrived in Copenhagen just in time for our son's birth-day. He lived with his partner in a municipal apartment block in the north of this beautiful city. We enjoyed some quality time with them.

On our way back to Frankfurt we stopped to visit my wife's aunt at Bederkesa, an ancient Viking village, and with her and her husband we visited Bremerhaven, an old hunting ground of mine from US Army times (the shark steak!). Details in "For All it Was Worth" at Amazon. She hailed, like my wife, from Rosslau. During the war she had met there a young soldier and they had fallen in love.

After the collapse of communist East Germany and the opening of the borders, and after both had lost their respective partners, she contacted him, and he invited her to join him in his large empty-feeling house. Very romantic and heart-warming! They were clearly very happy together.

Then we set off for France. We had made plans to meet up with our son and his partner in Lyon. He had phoned to say they would arrive a day late. This is the first occasion I can recall that we used a mobile phone. Luckily, my wife is rather tech-savvy. I still don't know how to properly use these newfangled contraptions. What was wrong with turning the handle on the side of the wall-mounted telephone? Never mind, I have to admit these peculiar things have their use, occasionally.

In the early evening we went exploring the neighborhood and found a small rustic restaurant, where we 'celebrated' my 70th with (for us) too much wine, returning to our camper giggling and bursting into song and dance. My wife denies this version strenuously, but she also was slightly tipsy.

Next day we went with our son and his partner sightseeing in Lyon. Afterwards, late in the afternoon, we went to the *Pont du Gard* where, for the only time in our twenty years of camping, we stood in front of closed gates of the camping ground: *"complète"* (full). Even without any knowledge of French the meaning was clear. In future we made sure to arrive at any camping place in the early afternoon, at the latest.

After finding another camping we then drove the next day to Avignon and parked the camper next to the impressive walls of these mediaeval fortifications and walked into town. A visit to the Pont d'Avignon was obligatory, and on the way back to the camper we hummed, probably all out-of-tune, the famous song.

However, we could not find our camper, despite the fact that we had correctly remembered that we had to walk along this huge wall. But we had made the mistake to listen to our son's expert advice, and we had chosen the wrong direction.

As a matter of fact, he still had a few French words and phrases from the time he had travelled in Europe after finishing school in South Africa. We, on the other hand, did not have a clue. Except, if a word showed a close relationship with an English, Latin or Italian one. It was all Greek to us.

Then we were on our way to Nimes, another one of the many towns in the south of France founded by the Roman Empire. The amphitheater was impressive, similar to the Coliseum in Rome. The French should really consider paying some hefty license fees to the Romans/Italians for all the tourist attractions left by the Imperium Romanum!

After the 'children' had returned to Denmark, we finally arrived at Agde, our destination for the next two weeks. The development of Cap d'Agde was started as a huge seaside resort in the 1970s by the French state as a project to improve the economy of the Languedoc Region. Here we stayed at the camping ground at the Centre du Naturism, the largest naturist village in Europe, which was only started in 1973. Two thousand five-hundred camping sites and one-hundred and eighty businesses (Wikipedia) comprised this large tourist development. Best of all were the deep sandy beaches which stretched for two kilometers along the gentle waves of the Mediterranean.

Agde was founded by Greek merchants in 525 BC (Wikipedia) at the mouth of the river Hérault. At the time this colony was a very important harbor and ideally suited for trading with the Gauls of its hinterland. Even at the time of Louis XIV it was still considered important. He had fortified a small island adjacent to the river mouth, which is now a popular tourist attraction.

Back in Margate, selling our Pinetown house was now not a problem and was finally achieved to our satisfaction. But for a long time I had to travel once a month to Durban to check on our four rental houses. We had to wait for the property market to pick up a bit more. Selling our four rental houses in Queensburgh was rather more difficult and took some time. Actually, it took up to the year 2000, but eventually this was also achieved to our satisfaction.

That only left the de-registration of our Management Efficiency company. The tax implications for the company, in connection with the sale of the four houses, had been sorted out by the auditors and we did not have to pay any tax on the capital profit. Finally, we were able to relax and concentrate on our next task, settling into our retirement home.

During this time we learned that the new owner of our Durban Stamp Auctions had become a 'crack' addict. Very quickly he had completely broken down. He eventually was murdered while trying to buy drugs in Hillbrow, the Johannesburg suburb, where we had first lived for a year, after arriving in this country. This area had by now gone almost completely 'African' and had unfortunately become a drug and criminal den.

This tragic event brought home to us how lucky we had been with our son who was of the same age group as this poor chap. His business now folded almost immediately, because in stamp dealing trust is of paramount importance.

In 1995, back in Europe again, we paid another visit to Dresden, but the hoped-for huge inheritance turned out to be a *fata morgana*. I could have claimed compensation for the land which my grandfather's apartment block, destroyed in the 1945 bombing of Dresden, had occupied. This land was after the war expropriated by the East German state. But the municipal fees, accumulated since the end of the war, exceeded the assessed land value. These real estate values were frozen at the 1934 level. In any case, no claim for compensation for the apartment block was possible, since the insurance excluded war losses. Nice bit of skullduggery, I thought.

This was the first year of the Schengen Agreement, which provided for free travel over the boundaries of the first five signatory countries (Wikipedia). From now on this saved us a lot of hassles, particularly as more countries joined in later years.

We spent another week again with our son and his partner in Copenhagen. We were sleeping in our camper, as almost always when visiting somewhere. One day the lock on the camper's rear door was jammed and had to be opened and replaced by a local plumber. An expensive experience!

A few months earlier our first grandson had been born. It was a moving moment for me when, lying on the bed, I held this tiny addition to the family in my arms!

One of the first things we undertook, after arriving again in Cap d'Agde, was to join a bus tour to Andorra. This being officially an independent state, people traveling there from France or Spain were allowed to bring back with them a limited quantity of tax-free alcoholic beverages. This explains why a very large bus was needed for this journey. French people go for bargains just as much as everybody else, apparently.

Andorra is sitting astride the top of the Pyrenees at a very high elevation. Coming from the seaside, we were not dressed for the cold we encountered there, and I had to buy a pair of jeans, in addition to a mediocre bottle of Andalusian wine. Leaving Andorra, the French customs ordered everything unloaded and confiscated a huge amount of alcohol, but they ignored our single bottle of wine.

Shortly after settling down in Margate again, my wife was lucky to receive from the SPCA a horse to take care of. Sunplume was elderly and had been abused. My wife now again had a baby to look after, and to take her on outrides, unfortunately mainly through the banana farms. The wild African scenery we had so enjoyed in Pinetown was just not available here within horse-riding distance.

The whole of the Natal South Coast area had been built-up over the years and had largely become a pensioner's reservation. Further inland we had a many kilometers deep strip of agri-cultural land. Only beyond this started the true African landscape, dramatic and breath-taking.

Lately, we had discovered in Margate a trendy small restaurant, *La Petite Normandie*. Unfortunately, the owner, a French lady, was murdered shortly afterwards, and the restaurant remained closed and the house appeared boarded-up since then. What a pity!

We now joined a group of hikers in their once a week nature walks and we joined them in their nature walks. Usually we were twenty to thirty participants, but there was not a single Non-European amongst us, even though they would have been very welcomed.

During the years, we had developed in Margate the habit of going for a standard walk of nine kilometers at least once a week, weather permitting. Standard, because we did not have a genuine choice of alternative walks. This consisted of a long walk down a valley to the beach. Then we followed the coastline to Margate. Along this stretch we passed a typical South African view; a beach swimming pool next to the surf. This was a large concreted construction, designed in such a way that the waves could spill over the sea-side wall at high tide.

On the way back our walk followed a small creek up to the dunes which the ocean had piled up eighty million years ago. Then we drudged past the Village of Happiness back to our own little paradise.

Up to now my wife had to use glasses with extremely thick lenses. The bottom of a wine bottle conveys a relevant idea! Laser treatment had now become available and the eye specialist was able to correct her severe problem by implanting lenses. I was very happy for her that she could now abandon those terrible spectacles. Next problem was still her hearing. The operations in Germany had improved things somewhat, but the middle-ear damage was too severe, and hearing aids became now indispensable.

We were not allowed to have dogs at our place, but because of all our overseas travels we could not have had one anyway. You have already made the acquaintance of the mole-rats which had dug a huge underground lair in our garden in Pinetown, which eventually caved in and created a substantial pit. As we soon found out, some similar little critters also lived on our new property. With our front door standing open in summer, one day one of them decided to investigate what goodies could be found in a cottage like ours. We had a heck of a time to persuade this veritable monster to leave our home again. For a casual observer it would have been hilarious to watch or attempts to persuade the unwanted visitor to get lost.

In 1996 we started with private French lessons. First with an Italian gentleman, who had studied in Paris. He grew up in Frosinone, where I had in my youth served as a soldier. Later we switched to a German lady, who had lived in France during the German occupation, probably as a 'Nachrichtenhelferin', a female auxiliary army volunteer. She was an 'esoteric' believer, who was convinced to have been a Huguenot in a previous life. She had some other believes, which were in our eyes rather peculiar. By now, we had joined a French conversation group, but we battled and after only a few sessions, we gave up.

We carried on with our weekly nature trails with the large group of like-minded people. Also, all our other more or less mundane activities continued as before. We still kept ourselves busy and reasonably fit. But we could not kid ourselves about the relentless march of time, meaning to get older.

However, we were lucky to be still healthy and able to do more or less what we wanted. It was also fortunate, that we did not have to worry much about the political and economic situation and future of our host-country. We figured, things would probably remain on an even keel during our lifetime. Touch wood!

Back in Cap d'Agde, we participated in a number of bicycle tours, including one of seventy-five-kilometers along the Canal du Midi to Beziers. There the waters of the canal were lifted, via eight lock chambers, across an aqueduct over the river Orb. This amazing construction was ordered by Colbert, the finance minister of King Louis XIV, and all this was accomplished in the seventeenth century.

This was one of the finest canals in Europe and a UNESCO world heritage site. It connected the Atlantic near Bordeaux with the Mediterranean at Séte. On its way it overcame a height difference of one-hundred meters by way of numerous locks. Cargo boats used to enter the estuary of the Gironde at Bordeaux, sailed up this river and then up the Garonne to Toulouse, where the canal proper started.

Beziers, founded 575 BC (Wikipedia), was the scene of one of the most horrific massacres of the Middle Ages (and there had been many of those!). In the thirteenth century a large number of Cathar heretics had found refuge there. A combined Papal and Royal crusade army against them committed the murder of twenty thousand inhabitants and the razing of the town, including all the churches.

When the commanding general was contemplating whether to storm or to burn down the cathedral, with hundreds of heretics sheltering inside, he asked the papal legate how to avoid killing the true Catholics together with the heretics. The priest is reported to have replied: "Let's kill them all. God will know who the true believers are".

Our usual stay of about six weeks at Cap d'Agde was uneventful otherwise. Thereafter we travelled via Nice, Monte Carlo and Ventimiglia to the Toscana in Italy. This road along the Mediterranean coast was unbelievable. Tunnel after tunnel, one hairpin curve after the other, and always the impossibly blue Mediterranean on our right.

One could have written a whole book, or at least a whole chapter, about the towns and landscapes of the Toscana, but I was in a dilemma here: how to balance volume with brevity? And this same problem existed throughout all our travels in Europe.

In 1997 we started the year with our second holiday to Mauritius and Réunion. Since the 'holiday' term is rather an oxymoron for pensioners, I therefore correct this to 'trip'. We were using Air Mauritius and flew direct from our Durban airport. We explored the island on foot, by taxi and by bus, but we also used the gym and a Jacuzzi at the hotel, and we went several times for a swim in the warm Indian Ocean.

We took a bus to the capital of Port Louis and wandered through the (smelly!) market and through town. Very British Empire-looking. We visited all corners of this tropical volcanic island. Remarkable was a large Chinese gambling establishment. The rather large Chinese minority on Mauritius seemed to be quite interested in this past time.

But we also visited the remote stretches of Mauritius, which presented quite a different picture; that of an Indian district whose inhabitants spoke a French dialect. We were able to use our sparse French, but we were happy to note that practically everybody also understood English.

The highlight for my wife was naturally the world-famous Botanical Garden of Pampelmous*e*. A huge area, with thousands of different indigenous and imported plants. I remember particularly well a large pond with huge waterlilies, but there were many more interesting and rarer specimen. A rather obnoxious but very knowledgeable Indian guide showed us the rarest plants of the Garden.

From Mauritius we flew to the island of Réunion, a short hop of just one-hundred seventy-five kilometers. We tasted fresh coconuts and other specialties, and we explored this smallish island on our second holiday there by hired car. We visited, among many other sites, the capital of Saint Denise and the plateau of the Plaine des Cafres, the 'Plane of the Kaffirs', the name referring to a settlement of escaped African slaves.

Next destination was the volcano Piton de la Fournaise, the 'Bellows of the Furnace', which was still very much active. It erupted quite often, when red-hot lava was flowing down a high and steep side of the volcano into the sea, as could be studied at the nearby museum.

Unfortunately, it was dormant during our visit. Driving over the lava cinder field near the caldera of this volcano one of our tires got slashed to ribbons. I almost suspected that the local tire dealers had arranged for the most recent eruption, to produce these vicious lava cinders. Crafty chaps!

The famous vanilla plants of this island we visited in a specialized commercial establishment. On our second holiday on Réunion we had picked up enough French by now to show our willingness to learn the language. And that made this time a huge difference to the attitude shown by the locals.

By mid-June we were off again to Europe, this time with a stop-over in Vienna. I was looking at some places I remembered from my involuntary stay in 1943. But this time we also visited Schönbrunn, the summer residence of the Austrian-Hungarian double-monarchy.

In Frankfurt we bought two bicycles. They were basic, with just three gears, which was all we needed. They also had what we used to term during my high school time "semi-balloon tires". In previous years I had two falls with the bicycles my brother-in-law had lent us, because of their narrow tires.

Next stop was Paris. Their municipal camping ground was in the Bois de Boulogne, next to the river Seine. Bus and subway brought us to the city center. During this week the weather was so horrible that we had to buy an electric heater, as I was worried about using the built-in gas heater. But we had one sunny day and used this for a boat trip on the Seine. Actually, these 'boats' are quite large ships, packed with tourists like sardines.

It would be impossible to list all the sights we visited. If you would look up a tourist pamphlet, we would have visited most of the ones listed there, including a very worth-while sight-seeing round trip on board a tourist bus.

Later this year we received in Margate the first family visit from Germany. Tante Hanni and husband stayed with us for a few weeks. We took them to our own South Coast gambling casino and entertainment complex, to a crocodile farm and to Durban. Finally, we drove them to the 'Thousand Hills' Zulu area. She immediately became friends with all the Zulus in the village, and only the color of her skin distinguished her from her new friends. No, sorry, they also wore, and some did not wear, very different clothes.

We also went with them to the 'Space Center' outside nearby Port Edward. This establishment had a collection of working telescopes on display, but unfortunately the sky was overcast. So, apart from a decent dinner, there was nothing much to see otherwise.

Then we went with them to Giant's Castle in the Drakensberg Mountains and to the Umfolozi Game Reserve in Northern Natal, where we saw giraffes, elephants, rhinos and plenty of baboons and monkeys, but unfortunately neither lions nor hippos.

In March of 1998 my wife's older brother and his wife visited us for a few weeks. We took them more or less to the same places we had visited with Tante Hanni. Another very enjoyable few weeks with members of the family.

After a direct flight to Frankfurt, we visited this year our son in Copenhagen again. Our grandson Frederik was now already three, and it became obvious to me that he would become a worthwhile member of the family. Was there any other 'work in progress'? Later this year our first granddaughter Amanda made her appearance on the family tree, greatly approved by her grandparents.

At about this time Paddy, a geologist residing in the area, started a group of nature-inclined people in the district. Since I was interested in geology, particularly in rocks and minerals, but also generally in natural activities, we joined them. Unfortunately, he was the only professional in the group, and only of limited help to me. Maybe every two or three months we participated in some meeting or other, and quite a few times we went on exploratory walks with this knowledge-able man, who also published valuable notes regarding these outings.

In 1999 we went to Spain and visited Granada and the Alhambra.

Both provided really unforgettable memories. Seville with her mixture of Muslim and Christian architecture and history was rather daunting, with the huge cathedral being oppressive (my wife's diary) rather than being beautiful.

Here a gypsy woman tried one of the oldest tricks in the book on me. As always, I had our valuables in my 'banana' bag in front of me. She pushed a piece of cardboard over my bag, which she pressed against my belly; and she kept babbling incessantly. When I turned away, she followed me like we were Siamese Twins. Eventually I had to stymie her advances with some choice English curses. It was always a good thing to propagate and teach the usage of English to the indigenous!

Then we spent some time in Gibraltar, going to the southernmost point in Europe and looking at the northern coast of Morocco and the Atlas Mountains. For some forgotten reason we did not ascend the top of the 'Rock'.

The town was a peculiar mixture of English and Spanish influences. Newspapers of both countries were on sale and the shops were full of goods from both. But at the border post things were different. There was a definite tension to be observed, due to the previous stand-offs between the two countries.

We had been to Mirabella and other places with large populations of British expatriates living in the south of Spain along the Mediterranean coast. There the people seemed to be completely relaxed with each other.

We, and particularly I, started to have more doctor appointments than before, and I needed to take more medicinal supplements. Now I started to have regular check-ups regarding weight, blood pressure, glucose and cholesterol levels, TG and prostate checks.

We also looked after our health in more natural ways, walking as much as possible, including going with our hiking group on long walks. The car was only used when we undertook our weekly shopping forays at a shopping center nearby. Or if it was raining or the distance was excessive.

With everything we always tried to follow a simple motto of mine: Everything in moderation; eating, drinking, sleeping, working. I suspect that there used to be something else, but I just cannot remember.

On Monday afternoons I walked to the Village of Happiness, about four kilometers both ways, to play chess as part of a small group of aficionados. My wife still enjoyed her horse *Sunplume*, but eventually gave my wife problems with her arthritis, when she could not be ridden any longer. This was a sad time for my wife, when she had to return the horse to the SPCA.

She (my wife) now started fabric painting as well. No rest for the wicked! During all these years I occasionally submitted stamp lots to various auction houses in Europe and here in South Africa.

In South Africa I had always missed the good old German rye bread. My wife had finally discovered one to my liking, the 'Berliner Landbrot', in a Margate supermarket. It was not exactly what we had been used to, but it was a huge improvement to the local brown bread, which for my taste contained too much air. To be on the safe side, because the supply was unreliable, we bought from then on ten loafs at a time and nine of them we placed in the deep freeze.

In late 1999 we awaited with interest the coming of the new century and millennium as well, just as most other people. The newspapers were full of heated discussions about when exactly they would start, in 2000 or in 2001. Eventually, the 'experts' reached agreement that 1 January 2001 would be the first day of the twenty-first century and of the new millennium.

6

MARGATE AND THE FIAT

Early in 2000 my wife's older brother from Düsseldorf visited us again with his wife for a few weeks. This time we went with them to Port Elizabeth, to visit their father's friend from Rosslau. For about five hundred kilometers the drive there was as untypically South African as possible; dense fog and rain almost all the way there. We also spent a few days with them in the Drakensberg, where we undertook some interesting hikes. Additionally, we showed them the famous local rock paintings by the Bushmen.

Later that year we visited the Saddle & Trout Resort, where I (foolishly) had bought a time-share. The stay was very dis-appointing for us, because there was no possibility of any nice walks, and no horse rides were available, either. And lazing around the pool or sitting in the bar was just not appealing to us.

This year, trading in the Peugeot, we bought in Frankfurt our new and final camper, a slightly larger Fiat. This time we also invested in a retractable awning with side-panels and a double bicycle rack on the back of the vehicle.

From there we went to Magdeburg, where we stayed with Tante Hanni's daughter and her husband. She had arranged for my wife to see an eminent professor in Halberstadt about her long-term hearing problems. They also showed us a unique feature: the world's largest structure to lift big riverboats from the *Mittellandkanal* into the river Elbe, and vice-versa.

Next, we went to Thyborøn, where our son had now settled-in with his family. He had earlier graduated from the university of

Copenhagen with, first, a Bachelor, then his Master and finally with his PhD degree. A fantastic achievement of his, and against all the financial odds!

He had obtained employment in this hometown of his wife, as a micro-biologist with Cheminova, the largest enterprise in this small fishing town. And there was another happy achievement to report; our second grandson William had established his presence in this world.

This year in Denmark I did not pick up any rocks, since there practically ain't any, except on the beaches. And these had been imported from Norway and Sweden fifteen thousand years ago by the glaciers of the last Ice Age.

On our way to the South of France I made the mistake of staying overnight with our camping car at the freeway rest area at Orange. While we were sleeping, somebody had opened the door of our camper and had stolen our blank checks, bank cards, cash and, apparently, our passports.

I suspected a grandfatherly man, who had been sitting with a boy of about ten in the restaurant. Panic buttons, but our loss was limited to several thousand German Mark. We had called the police and they were helpful, but unsuccessful. Amazingly, I was able to communicate with them in French. To our great relief we found on the next day our passports amongst our music cassettes.

In 2001 we met Andrew on our nature walks. He was a general geologist, as opposed to the highly specialized mining variety one usually met in South Africa. His practical knowledge and experience were fantastic. When I had started to properly collect rocks, he became my mentor.

This year in Europe we went to Italy again. On the freeways we noted something peculiar: in Germany everybody used to always complain about the Italian 'racing' drivers, but here we spotted a number of very slow-moving cars. Going at an annoying sixty kilometers/hour, where one hundred-twenty km/h were allowed and were easily possible.

The Forum Romanum and the Coliseum were not only impressive, but were so full of historical importance, that the mind she boggled. As a schoolboy I had seen pictures of Trajan's column in our history book, but the real thing was much more intimidating. Naturally, we had to visit St. Peter's Cathedral and the Vatican, the Pantheon, the Trevi Fountains and the Spanish Staircase as well. But we also went to the Roman flea market, the largest one we have ever been to.

On our way again, we stopped at Frascati and Tivoli, and I wanted to have a look at Polombara Sabina, my old stomping grounds of the last war. But I recognized almost nothing. In the place of the trattoria, where we had occasionally partaken a few drops of wine, was now a high-rise apartment block. Disgusting! Similar my lack of recognition of anything in Fara Sabina.

We carried on to the Rimini area, where I had fought as a soldier, and had been locked-up as a Prisoner of War. But our camp complex at Bellaria had been swallowed up by the local development juggernaut and sported now an ugly indifferent shopping center.

We then invaded the nearby tiny Republic of San Marino, which fortunately was still unchanged since the Middle Ages. After climbing the steep approaches, we had a fantastic view of Rimini and the Adriatic Sea. In Ravenna I wanted to visit the mausoleum of Theodoric the Great, a picture of which I had also seen in our history book. Here, for a change, the picture had looked more impressive than the relatively puny original.

Back home, my wife's younger brother and his partner (from the Spessart) came to visit us for two weeks. We had booked them a room at the 'Cote d'Azur', a block of holiday apartments in Margate, close to the beach and to a natural tidal pool.

We went with them for a week to the Drakensberg, the mountain which forms the several hundred kilometers long geological backbone of Southern Africa. This typical African environment with far-reaching views impressed them very much.

Naturally, we also showed them Durban with the Indian Market and on the way, a crocodile farm with hundreds of fully grown and thousands of baby Nile crocodiles.

In 2002 we had left home for Europe already at the end of May because we joined my brother-in-law and his partner for a two-week tour of the Greek Islands, which our future sister-in-law had arranged. First stop was Santorini, the island which consisted of half the remnants of the walls of a huge volcano. Its explosion had in the antique era destroyed much of the pre-Greek civilization.

We enjoyed a pleasant walk of ten kilometers along the rim of the ancient volcano caldera and admired the brilliantly white-and-blue houses and churches, splendid against the unbelievably blue sky and the sparkling Aegean Sea.

Back in Germany our camper trundled us first through Thuringia, where we explored Eisenach, the birthplace of Martin Luther, and then to Weimar, with the surprisingly small houses of

Goethe and Schiller, the two German poet princes. We then visited the son of Tante Hanni, who took us to the Colditz castle, famous for the successful escapes of Allied air force personnel during World War II.

Thereafter followed visits to Waldheim and the Kriebstein fortress, as well as the village of Ehrenberg, where I unsuccessfully attempted to gain some background information about the family of my paternal grandfather. The unfriendly counter personnel (of the recently deceased infamous GDR) were not interested to help the despised capitalist Westerners.

After visiting the family in Denmark again for a short while, we loaded the camper onto an overnight ferry and sailed from Esbjerg for England. Staying a few days near Oxford, we boarded one of the red double-decker busses and enjoyed the imposing old college buildings of this famous university, which we had often marveled-at in the Chief Inspector Morse TV shows. Yes, I had loved this series, with this crusty old scoundrel.

Next stop was Stratford-upon-Avon, where we were impressed by the house where Shakespeare was born. The size of the rooms and doors were quite similar to what we had earlier seen at Weimar in Germany, when we visited the houses where Goethe and Schiller had been born, but almost two hundred years later.

Apparently, the average height of the people in Europe had not much increased during this period. Probably, because they were weighted down by the heavy responsibilities of having to replenish the population after the Hundred-Year-War between Britain and France, and the Thirty-Year-War in Germany between Catholics and Protestants, as well as the numerous outbreaks of the 'Black Death' and other, similar plagues.

Arriving finally in the Canterbury area, we were pleased to see that the English had named their towns of Margate and Ramsgate after our homologous villages here in South Africa. A nice welcoming gesture towards the South African tourists. The Archbishop wasn't at home at his Cathedral, so we proceeded to Dover and caught the ferry to Calais, and back to Europe proper.

After our return from Europe, we had a candle-lit dinner with a German couple living in our village. The lady of German-Estonian parentage was always full of *joie de vivre*.

Sadly, our friend's husband soon showed advanced symptoms of Alzheimer's Disease. This very dehumanizing illness had severe consequences for her husband, but was even more debilitating for her, particularly since his suffering lasted for almost ten years. She was forced to engage two nursing helpers to assist her.

My wife's diary entries remind me that at this time we still had our internet connection via our telephone line, resulting in being without a phone while on-line. The connection was poor and often broke down. It was also expensive, because of our phone company Telkom having a monopoly.

We had coincidentally discovered in our neighborhood another attraction; a butterfly farm. This establishment housed not only most of the indigenous butterfly and moths species, but they also bred them for later release into the wild. Considering how important butterflies are in nature, this was a very commendable enterprise and had to be admired and supported.

Early in 2003 the hard drive of our computer had crashed, and we had to buy a new machine. I insisted that the dealer installed Windows 98 because, according to our son, the now available versions (Millennium and another one) were not stable enough. This older and trusted operating system served me very well for many years.

The partner of my wife's younger brother from the Spessart phoned one day, after they apparently had had a few drinks, and told me that they planned to visit us on my wife's birthday, but for me to say nothing to her.

On the day of their arrival at the Durban airport I told my wife that my new computer was ready for collection in town. After I had attended to that, I collected them at the Arrivals Gate and on our return to Margate, my wife's eyes were like soup plates, when she saw our guests. It was a wonderful birthday surprise for her.

We celebrated at the 'Cavern Hotel' in the Drakensberg, where we had a very enjoyable stay. A long and hot walk (thirty-two degrees Celsius) brought us to the Cannibal Cave near the top of the mountain. The view was marvelous. We had an expensive bottle of red wine with us, which on my back did get heavier and heavier along the way. After a leisurely picnic we skinny-dipped in a natural pool within a small stream and subsequently fell exhausted into our beds.

At the nearby 'Royal National Park' (less than one thousand kilometers away!) we admired the prehistoric Bushmen rock paintings and visited the Tiger Falls (tigers in Africa?).

On the way back we stopped at the private Tala Animal Reserve, but this was too touristy for our liking, even though there was much to see. Next day, we visited with them a Zulu *sangoma*, an African shaman, who gave us a remarkable performance. He tried to metamorphose my brother-in-law into a lion or something, which unfortunately did not work out.

Another surprise for my wife followed. I had booked flights for all of us to Cape Town, which was a first for them. Table Mountain was the thing to do. The ascent by cable car was spectacular, as was the view from the top.

The Waterfront development was another must-see, with restaurants, shops, night clubs and other attractions. This modern development was the rejuvenation of the old and rather dilapidated harbor quarter.

We rented a car and drove to The Boulders, where hundreds of penguins had established their home amongst the beach rocks. To observe them was a special treat. They were not tame but had rather got used to people. After a short stay at Hermanus and at Hout Baai we continued to Cape Point, the peninsula which separated the Atlantic from the Indian Ocean.

At least, this is, in my opinion, the correct definition, because here the waters of the two oceans meet. But this claim is open to interpretation. According to a different viewpoint, the separation of the seas happens at Cape Agulhas, because this is the most southern point of Africa.

During a previous visit of this locality I was fascinated to watch how the cold northbound Benguela current of the Atlantic had flowed alongside the warm Indian Ocean southbound Agulhas current, but moving in opposite directions. Unfortunately, I was not able to show our guests this natural phenomenon. Apparently, this could be observed only under certain circumstances.

A further highlight for all of us was an open-air concert in the Botanical Gardens of Kirstenbosch. This park had been established hundreds of years ago by early Dutch settlers. It consisted not only of a practically complete collection of the indigenous local flora, but also of numerous remarkable exotic plants, primarily those from Indonesia.

The famous wineries of Stellenbosch were admired as much as the historical Fort of Cape Town and The Gardens. These were established by the very early inhabitants of the Cape as their vegetable patch, which also produced for visiting fleets and lone ships. Thereafter, our visitors boarded their return flight to Frankfurt.

Before departing for Europe again, a note in the diary reminded us to pack any scissors into the suitcases, because anything sharper than my tongue in the hand luggage would be confiscated by the airport *Gestapo*. 9/11 has really changed international air travel, to the extent that many of the safety measures bordered on the ridiculous, such as the plastic eating implements on board, or the confiscation of tiny nail or skin scissors. Has nobody explained to these jokers that it was easier to kill somebody with one's bare hands, than by using these forbidden 'terrorist' implements?

This year my wife's younger brother married his partner of many years on the Isle of Rügen, in the Baltic Sea and off the German coast, and we had been invited as witnesses. There we did not have one, but two scary experiences. No, not in conjunction with the civil nuptial procedures!

First, when we were walking under some old oak trees, a sudden violent gust of wind broke off a very thick branch, which crashed to the ground not two meters behind us.

An hour later, we were walking below the famous white chalk cliffs of Stubbenkammer, where I was looking for a nice specimen of chalk rock for my collection, when a teenager, whom we clearly could see standing at the top, threw down a boulder, which landed very near to us. What a bloody idiot!

During the next visit to the family in Denmark we went all together to a holiday resort site, where our son tried to teach his younger son how to fish. While the father was busy with the rest of his family, William was trying to wash the live bait worms. Leaning more and more forward, he suddenly was under the water, and my wife was the only one to notice the mishap. She jumped in and rescued her grandson, forgetting about the camera in the pocket of her shorts. Ah, well, she claimed she needed a new one, anyway.

Back in France we visited Puy-en-Velay, which has one of the most spectacular rock formations in Europe. A vertical granite column rising about eighty meters above the ground, with a footpath encircling this intrusion of thirty meters diameter, leading up to a tiny chapel on top. The view from there must have been unforgettable!

Now back in South Africa, we enjoyed watching the cavorting babies of the monkeys in our garden, and occasionally we saw on our walks some dolphins wave-riding the surf.

Every two years, after we had returned from Europe, we had our car serviced by a one-man mobile service firm. There was no such thing as a TÜV in South Africa. Such check-ups were left to the sense of responsibility of the car owners.

I was also repeatedly reminded that the old equipment needed more and more repairs and maintenance. Yes, the car, too. But I was referring to myself. Now I realized that I needed new glasses.

Our neighbor Anna turned ninety this year. An unlikely advanced age only a woman could hope to reach. And quite rightly so: they are kept in constant survival training, as they have to cope with men all their life. She actually managed eventually to reach her one-hundred mark. Bravo, Anna!! I wondered, how people were able to achieve such an accomplishment.

My wife kept herself busy with craft workshops, allowing me to read my French newspapers, books and magazines which I had brought back from France, and work through the chess magazines brought from Germany. The lifestyle of pensioners was quite stressful.

I just see in the diary that Richard had helped us already in this year with our computer problems. Ten years later he was still at it. Only the computers have changed.

For this year's New Year's Eve Party we stayed overnight at the home of my former boss in Kloof near Durban. Maybe a bit too formal, I thought. We definitely did not really enjoy the occasion and did not repeat the performance. But then, we were not exactly the proverbial party goers!

In March of 2004 we flew from our little airfield in Margate to Namibia, the former German colony of German-Southwest-Africa, and later the South African Protectorate of South-West-Africa. Through the travel agents we had booked a small rental car.

Sightseeing in Windhoek should have been the first task to be marshaled. But first we had to solve a major problem; we were trying to draw some local cash. The ATM did not accept our South African cards, and the bank cashier did not want to cash our check. Even though the country had created its own currency, which was linked to the South African Rand 1:1.

It took several phone calls to our bank in Margate, and two visits to a local bank in Windhoek, to obtain some local cash. Surprisingly, I do not remember any similar problems later. Did we draw enough cash for our whole stay in this country, or did our complaint break a logjam? The ridiculous part of this situation was the fact that we could easily have paid with our own money, since the South African Rand was accepted everywhere in the country.

The background for this situation was political. Namibia had just recently obtained its independence, after the collapse of Apartheid in South Africa. Logically, the two now liberated countries should have been close friends, but there were a few hiccups, possibly due to lack of political experience on both sides.

This country had only about one-and-a-half million inhabitants, and South Africa had more than fifty million. And Namibia insisted to be treated as an equal partner. On the one hand, this country had just, after many years of bloody fighting, obtained her independence from South Africa, but on the other hand, the two newly liberated countries were now supposed to be friends.

The question of the isolated South African enclave, with the harbor of Walvis Baai on the Namibian coast, had developed into an open conflict. The British had built this harbor before World War I as a counterweight to the neighboring German colonial harbor of Swakopmund. Even after South Africa had voluntarily relinquished her priced possession, the relation-ship between the two countries remained frosty, as Namibia was suspicious of the big brother.

In-between all these hassles we saw the *Christuskirche*, the *Reiterdenkmal* and the *Alte Feste*, all remnants of the German colonial past. The climate was very dry and hot, thirty-five Celsius. At *Café Schneider* we felt right at home, with German bread rolls and cakes. Yummy!

Off we went in our hired car to the one-street 'town' of Rehobot, then on to Mariental and Keetmanshoop, where we enjoyed sitting in *Uschi's Café* (my wife's first name). I had the car's clutch adjusted there and we carried on to the Fishriver Canyon, a deeply incised cut into the surrounding plateau and a further touristic must

After organizing a B&B we visited next morning the Giant's Playground, a wide field of large boulders strewn around and piled up helter-skelter. After that followed the Quiver Forest. These quiver trees were growing in such a way that their branches were used by the Bushmen as quivers.

We only found three tarred roads in the whole country. These main roads were so devoid of traffic that each passing car was greeted with waving hands or flicking headlights. The rest were badly corrugated sand and gravel roads. These corrugations across the roads lead to a terrible shaking of the entire car as soon as one exceeded sixty kilometers per hour.

We were by now traversing the Namib desert. Surprisingly, a large herd of feral horses survived here, remnants of the fighting in the Great War. In Aus there were just a few houses, but a large *Bahnhofshotel* from German times. It was obvious in many instances, that this colony was meant to go places, but after the German colonial administration and army had left, any development came to a dead stop.

After arriving and sightseeing in Luderitz, this very German-looking town, we drove out to the ghost village of Kolmanskop. This is the location where the first diamonds were found in this colony before World War I. The settlement was gradually being reclaimed by the ever-shifting sands of the Namib Desert. Many of the houses were already half swallowed-up.

We now left the main road and went to Gibeon. Eighty-two thousand years ago a huge fifteen-ton meteorite had hit here and had shattered into seventy-seven large fragments over an area of 360 by 110 kilometers. Several of these, including the largest one of six-hundred and fifty kilograms and nine cubic meters, were exhibited in the middle of this small town, where this information was displayed. Several other fragments are on display in Windhoek.

Driving on some secondary road off Maltahöhe, one of our tires was completely shredded by the road corrugations, and when changing wheels, we found that the spare tire had a large bubble in the side wall. From now on slowly - slowly, until a new tire could be bought in Mariental. Finding any suppliers outside the capital was quite a problem in a huge country with just one and a half million inhabitants.

We wanted now to go north, but because of the huge *Sperrgebiet*, the famous blocked-off diamond fields, we first had to go all the way back to Windhoek. After passing the capital town, our next stop was Okahandja, the cleanest and most prosperous-looking small town of the country.

From there we drove to Usakos, where we just avoided running-over a warthog in the middle of the road. There I bought on the side of the street some minerals from a native. I did not want to miss the huge uranium mine at Rössing, but could not get in. *VERBOTEN.* But I found some interesting mica sheet minerals just outside the main entrance gate.

Swakopmund is another one of the modern and clean typical German-looking towns in this country, with German pubs, street names and surnames everywhere. From there, a short trip brought us to the former British colonial harbor of Walvis Bay, or Walvisbaai in Afrikaans, were I collected some sea salt crystals on the beach.

Then we had to haul us all the way back to Windhoek, to catch our flight back to Johannesburg. In these ten days we must have driven about two thousand six-hundred kilometers.

When I had to go through customs, the inspector was baffled by two large shopping bags filled with rocks and a few minerals, each wrapped in a piece of paper, with notes regarding its provenance. He jokingly enquired how many diamonds were in there, but he was satisfied with my disappointed negative reply.

Back home in Margate we had quite a few hassles with the travel agents, until we were finally reimbursed for the costs of the tire and the clutch readjustment. They were not exactly customer friendly, but dealing with a foreign country to get reimbursed was probably no fun for them, either.

This year in Europe did not warrant special mention, except for another two weeks in Paris. We just could not get enough of this place! But a person's capacity for memorable impressions is limited. On our drive out of Paris a suicidal 'Speedy Gonzales' driver shot out of an on-ramp onto the freeway, inches in front of our camper.

On another sector of the French freeway grid, a car lost a bicycle mounted on its roof which crashed down right in front of our camping car. Both these incidents could have had serious consequences!

Before leaving for home again, we were walking one afternoon through the fields outside of Frankfurt, when I re-discovered the small former US Army airstrip of Bonames. From here I often used to fly to my assignments as a management consultant working for the US Army, to Army Posts all over the northern part of the US Zone of Occupation of Germany. Sometimes, neither sitting in the helicopters nor in the small planes were particularly pleasant memories.

Now we were already in 2005. From my early days onwards, I had often problems with my weak ankles, as you may remember from the very early chapters of this story in my first book '*For All it was Worth*' on Amazon.

Sometime during this year I had become aware of somebody offering to fabricate orthopedic inlay soles, individually made for the customer's feet. They solved my problems miraculously. A bit late, one has to admit, but better late than never!

This year we had a stop-over in London on our flight to Germany. As usual for us, we meandered through the streets of this city in bitterly cold weather (for us, probably it was just under twenty degrees Celsius). Walking past Trafalgar Square and the South African embassy, we saw Big Ben and the 'Eye', about which the locals were arguing bitterly.

On our way back to the hotel we were snared by the sign of a Sherlock Holmes Bar and we ordered a "hot toddy" to get warm again. Incredulous looks by the barmaid. When we asked for a Sherry, we were likely the first in fifty years to ask for such an outlandish drink. Except if they had some South African customers, who practically lived on these beverages. We were not deterred by such lack of knowledge about the finer things in life and giggling stumbled our way back to the hotel, ignoring bravely the depressing thoughts about the extortionist prices we had just paid.

From London to Frankfurt, and we were off on another jaunt of ours, this time to the United States, for a combined two-week air and bus travel. We started our first week of the guided tour on the East Coast. On arrival in New York only my wife was photographed and fingerprinted. Apparently, I was considered too decrepit to be 'a person of interest'.

A guided bus tour of the city was instructive, but the impressions were simply overwhelming. At the Empire State Building we got off the bus and walked to Central Park, where I found a beautiful specimen of Pitch Rock, and further to Broadway, Wall Street and Times Square. Exhausted, we skipped the ascents up the Empire State Building and the Statue of Liberty.

Then we carried on to the Niagara Falls at the border between the USA and Canada. An unforgettable experience! A short boat ride below the Falls landed us completely soaked, but what a view! It was very interesting for me as a hobby-geologist to hear that the Falls were relentlessly wandering upstream, because the river current was reducing the rocky sill of the Falls more and more.

Something we experienced at this occasion had us flabbergasted. An Afro-American "lady" was checking the passports in such a way as we had previously only seen in the GDR, the German Democratic Republic, and in the communist Eastern Europe before 1990.

Now we left for Intercourse (did they have to be so graphic?), a small town in Pennsylvania, to experience the lifestyle of the Amish people. They were the descendants of a German religious sect who had emigrated to the States in an earlier century. They shunted all modern appliances, like cars, telephones and the like.

A short visit to Washington, DC followed, staying at the Hilton Hotel. We did not want to bother the President, but we had a look at his home, the White House. We also visited the Lincoln Monument and the Congress Building. The huge impressive Arlington cemetery, with the Vietnam Memorial, was gut wrenching for me.

After flying to Las Vegas, we wandered along the main road, and my wife tried her best to drive us into financial ruin, by losing ten dollars to the 'one-armed bandits'. We were dog- tired by now and fell early into our beds. So much for our excursion to the 'sin city' and the fleshpots of Las Vegas. We wondered, if something was possibly wrong with us!

Now we flew in a small plane towards the East again. On the way we glimpsed the Hoover Dam, Lake Mead and then we flew over the Colorado River, which had over hundreds of thousands of years chiseled-out from the huge Colorado sandstone plateau the marvelous Grand Canyon. We landed there and stayed for a few hours. A further must-see on this trip. The bleak impression of this wonder of nature will be remembered forever by me.

At the Yosemite Park I was able to collect a few interesting specimens for my collections of minerals and rocks. A further stop-over was Calico, a mining ghost-town. There my wife took a photo of a sheer cliff, about a hundred meters away and across a deep valley, which was suited ideally for my book "Rock ID". This was intended to facilitate the identification of rocks by the collector.

Finally, we approached the West Coast of America on our way to Sacramento, the capital city of California. The ambience of this picturesque town was much more to our taste than Las Vegas, the 'capital of tourism'.

San Francisco found us rather chloroformed from all the impressions. After 'digesting' Fisherman's Wharf we wandered by chance into Chinatown and we found a simple place to eat, with mostly Chinese customers. My wife, brave as always, used the chopsticks, but I, as usual, backed away from such outlandish and undignified behavior.

Our last stop was Los Angeles, with Hollywood the main attraction. I refused to leave my handprint in the concrete. As you probably have noticed, my recording has become more and more erratic, because of complete exhaustion by now. More dead than alive we arrived at LAX, the Los Angeles airport. This whole excursion was wonderful, but we were happy to be back in Frankfurt.

When we eventually had reached Cap d'Agde, we went after a few days by bus to the Camargue, which is home to hundreds of semi-wild white gray horses. They are not feral animals, because the owners keep an eye on them and look after these magnificent beasts.

Nearby was the walled medieval town of Aigues Mortes (Dead Waters). The name referred to the fact that the river delta of the Rhone had sanded up the harbor of Roman times. In the Middle Ages it was still fully operational, and the French king *Saint Louis* had started one of the most important crusades from here. This is how Louis IX earned the

'Saint'. The town was still largely intact. The huge expanse of empty space in front of the towering walls all around the town was most impressive.

A few kilometers further along the coast we went to *Saintes-Maries-de-la-Mer*, the town of the Holy Maries of the Sea. Legend had it that the mother of Jesus, shortly after the crucifixion of her son, was fleeing Palestine with her name-sake servant. They were shipwrecked on Malta, from where they made their way to this harbor. The twist in the tail is the fact that the European Gypsies believed that this servant was one of theirs. Every year thousands of them congregated here in honor of this perceived illustrious ancestor.

Back in Margate, some of the recurring events were the repeated cries for help to our computer consultant. It seemed there were always new problems, or I had forgotten previous solutions. In the meantime, we had realized that the digital era had bypassed us, or expressed differently, that we were simply too old for these developments.

Also regularly appearing were entries in my wife's diaries about our nature walks, and the handicraft afternoons for my wife and the chess club meetings for myself, indicating that our pensioner's routines were still in place.

In Margate we may have been living in the darkest Africa, but we also had a *Mardi Gras*, together with the annual meeting of the Harley-Davidson motor bikers from all over the country, and even from some neighboring states.

Now our study had suddenly doubled in size. No, I had not experimented with gun powder. With my years advancing relentlessly, my wife would have been burdened with an impossible task if she herself had been forced to dispose efficiently of my still very large stock of stamp and coin auction lots.

I took the plunge and placed my remaining stock with a specialized auction firm in Johannesburg. They supplied some-thing like two dozen folding cardboard boxes. When we had packed up everything, they sent a courier to collect the lot and to take it to their offices.

Overnight, the cramped study had become an airy and pleasant room to work in, after one of the ugly big shelving units had been banished into the garage, and the dehumidifier unit had been sold back to its supplier.

By 2006 I also had (sort of) learned to play snooker, and we had once a week a few games with a group of four to six gentlemen. Sometimes one of us, I mean one of the others, had a senior moment and had forgotten who's turn it was, or which ball to play.

After the customary few days in Frankfurt and the Spessart, we set off, on our way to France, for Salzburg, Austria. These were also old stomping grounds for myself from the time, after we had escaped as Prisoners of War from Italy, but I did of course not encounter any acquaintances.

Mozart's house and workplace were visited, together with one or two churches and the fortress of *Hohensalzburg* high above the river Salzach, but I skipped visiting the local prison, which I knew only too well, anyway.

In Margate, as you may remember, we even had a gambling casino nearby. Despite my previous youthful bout of gambling addiction, I never gambled again. Just watched my wife, and sometimes our guests, to feed the one-armed-bandits, while the two-armed-bandits sat in their offices and watched the crowds and the growing of their bank balances.

Once in a while we visited the local so-called Saturday flea market, which unfortunately was not a proper flea market at all, but just a weekend open-air craft market and a place for a group of sellers of new goods. A European-style flea market I have only seen once in this country, in Cape Town.

Later we travelled with my geologist friend and his wife via Kokstad and Umtata to Koffeebaai in the former Transkei Homeland, and visited the Hole in the Wall. This was a vertical free-standing thin slab of shale rock, maybe forty meters high and sixty meters long. The waves of the Indian Ocean had chiseled a large hole through this massive rock, through which the waves were spectacularly breaking, sprouting a pulsing strong jet of water.

Then we continued through Port St. John and Lusikisiki to the quaint holiday resort of Mbotyi Lodge. On our way back we travelled to Flagstaff and stopped at Bizana, the ancestral home of our friend's family. His father had been a doctor here. He told us marvelous stories about life in a distant place like that in the outgoing nineteenth and the early decades of the twentieth century.

In December we had to drive from Margate to Durban to renew our passports at the German Consulate for another ten years. Was this for the last time? It was probably just as well that we do not know what the future will bring!

2007 started out with a visit to the local geological society. I went there a couple of times, but later stopped going because I was not able to get the kind of help and advice on my mineral and rock collecting endeavors which I had hoped for and expected. But I had probably been too optimistic.

Europe saw in this year our usual jaunts through Germany and France on our way to Cap d'Agde, including a short stay in, you would never guess, *gay Paris*. In the intervening years our knowledge of French had come on nicely, but it was still not good enough for an easy free-flowing conversation with the locals.

Some of the lasting memories during the last twenty years have always been our hiking trips in the marvelous German *Mittelgebirge*. This term refers to all the mountains in Germany, save the Alps. All types of woods, natural or planted forests, historical and mythical castles, fortresses and medieval towns and picturesque villages; and lakes and remote hiking trails with nobody about could be experienced in many places.

Not to forget the best of all this; the small village pubs where one could find the best food in Germany, usually prepared by the publican or his wife. Yes, I know, no Michelin five-star establishments, and therefore of no interest to the modern luxury-conscious and demanding globetrotters.

After our return from Europe we took part in a bus tour organized by our retirement village. We went to the Orange Free State province, where we enjoyed the Cherry Blossom Festival at Ficksburg. This dealt with European trees, but the taste of the cherries was not the same. However, we were lately able to buy beautiful dark red (imported?) cherries in our supermarket.

Then we went on to Lesotho, the enclave of an independent state within South Africa. The alpine landscape, with the rounded tops of the mountains, showed their age of more than two-hundred million years, quite a different impression from the pronounced peaks we had seen at the European Alps, with their age of just forty-five million years.

We then visited the Katse Dam, the huge water storage reservoir and hydro-electric installations. It almost single-handedly powered the Gauteng industrial heartland of South Africa, and it also provided most of the water supplies for this province.

2008 was for me the *annus horibilis*, when my wife went with three of her lady friends from the village on a two-weeks car tour all the way to Cape Town, more than a thousand kilometers away. And she forgot to tell me how to open the fridge! But a dozen or so of the single ladies in the village looked after me, but we better don't tell my wife.

Back in Europe, saw us this year again in Andorra, the tiny 'independent' state on top of the Pyrenees. The scenery was naturally magnificent. Historically, this country was jointly owned (but not ruled, anymore) by the French state as successor to the Counts of *Foix*, and the bishop of a nearby Spanish diocese.

This is the only country in the world where Catalan is the official language, very much to the chagrin of the Spanish government! This language was spoken by the overwhelming majority of the inhabitants, if one ignores the army of Spanish and other lawyers and notary publics domiciled here, who earned their meagre income by operating letter-box companies, arranged tax havens and offered other worthy activities. This, at least, was what the locals told us.

On our way to Carcassonne, which we had already visited some years earlier, we passed the castle of the *Contes de Foix*, situated in the middle of a torrential mountain stream. The *Tour de France* circus had just arrived in town. Looking everywhere, except where I was going on the main street, I had a bad fall and my arm was bleeding like a stuck pig, as us kids used to say. Bandaged like a war casualty, I duly felt sorry for myself and tried to figure out whose fault all this was. Surely not mine!

South Africa was swamped with tens of thousands, and possibly hundreds of thousands, of illegal firearms. At this time our government had come up with a novel idea. All gun licenses were scrapped and had to be reapplied for. This process was going to be a costly and time-consuming exercise. Except for the criminals, of course, who did not bother with such cumbersome niceties. I did not bother, either and reluctantly handed in my expensive gun at the local police station. If I had held on, I could later have sold it for a considerable amount, but at the time nobody was interested to buy, because the market was drowning in second-hand guns.

This year we traded in our ten-year-old car and bought a Toyota Corolla, a second-hand, sorry, a pre-owned one. I always bought one-year old cars, because I figured that by then the previous owners had suffered through all the kinks and troubles of the marvelous products the car manufacturers sold us, and that by then the original owners had corrected and repaired all the inherent problems.

Early in 2009 (our late summer and early autumn) we went for a few days with friends to a camp in a nature reserve near Port St. John, about fifty kilometers further south from us. A very rustic affair, with several species of wild animals wandering right through the camp. Most conspicuous were the Wildebeest, a close relative, also in size, of the smaller breeds of cattle. They lived wild, but by now they were accustomed to people. Both species of wild animals were keeping carefully out of each other's way.

In Europe the year started with a trip to Ketzin, where my wife's family had a holiday stay when she was still a kid. As is usual with this kind of situation, her memories were simultaneously strong and weak. But the return visit was enjoyable for her, and this was the important point. Nostalgia is a very strong emotion, as I also have learned in the last several decades.

Next, we visited the town of Brandenburg (remember the Division Brandenburg from my first book?). This was a disappointment for us in so far as the town was still almost as gray and shabby as it had been during the communist rule of East Germany. In other places in the former GDR we had seen some renovations and/or new developments, but there was very little of this to be seen here.

Now we were again on our way to France. We stayed a day near Verdun, where in World War I my father had been fighting and suffering for his survival. And where the German and French armies had almost annihilated each other. Absolute stupor!

Most Europeans have still not grasped the most important promise of the European Union; to make such folly impossible for the future! The Common Market, the Euro, the European Parliament and the Schengen Agreement, they were all very helpful, but the elimination of inter-European wars was, in my opinion, by far the most important achievement of the two visionary political fathers of the Union, de Gaulle and Adenauer. As a beneficial by-product, the centuries-old animosities between the French and the German people have also largely dissipated.

If we would dream about the future, the abolition of national defense forces and the election of a government by the European Parliament, at least for the Euro area, would in my opinion be the crowning and final achievements for the foreseeable future of Europe and its inhabitants.

No, I am not yet campaigning for the European Parliament, there is still plenty of time for that.

On our return from Europe that year, my wife noted in her diary: "shopping in the rain, flu, cough, cough, rain, rain". What had happened to this country of permanent sunshine during our absence?

My wife was now also needing the kind of inlay soles I had been using for the last few years, and fortunately they helped her as well. We may have damaged our feet with our long and frequent beach walks in France.

This year my former boss of the group of building companies came with his wife to visit us. He was clearly under-whelmed by our modest bungalow, because he had, for most of his life and during recent times, lived in huge houses. He was a typical self-made man from a modest background, who loved to show his achievements and his affluence. We went with them to Oribi Gorge, a spectacular canyon-like, cut more than one hundred meters deep through the sandstone layers, and with a typical African wild scenery.

Every year we visited the local German *Weihnachtsmarkt*, the Christmas Market, organized by the strong local German church community. Their ancestors had arrived here in the nineteenth century, mostly from the area around the *Lüneburger Heide* in northern Germany.

They still speak perfect German, probably because of the strong connection of their local church parish with their counterparts in Germany. But they have nevertheless developed something like a local dialect, with a few inserted local expressions, borrowed from Afrikaans, English and some even from the local Zulus.

Up to now I had shown very little interest in alcoholic beverages of any kind, but lately I had acquired a taste for whisky. In line with my attitude towards the maxim of "all in moderation", I had decided to make sure that I did not become an alcoholic in my old age and had settled for a double-one on Tuesday and Thursday evenings, the days when my wife went on her botanical excursions. On Saturday and Sunday evenings I usually had a glass of white wine, even though weekends were really rather meaningless for retirees.

Now, I have to admit that my computer problems did not exist in isolation. There was another area of expertise where I was rather useless with these newly fangled gismos of the TV and our VCRs, while my wife has always been very knowledgeable in this regard.

The discrepancies in our respective capabilities and short-comings were even greater when dealing with our mobile telephones. She was now managing a smart phone without any problems, whereas I could still not make or receive a simple call with her old 'steam' mobile passed down to me, without having my notes in my hand! And even this did not work most of the time.

To send or receive a simple SMS was beyond my capabilities. This illustrated rather drastically the influence of the generations. But even my wife was stumped whenever we had a more serious computer problem. Surprisingly, in a few simple cases I did know what to do, based on previous trial-and-error attempts on my laptop.

We had now started in South Africa to have for many years frequent power failures because Eskom, our electricity mono-poly, was unable to produce and distribute enough power to satisfy the demand. Our government had since the end of Apartheid neglected to main-tain properly the aging old plants and distribution networks. Despite warnings by the experts, they also failed to build new generating plants, which needed many years of planning and construction.

The irony of this latter point was not lost on us, because one of the most pressing demands of the ANC had been to provide afford-able electrical power to the masses. Such demand in addition to what industry would require in future.

The natural results of these shortcomings were frequent disrup-tions of the power supply, usually two or three times a week for two hours each. A new term was even created here: "power shedding". We had to buy emergency battery lamps, which allowed my wife at least to prepare a cold dinner, and for us to read a book. Some people even bought small generators, but I left this idea alone.

A heated meeting in our Community Hall was called to discuss the possibility of installing a large communal generator to bridge the 'power shedding' periods. Because of my hearing problems I did not attend but was told that our managing director claimed that it would cost each cottage more than three-hundred Rand every single month, if this would be done. This fictitious claim ensured that our people rejected that idea, because they omitted to think this through logically.

This was just an obvious smokescreen, because the administration shied away from the capital expenditure involved. Nobody could fore-cast, or even realistically speculate, for how many hours a month such a generator would have to run. Therefore, no monthly costs could be predicted by anybody. But I kept my big mouth shut, because I knew nothing about the subject of management, anyway.

I could not find anybody to argue with (the wife was out of bounds - I'm not suicidal), so I picked a fight with our Medical Aid Scheme, a sort of hybrid health insurance company. We paid hefty monthly contributions, and when going overseas for three or four months my wife was covered but, due to my age of over eighty years, not me.

I wrote to the ombudsman of Medical Aid Schemes and complained about this blatant discrimination. The scheme's excuse was that due to my advanced age their risks were increased. My reply to this flimsy reasoning was that their higher risks also applied if I stayed in South Africa.

Surprisingly, this erudite argumentation was not successful. Alternately, I then argued that they should at least have credited our account with the three or four months of contributions which they had not earned, since they did not want to insure the risk. This time I was successful, and the restriction was cancelled by the supervising agency.

By 2010 I had finally completed the manuscript of my first book *Geophysical/Paleontological Parallel Developments from the Big Bang up to 3 000 BC = 5 000 Years ago* which our son has published on Amazon.

Quite a mouthful, but this has been a work of love for thirteen long years, because I have always been interested in the subject of the interaction over time between the various components of nature: Cosmos, Geology, Ecology, Botany, Zoology and Anthropology.

Many publications on these individual subjects existed, but I my specific interest has always been the 'cross-pollination' and inter-linked developments of these various elements. The book presented a compendium of details cleaned from many different quoted sources.

Our son had published a first version of this already many years earlier on his webpage, but now he had organized the publication as a printed book in addition to the e-book version. A marvelous feat and very welcome help for a digital fossil like me.

One of the highlights for us had always been the occasional phone calls with the family in Denmark. Our grandchildren grew up so quickly. The family birthdays we had been used to for a long time, but now the confirmation of our oldest grandson was a stark reminder of how fast the time was passing.

This year saw a very different visit to Paris. We had arranged with our son to meet him and his family at the Paris Disneyland. Since this type of establishment was below the bottom of our to-see list, we had during our multiple previous stays in Paris not visited there before.

Getting established at the Pommeuse camping ground near Paris elucidated in my wife's diary this entry: 'rip-off!' Ah well, only to be expected near a world metropolis and next to the even more exalted Disneyland.

Some years back our son had given us a GPS gadget as a Christmas present. We set sail and ventured with our camper into the Great Unknown. And what had to happen, did happen. The GPS led us a merry-go-round through the *Isle de France*, but not to our destination. Fortunately, the mobile phone had been invented already. This enabled us (meaning my wife and our son!) to finally unite our family.

The poor grandchildren were near to starvation, because they had neither had a burger, nor an ice-cream, nor a coke, nor this and nor that for about half an hour. But this act of flagrant child abuse was promptly remedied upon our arrival. After the 'feeding of the animals' we proceeded to sample the offerings of the 'American Way of Life'.

Back at the camping ground, after the kids had been saved from another terrible fate of terminal starvation (half a dozen or so burgers and Cokes did the trick) we had a nice chat and our son had made a recording of some of my memories, an economy version of these writings, I suppose.

After our return from Europe we attended to our various duties and hobbies as before. Life went on, even at the pedestrian pace of old-age pensioners. We were grateful for all the diversions we had here for both of us. There was never a dull moment in our lives. As a matter of fact, we sometimes felt almost stressed, which was of course slightly silly. Between our hobbies and our walks and meetings with friends we were fully occupied.

We never had time to feel sorry for ourselves because we grew older and, in my case, starting to get wobbly legs. However, we had to make a few adjustments to our lives. The hiking group which we had joined back in 1994 already, and which had afforded us many interesting and enjoyable walks, we had to leave because of my weak and painful ankles. After I had discovered my inlay soles, we should have rejoined them, but for one or the other reason we did not do this. A pity, the walks had been good for our health and had always been very interesting.

Our son and the mother of their three children were now together for twenty-four years already in Denmark. The fact that they had never married seemed not to be important to them, in line with what appeared by now to be quite normal in their country, as we had discovered during our frequent family visits there.

The only fact important to them, and to us, was that our grandchildren grew up in a happy and caring home. Watching them it was clear to us that the 'science' of bringing up children had changed very much since we had been young ourselves. Today's parents obviously had approaches and values quite different from those of our parents, and also rather different from our own attitudes.

After our son had gone to Europe and Israel, we had accepted that he now was leading his own life. We had adopted a hands-off approach to our son's family and the upbringing of our grandchildren and, we hope, everybody was as happy about that as we were.

Thinking about changing attitudes reminded me of the fact that neither my wife nor myself showed much interest in our present-day hobbies when we were young. In those days, survival was the top priority, and there was not much leeway for extraneous interests, which were a luxury we could not afford to indulge in.

We had earlier detected near our village a mulberry tree with large, sweet fruit, and we harvested enough of them for my wife to make a delicious mulberry jam. The berries were not quite as large as the ones I had encountered in the Italian countryside sixty years ago, which had so forcefully demonstrated to me their purgative and laxative powers. But they were much better than those of many other trees of this genus in South Africa.

Originally, all these trees probably came with immigrants from Italy, and there existed several species of them. As a matter of fact, many mulberry trees here bear no fruit at all. They are only used as ornamental trees.

Once a year I was still having my regular medical tests done. Because I had recorded the individual results over the twenty years of our stay in Margate, it became clear that things were moving on an even curve, albeit a slowly downwards pointing one. Which was only logical, after all.

Every morning at breakfast I took five different health supplements. Many years ago, I had read that the Americans were daily 'pissing away' a fortune in the form of such supplements. That may be so, but I still thought that a moderate use of them was justified and advisable (now I'm a doctor as well!).

Additionally, I drank three large glasses of tap water during the day. I never trusted bottled water, after I had read in a German consumer magazine that in a comparison of the purity of all the bottled waters on the market, they all had fared worse than the local tap water, even the famous branded ones.

A long time ago I had developed some scabs on my scalp, which I was told were symptoms of psoriasis. I am pretty sure, that these scabs evolved after I had banged my head a couple of times against the door frames of our cars. But I must not upset the medical profession by giving away the secrets they do not want us to know about.

When I looked up this subject on the internet, I read that such eczema would primarily appear on the elbows. Well, mine looked as pristine as those of Brigitte Bardot's back in the 1950s. No, to be honest as promised, I did not check up on her elbows. There surely were other areas of interest to keep an eye on.

Generally speaking, my mind was still reasonably in shape at this stage. Sometimes, I could not retrieve a word which was at the tip of my tongue, but most of the time it would pop up later. Things were not too bad, however. I was even playing with the idea to find out what my IQ was. I know, a bit late, but as usual, I was just curious, and in the end, I did nothing about it.

Chessmaster 10 was the chess program on my computer. No harm in doing some advertising for a good cause, particularly as it is now available free on Google. I have used it regularly, as it was very good and sophisticated. It utilized, among many other useful features, a system of awarding or deducting points, depending on whether the player had won or lost a game.

My point count (my chess rating) during the almost twenty years of my usage of this program always fluctuated between 1300 and 1600. When I previously had played at the Durban Chess Club, my rating was most of the time just above 1400. It appears, therefore, that the program's balances are reasonably realistic.

An amazing thing that I noticed was the observation, that over the last few years an increase of about twenty to thirty points in my ratings had happened, since I regularly took a Folic Acid tablet every morning. Again, some underhand advertising, but the truth can be told.

Early in 2011 I had to have double cataract operations. Now I could do away with my bi-focal glasses, which I had needed for driving, reading and watching TV, for instance, and could replace them with simple reading glasses. This made the com-plicated life of an old-age pensioner much easier.

My wife undertook, with three of her friends, a three-day trip to Balito and Umhlanga Rocks on the Natal coast north of Durban. They stayed at a timeshare establishment, using the account of one of the ladies. The diary only recorded that they had breakfast at an Italian restaurant, but it was doubtful that they would have driven three hundred kilometers for just this purpose. Maybe they had the odd natter as well.

Also noted was the first purchase of internet data for the laptop. This probably happened in conjunction with our son's arrival with his family in Margate. We had booked them all into a pleasant holiday cottage in a little camp on the shores of the Indian Ocean. We thought they would enjoy this experience. Yes, they went into the sea, once.

The remaining two weeks they would have liked to lie next to the admittedly very nice swimming pool. But the old man put his foot down and dragged them screaming and performing (only the kids) along the beach into Margate for breakfast. End of screaming, start of gobbling up burgers and Coke and ice-cream and....

After they had settled down, we drove to the Natal Midlands, where our son had attended the Agricultural College at Weston. Being an alumnus, he had a chat with the present-generation staff. At the nearby Sierra Ranch, where we had often stayed with him on his weekends off, we spent an agreeable afternoon and night there.

From there we went to Giant's Castle, a nature reserve in the Drakensberg Mountains, with a highest elevation of almost 3 500 meters (Wikipedia). We had booked a large chalet for our immense family. This was a real pleasure for our grandchildren from mountainous Denmark, with a highest elevation of 50 meters above sea level (my estimate), particularly for our oldest grandson, who was visibly moved by this tranquil and picturesque experience.

After our return to base they spent a few days - you have guessed it - next to the pool, and then we were off again and went to Hluhluwe, a wildlife reserve of note in northern Natal. We did not see all the species of animals present there, but it was nevertheless worth-while for the kids, whose only contact with wildlife, apart from cats and dogs, was the occasional mouse and a sparrow or two (just kidding).

While again in Northern France this year, I pondered the fact that the Arab invaders out of Spain in the early Middle Ages had in the eighth century progressed to well north of Paris, before they had been defeated by Charles Martel in the bloody five-day battles of Tours and Poitiers in 722 AD. Europe could easily have ended up as a batch of Muslim countries! Amazingly, there were virtually no traces of this invasion left in today's France.

Very impressive was for us the field of massive prehistoric megaliths at Carnac near the Atlantic coast, standing like soldiers in long ranks and files. It is absolutely amazing, how these people of the distant past managed these feats without any equipment to aid them in this back-breaking work.

Now I realized a long-held dream of mine: to visit Mont St. Michel on the Atlantic coast. My father had been there during the second World War. Why was I attracted to this place like that? No logical reason for somebody who always has considered himself being rational and completely unemotional. Strange!

This well-preserved medieval town on a tiny island, or a peninsula, depending on how high or low the tides had risen or fallen, provided a fascinating insight into what life was like for the people in the High Middle Ages.

In 2012 we explored Germany again, in addition to France, and had an experience which was both, funny and worrisome at the same time. We had set off on a walk from a camping ground, across fields and woods, until we came to a T-junction where we had to decide whether to turn right or left, to get back to our camper. As an obedient husband I accepted my wife's certain knowledge that we had to turn right, even though I was convinced we had to turn left.

The woods we traversed were badly damaged. They used to be a training ground for the East German infantry, artillery and tanks. Eventually, we landed up in a small village. By now we had realized 'our' mistake and we looked for a bus, or even a taxi, to get us back to our starting point. No such luck! So, we trudged back and completed an involuntary five-hour march of twenty-three kilometers.

The next day we were not even particularly tired, even though we had suffered through a thirty-three Celsius heatwave. And in the following night we experienced a terrible thunderstorm, which ripped off one of the small side windows of the 'bedroom' of our camper, probably to round off our mixed memories of this place. Surprisingly, we made it without any further mishap to Moritzburg, after we had provisionally covered the open window space with some plastic sheeting.

We had booked there a chalet for our son's family well in advance. Happy reunion with him and our grandchildren. Next day we went to Dresden, a half an hour drive in our son's car, and obtained a replacement window, which he fitted perfectly. He also did some repairs to our bicycles. I knew, why I had wanted a son!

In Dresden we walked through the rebuilt Old Town and I showed the family the sights which I remembered so well from my childhood. In particular the Frauenkirche, which had collapsed after the bombardment of Dresden in February of 1945. The ruins and the rubble had been preserved as a memento of the ravages of the war.

A few years earlier, after the reunification of Germany, the ruins of the church and the preserved sandstone blocks were meticulously catalogued and the church was rebuilt block-by-block, according to the original plans, which were luckily still available.

In the evening we landed up in a modern shopping center, where I used for my laptop, for the first time in my life, the free WiFi connection available there, with the necessary assistance provided by my elder grandson.

Back in Cap d'Agde suddenly panic stations: the camping gas bottle was empty! With all the talk by the politicians and bureaucrats of the European Union about the Common Market, camping gas bottles were still not interchangeable between the European countries. Instead, they had standardized the toilet seats and decreed to what degree cucumbers for sale were allowed to be bent. I'm serious!

Electrical plugs and sockets were still found all over Europe in a rich variety of designs, varying from country to country, and driving travelers around the bend. But to be fair, they had introduced a standardized set of Euro plugs and sockets, but it will probably take decades, until the national gizmos disappear, but most of the camping grounds had installed the standardized Euro equipment.

At the end of August we sold our faithful camper, to be collected by the buyer from the Frankfurt camping grounds on the day of our return flight to South Africa. The last few days of our stay we used for some bicycle tours, before they also had to be left behind. Our sister-in-law from the Spessart came to collect from the camper a number of things for which she found some use. We then had to squeeze our second household into our two suitcases. Luckily, we each had a thirty-kilogram luggage allowance with Emirates Airlines.

Our son came from Denmark to stay for the final few days with us in the hotel next to the camping ground. This was very helpful, and we had some quality time together, during which we were able to give him a parting gift for himself and our grand-children.

An era had come to an end! Let me quickly get a bucket and find another box of tissues. Apart from the occasional mishap, which is only to be expected when traveling in the European wilds, we did have a wonderful time during our almost twenty years in and with our camping cars. These valuable memories will be saved forever on the hard drives of our brains.

As a former Director of Finance and Administration I could not abstain from calculating the financial effect of having made use of our camping cars. The position regarding these almost twenty years looks like this:

$$\text{Depreciation of the Peugeot: } 25\ 000 - 10\ 000 = 15\ 000 \text{ DM}$$
$$\text{Fiat } 80\ 000 - 10\ 000 = 65\ 000$$
$$\text{Diesel etc.} 1\ 500 \text{p.a.} \times 20 = 30\ 000$$
$$\text{Camping ground fees} 40 \times 30 \times 3{,}5 \times 20 = 84\ 000$$
$$\text{Tax, insurance, tires} 400 \times 20 = \underline{8\ 000}$$
$$202\ 000 \text{ DM}$$

This translated into about DM100 or 50€ per day (202 000 ÷20 ÷

3,5 ÷ 30). Without utilizing our campers, it would have been completely impossible to finance our gallivanting in Europe at such low cost. The only alternative would have been car hire and hotels, B&Bs, back-packers and the like. More expensive and much less comfortable!

And this applied, quite apart from the important side-effects of this type of holidaying:

- having at all times an almost complete second household available to us,
- not having to lug around heavy suitcases, apart from the airports, where suitable trolleys were available,
- not being dependent on hotel bookings,
- enjoying complete freedom in the planning of our travels during these three or four months.

7

MARGATE, FINALLY SETTLED DOWN QUIETLY.

But even when we were not gallivanting around the world anymore, we had some beautiful places to visit, right here on our doorstep. Early in the year we went again to the Oribi Gorge, the Leopard Rock and the Lake Eland Reserve. A day well spent and easily comparable with many of our earlier overseas visits.

My wife kept up twice a week her diligent study of trees, grasses, flowers and ferns, while I was less involved with my chess meetings once a week. But I also kept myself busy with my collections of rocks, minerals, and to a lesser extent, of fossils. The latter one was not really a collection, but rather an accumulation of bits and pieces acquired over the years, without forming a proper structured collection.

We both also kept up our walks of nine kilometers around Margate at least once a week. To be as honest as I rashly promised to be, in the last few years we never managed, or even aimed for, more than one walk per week. Therefore, the term "at least once a week" is too ambitious, if not plain wishful thinking.

These walks were, in a way, rather boring, but they were nevertheless good for our fitness. My wife found sometimes a grass or bush, or a creeper, of interest to her which she attempted to identify afterwards. Occasionally I also found some interesting-looking rocks which I took home (my wife refused to carry them for me, even after I had offered in turn to carry her grasses etc.; highly uncaring of her!). After their obligatory cleaning I usually threw away most if not all of them, because they were not what I had hoped them to be.

Occasional entries in my wife's diary mention that there was no power, and at other days, that there was no water. Undeniably, we lived in Africa, but we were happy to be here, in spite of these annoying shortcomings.

Even fossils like us needed to renew driver's licenses, had to see doctors and had to perform similar duties to keep the State and the professions in clover. It was all such a nuisance, particularly when you were much too busy as a pensioner to waste your time like that. As I have remarked previously, I often wondered how I ever found, prior to my retirement, the time to go to work.

We now had discovered a proper German restaurant in Margate, the *Münchner Haus*, where we sometimes went and indulged in an *Eisbein* or a *Schnitzel* dinner, with a glass of a German-type white wine. Many of the South African wines taste similar to German ones, and German names abound in this field, like *Riesling, Liebfrauenmilch* and many others.

An annual highlight at this time of year was always the German Christmas Market of the local German church community, where we could buy all the things one doesn't really need. But it was all for a good cause. And occasionally a treasure could be found on the shelves stacked with German and English books. One such find was a copy of *Dufresne-Mieses, Lehrbuch des Schachspiels*. I used to have a copy of this book, which I had given to my son, and I had not expected to ever see another one. Also, I found there Christopher Andrew, MI 5 and *Heinz Höhne, Canaris - Patriot im Zwielicht*.

For a few days my wife went with like-minded friends for an inland trip up to Ingeli Forest Lodge near Kokstad in the Drakensberg foothills. This was a nice break for her. She could rummage for hours in the vegetation and argue about the classification of the local plants, and I could read my books and play chess against my computer programs (and pinch some chocolate out of the fridge).

I must now rectify a serious omission in my tale. Often I have mentioned my collections of minerals, and especially the one of rocks. Not being a geologist myself, I was lucky to have met Andrew, as mentioned earlier. He was an experienced geologist with a broad spectrum of general knowledge in this field. Most other geologists I have met in South Africa had been specialists in mining geology or some other specific subject within this science.

He had worked in many parts of southern and eastern Africa, surveying the geological composition of the districts under investigation. He was as well involved in Syria during the war, trying to find subterranean water sources in the dessert.

In many sessions with him I asked for his advice on the classification of my rocks, which I would never have managed without his help. His assistance enabled me to compile a manuscript of hints for the classification of rocks *Rock ID, the Identification of the Rocks of the World* which my son has also published for me on Amazon.

To wrap up the year, we went with our geological group to a limestone and dolomite rock quarry, where I found some large crystals of limestone and of dolomitic marbles. We also visited a coffee farm with a few hundred trees, which a Belgian immigrant had established here. Smart as these people were, they had added a café, where they sold, in addition to the coffee beans, also coffee and cakes. Pastries were also on sale, the real reasons why I wanted to go there.

2013 started out with ordering a mosquito screen-door for our rear entrance. This finally enabled us to leave the back door open during our summer months, when temperature and humidity combined to make our life rather miserable. The benefit of this small investment was such, that in the autumn we decided on the much larger outlay for a similar screen-door for the front entrance of our cottage. Now, the air finally could circulate freely through our lounge.

This year, we flew from Frankfurt to Billund, the medium-sized regional Danish airport of Jutland. The occasion for our visit of two weeks was the confirmation of our only grand-daughter. When our son and Amanda collected us at the airport, the two were waving Danish flags to welcome us, a not unusual occurrence, as we could observe with other arrivals. Then they brought us home to Thyborøn.

After the festivities, on the way back to the airport, we stopped at a museum honoring the Vikings. Their history is vicious and colorful, barbaric and poetic, all at the same time. They pillaged and burnt-down towns, cloisters and castles all around the North Sea, but they also ransacked Paris and Constantinople!

The various versions of the Icelandic *Edda* had been created in the tenth century, the pinnacle of Viking culture. They were at first only passed-on verbally, and they were only written down in the fourteenth century, we learned at this unique place, where we also saw some authentic runic Viking inscriptions on two huge boulders.

In Margate we bravely carried on with our various activities, but particularly my wife. She has really developed into an experienced amateur field-botanist. Her enthusiasm is a pleasure to watch – from my easy chair. But I also did my little bit, with chess, my mineral and rock collections and now with jotting down my memories and suggestions on how to improve the running of the world. After all, somebody has to do that, if we do not want to find ourselves back in the Middle Ages. Or would you prefer to read this marvelous book in the light of a flickering candle?

But now, preparing my six books for publication by our son, demanded absolute priority. Everything else, from my collections to chess, was relegated to a back seat. Rather than playing daily two or three computer chess games, I restricted myself to one game on Sunday afternoon. Terrible, the sacrifices one has to make in one's old age, if one has to improve things in this world all by oneself.

Early in 2014 my wife went with her small group of botanical enthusiasts for three days to a Pondoland homestead, to survey and record the local flora. This district was just south of our area, in the heartland of the African tribe of the Pondos.

They slept in one of the African huts and lived rustic, like the locals. This must have been a sobering experience for them (the Europeans, I mean). What the rural Africans, who had possibly never seen White people before, thought about this occasion was not recorded.

Unfortunately, Africans, by and large, have no particular appreciation for the beauty of their land, the wild animals and the prolific plant life. But there is hope. A few young people are now being trained and their interest nurtured in preserving the indigenous fauna and flora of this astonishing country.

Shortly afterwards we went with another botanical group to Himeville, on the way to the Sani Pass on the border between South Africa and the mountain kingdom of Lesotho. There I had a unique experience: We had a three-some and I slept with my wife's best friend and fellow botanist. No, you got it all wrong. What I'm talking about is the fact that all three of us slept in the same pokey little room of a back–packers hostel. Shame on you!

Next morning after breakfast we mounted one of the 4x4s provided by the 'hotel', and we were on our way to one of the higher points of Southern Africa. From the South African border post, at an altitude of 1 544 meters, along a nine-kilometers-long so-called road, we travelled to the Lesotho border post at 2 876 meters, for a vertical rise of 1 332 meters (Wikipedia).

If you were thinking of a pass road like in Europe or North America, think again. This goat track was only passable by 4x4s, and ours got even stuck on our way up. We had to disembark, and we attempted to walk up to the top. For some reason, I only managed about fifty meters or so, when I suddenly felt dizzy. I had to hitch a lift with another of these mountain vehicles to the top of the Drakensberg.

My wife soldiered on and, upon arrival at the summit, went botanizing with her friend on the mountain meadows. Waiting for her, I had recovered quickly and explored the area, but apart from sandstones there was nothing of interest to see for my rock collection.

We were supposed to walk down again to the South African boarder post, but I only managed a few kilometers and had again to catch a lift with one of the returning trucks. Yes, my wife outperformed me easily anew.

Our younger grandson was now at age fourteen and celebrating his confirmation. Time just flies. In July we also were flying, but not to our camper, as in the last almost twenty years (where is my handkerchief?). Instead, we were in Europe to also celebrate my 90th with the family.

We flew from Frankfurt to Mallorca, part of the Baleares Isles of Spain in the Mediterranean Sea, where our son had booked us into an extremely nice holiday resort on the south-eastern coast of this island.

The accommodation was first class, as one could expect from such a posh place. The food was even better and included free drinks. Surprisingly, there were (apart from us) no drunks falling about. Sorry, silly joke.

Our son's work-related commitments did not allow us to celebrate on the correct date. But finally, the day of the pre-birthday party had arrived. He had booked a large table and I sat down, not knowing what to expect, and I was pleasantly surprised to receive an expensive bottle of whisky, which I would never have expended on myself. I did not open it there and then, but I took it home to South Africa with me, to enjoy in peace. We had a very pleasant evening, with marvelous food and drinks and fun with the family to round off this day.

Upon our return to Frankfurt we had arranged a get-together for my 90th birthday with my wife's brother and his wife, who had suffered our visits for so many years. We met at an open-air restaurant near the *Sachsenhäuser Warte*, a medieval watch tower in an elevated position above the fortified town of Frankfurt, serving in the Middle Ages as an advanced warning post.

It was in a way a rather sad event, because we all realized that we would probably not see each other again. They were getting on in years now, having reached their early seventies, and they cannot keep up with a youngster like me! Sad, but life has to go on, as everything has to end eventually. As also, incidentally, this story, in regard to our travels in Europe, ends herewith.

After our return we went in August for a "holiday from our permanent holiday" to the Ingeli Forest Lodge, to celebrate there our 50th, the Golden Anniversary. We had some nice nature walks through the woods. This was something special here in South Africa, since we did not have the many natural woods as in Europe. If anything, we are usually settled with planted forests. Luckily, I found another couple of mineral and rock specimen for my collections.

Back home we celebrated with my geology mentor his ninety-fifth birthday in a new café in the Village of Happiness where he now lives. Unfortunately, he was by now rather frail, but mentally he was still on top of the world, and only his legs were not doing their job anymore. Of course, we still kept in touch and visited him sometimes (not as often as we should have!) and we took him sometimes on an outing to somewhere nice and interesting.

But he was not the only one who had been leaving his teenage years behind. In addition to the slightly frightening experiences at the Sani Pass, I also had the occasional dizzy spells. But I am not complaining about minor worries like that.

More serious were the constant complaints that I should get some hearing aids. I should have ignored these niggles, but who can resist the Chinese Torture, also camouflaged as "married bliss".

To be on the safe side, we bought Swiss products, and after a horrendous investment I now sported two hearing aids – for about three hours per month. My hearing with them was only marginally improved, and I used them only in the company of two of our friends, who both spoke extremely softly. Ah well, one must do one's bit to grow the GNP, employment and import/export volumes of two countries.

Going through my wife's diary while working on these notes, to check and to prod my memory, it was sad to come across the many names of our Margate friends and acquaintances, who over the years have passed away. There is now virtually nobody left here from the time we moved into our cottage only twenty years ago.

Sorry, I have to interrupt here for a moment. A group, or rather a riotous horde, of about twenty Vervet monkeys who caught my attention while slaving on my computer is cavorting in our little garden in front of the window of our study.

The acrobatics of the babies make anybody smile, even a grumpy old man like me. The teenagers play and cavort around much more spectacularly than any group of kids would, and the mothers and other adults tear off my wife's flowers, taste them and throw them away again. But one cannot be angry with them. They are so funny to observe.

Anyway, we are the intruders here, and they are just retaliating and trying to survive. And they clearly enjoy doing that, particularly when people were careless enough to have left fruit on their kitchen table and left a window open just a crack. It is getting dark now (quarter to six) and our visitors are going home to wherever they retire to for their night's rest.

The very next day my wife had raised the garage door for a frail friend, whom she took shopping once a week, to let her enter our car this way. As recorded previously our garage was connected to our kitchen, and the connecting door was most of the time left open. When I entered the kitchen, I saw a monkey sitting on the kitchen counter right next to my wife, who was working there but had not noticed her visitor.

The monkey had stolen a banana out of the fruit basket and had carefully peeled it. My appearance had interrupted his breakfast and upset him badly. I was almost run over by the little horror, fleeing at an accelerated short retreat. But then he was calmly sitting under the raised garage door, completing his interrupted breakfast.

As one can see, wildlife is healthy where we now live, even without the unlamented "Durban Prawns". We also often had an interesting selection of birds in our little garden. They were enthusiastically using our two bird baths, particularly the Bulbuls.

Our neighbor was feeding every evening a family of three woolly-necked storks. One of them had its leg damaged, but it managed. In the late afternoon they congregated in front of our cottages, patiently waiting for their supper. If they were worried that they had been forgotten, one of them picked with its beak against the glass front door to complain about the slow service.

A family of Hadedas, or Sacred Ibis, had caught on to this feeding scheme and they had jumped onto the band wagon. The members of this species were past masters of producing tortured cries which imitated bitter complaints by human babies.

PART III

APARTHEID - THEN AND NOW

1965 TO 2014

8

RACISM PRIOR TO 1948

Now we have to go back quite far in history, in order to understand the complex background of Apartheid. This system originated from the fact that the European colonial powers had for centuries looked down on the colonized peoples as racially inferior. They always maintained their distances from them, except if it suited them to act otherwise, when they wanted to utilize their land, their minerals or their labor.

And in most cases there was something else to use: their women and girls! In spite of their feeling of superiority, one could observe in all these colonial empires throughout the centuries the same thing: many of the colonists were busy proving that the autochthonous females were also members of the Homo sapiens species, by producing plenty of off-spring of mixed blood.

They usually practiced their aloof attitude as a form of social differentiation. Generally speaking, all colonial powers all over the world were racists, starting with the Spaniards and Portuguese in America, through to the modern colonists like the Dutch, French, British and Germans.

The underlying reason for this racism, apart from their superiority complex, was the subliminal "fear of the great numbers". The Europeans in all these empires were worried about their personal security, the safety of their possessions, but also about the integrity of their cultural identities. The direct outcome of this mind-set was the White minority rule, and the concomitant suppression of the Non-Whites in their colonies.

Among the modern Homo sapiens, the Khoi-San group of people were the original inhabitants of Southern Africa. With their light-brown skins, they actually consisted of two quite different populations, but probably of a distant common ancestry. The early Dutch colonists combined them under one name, either for simplicity's sake, or because they did not know any better:

The San were the first group to arrive in Southern Africa. The early colonists usually called them "Bushmen". They lived throughout Southern Africa and they were hunter-gatherers and therefore they were generally nomads.

In Natal the San people had been forced to retreat into the remote Drakensberg, after they had been driven off the more accessible lands between the coast and the mountains. The "Bushmen", as they were called also here, had already been eliminated long ago by the European settlers and the slowly from the north intruding African tribes. The large herds of these two groups of invaders were popular attacking aims for the San hunters.

The Khoi-Khoi were the next arrivals here. It appears that they immigrated from today's Botswana, and that they lived primarily in the Cape Province. Often, they were described as "Hottentots", because the colonists were unable to pronounce the name of their nation. The Dutch chose this designation based on the cries the Khoi-Khoi uttered during their trance-like dances.

They were cattle herders and as such they were semi-nomads, following their herds from pasture to pasture. This necessitated a life in many small groups, one of which apparently was the Nama tribe in Namaqualand of Namibia. Another one was probably that of the Griquas, a mixed-blood clan of Khoi-Khoi and some wayward Dutch herder's extraction.

In the seventeenth and eighteenth centuries a substantial group of Indonesian slaves had been imported by the Dutch-East-India Company from their Batavia colony, the present-day Indonesia, to their colony here at the Cape. The term 'imported', usually reserved for commodities, is justified here, as these slaves were considered and treated as commodities.

In spite of their European supremacy complexes, the same phenomenon of the mixed-race offspring could be observed in all these colonized areas, including the Cape of Good Hope; many of the lonely European men, due to an acute shortage of White women in the colony, were producing many mixed-blood children, either with the Khoi-San women or those of the Malay slaves from Batavia.

The descendants of this particular group of people of mixed race had always been referred to in South Africa as the Cape Malays. They were Muslims or believers of some heathen natural religions. Their un-Christian beliefs were ignored or ridiculed as hocus-pocus by the settlers. Their later off-spring intensely mixed further with the surviving Khoi-San. They all later adopted the Dutch language. Which, however, did not save them from the racial separation and the later Apartheid oppression, when the Cape Malays were classified as 'Coloreds', and they suffered very similar fates as the Africans.

I guess that there must be something like a million of them by now. The Apartheid regime could not deny the obvious fact that the Cape Malays were the result of racial mixing mainly between the Dutch and women of this group. During the Apartheid era there were repeatedly heated arguments amongst the Afrikaners, who of their group were tainted by this 'bad blood', and quite a few proud members of their group were technically Coloreds, including some 'Honorable Members of Parliament', and even a cabinet minister!

In the 17th century the Dutch colonists at the Cape of Good Hope were seriously discussing the question, whether the indigenous Khoi-San people were human beings or not. At best, they were considered by them as inferior specimen of the human species, who could only be utilized as slaves or as menial laborers.

Here it must be admitted that these indigenous people at the Cape were looking quite different from others the Dutch had met elsewhere. They sporadically still exist in the Cape Province, and slightly more numerously in the near Namib desert of Namibia.

There have recently been interesting discussions among experts, whether the Khoi-San, or either one of the group, were direct descendants of the original five-hundred thousand years old Homo sapiens species, or whether they were part of our own two-hundred thousand years old Homo sapiens sapiens sub-species.

The Dutch settlers at the Cape practiced their form of social separation based on race, religion and culture, but mainly on their firm belief of their own superiority over the 'savages'. Considering their horror of close contact with these people, it is amazing to realize that practically all their children were brought up by nannies of these same 'savages', particularly on the farms. To a large extent this still was, as we often could observe, the practice even nowadays, except that the present-day nannies were usually African women.

The Dutch settlers, and later their descendants, the Afrikaners, truly believed that they had a spiritual sending; that they had received from the Almighty the mission to Christianize and to civilize the Non-Whites, to look after these indigenous people as their masters and to make use of them as servants, the menial providers for their farms and households.

Interestingly, these two terms of 'masters' and 'servants' still appeared in the South African legal texts until very recently. The legal system of the Dutch was based on Roman-Dutch law, which in turn was partially a derivate of the *Sachsenspiegel*, the codex of the Saxons of north-western Germany.

The original European settlers of the southern tip of Africa were Dutch people, who had been sent to the Cape of Good Hope in 1652 to create and provide a staging point for the ships of the Dutch East India Company on their long travels between the Netherlands and their far-flung colonies in the present-day Indonesia.

But soon they developed their own commercial and agri-cultural interests, and they became merchants and farmers, but also hunters of major wild animals, and some turned to itinerant pasture-farming.

Later the Huguenots arrived, the religious fugitives from France, who were Reformed Protestants, just like these earlier Dutch settlers. Still later, a large contingent of settlers from Northern Germany came here, particularly from the *Lüneburger Heide*, an area of little agricultural promise, who also belonged to this same family of Reformed or Evangelical churches.

Nowadays, it is not easy to understand, how important was in those days the adherence to any of the various confessional groupings within Christianity. One just has to remember the Puritans of the Mayflower, the Pennsylvania Dutch, the Quakers and many more of such religious emigrants, who left their homes in Europe for confessional reasons.

Over time all the new arrivals accepted the Dutch language spoken by the first settlers. In the late nineteenth and early twentieth centuries the term 'Boers' became established for them. Their language metamorphosed over the centuries into the present-day Afrikaans. Likewise, the Dutch and the other immigrants over time became the Afrikaner nation.

When in 1948 they took over the government of the country, they insisted on the term 'Afrikaners', which is still current today. This terminology revealed a kind of schizophrenia; on the one hand they insisted that they were Europeans, but on the other hand they wanted to be recognized as true inhabitants of Africa.

When the British had snatched this colony from the Dutch during the Napoleonic Era, nothing much changed right away. During the British colonial era, the racial question was officially ignored by them, and therefore the problem did not exist. But unofficially, racial segregation remained nevertheless very much in place, just as before, and also just like in the rest of the British Empire.

The new rulers largely ignored the indigenous people. Their attitudes of superiority and racial prejudices were the same as those of their predecessors in the governor's mansion, but they apparently did not sleep around quite as much. But even so, about twenty percent (my guess) of the Cape Coloreds have British names, as opposed to the majority with Afrikaans ones. Another estimated ten percent of these people have French names, inherited from the Huguenots. A comparison with the Southern States of the US appeared obvious in this regard.

In 1910, the establishment of the Union of South Africa took place, consisting of the original British colonies of the Cape of Good Hope and Natal, as well as the former Boer republics of the Transvaal and the Orange Free State, which had become colonies in 1901, after the end of the Anglo-Boer War.

A paragraph of the former constitution of the Cape Colony was incorporated into the South African one, reserving some seats in the legislature for the Cape Coloreds. Naturally, they had no vote. The few seats to 'represent' them had, of course, to be occupied by Whites. After all, one could not possibly have 'Coloreds' sitting in one's own sacred Parliament!

The much smaller group of the Natal Coloreds were fathered mainly by British settlers, officials, soldiers and seamen. They all carried British surnames, but they were discriminated against just like all the other Non-Europeans.

This community spoke English and lived mostly in and around Durban, from where many later migrated to Johannesburg and other inland centers. However, on their way north they were not allowed to enter, or to live, in the Orange Free State, an Afrikaner stronghold, which after 1901 had become the Orange River Colony.

A remarkable feature of the British settlers in Natal was the fact that a few of them had turned 'native'. They took one or more African wives and lived like the Africans, and their descendants subsequently also became the Natal Coloreds. At least one of these Black-and-White settlers, Fynn, was made an African Chief by King Shaka of the Zulu empire. After the end of Apartheid his descendants successfully laid claim to their ancestral land. It was returned to them by the New South Africa, after it had been taken away from them under the Apartheid regime.

Still another group of Afrikaans-speaking Coloreds lived in and around Kokstad in inland Natal. They had migrated under their 'Kapitaan' Adam Kok from the area around present-day Kimberley and Bloemfontein in the central region of South Africa. Their ancestors came into being when Dutch hunters of the major wild animals or itinerant farmers with their herds had ventured into these central regions and had encountered indigenous populations there.

It was noteworthy that no Africans were living in the Cape at the time when the first settlers had arrived from Europe. During their slow-moving wanderings from East Africa toward South Africa they had just recently (in a historical time frame) reached the Kei river, north of present-day Port Elizabeth. For centuries this river was the *de facto* border between the Africans and the Europeans.

This constellation inevitably led to a number of bloody border wars and skirmishes between the settlers and the Xhosa tribe. They all ended indecisive, but the black warriors attacked again and again, with both sides consequently suffering badly.

The Africans of this country now consisted of a rather large number of tribes within the Nguni language group of Eastern and Southern Africans. Each had its own distinctive language and tribal customs. The two largest of these were the Zulus of our province of Natal and the Xhosas of the Eastern Cape Province.

These different tribes of Black Africa were still of great importance and relevance to the Africans, and not only in the rural areas. Repeatedly, there were inter-tribal conflicts with sometimes hundreds or even thousands of victims. The recent Hutu massacres in Ruanda are a telling example, with reported up to eight-hundred thousand viciously butchered victims.

The disenfranchised Africans in this country eventually started to organize themselves politically. In 1912 they founded the African National Congress, the ANC, and some years later the Pan Africanist Congress, the PAC.

As the names indicated, these were not conventional political parties, and neither was ever able to enter Parliament during Apartheid, because the Africans had no vote. The names also made it clear, that both movements were specifically for Africans only.

Both of these groupings protested for more than eighty long years unsuccessfully against their discrimination, and particularly against the fact that they did not have the vote in their own country.

In 1904 the first sixty-two thousand so-called 'indentured' laborers from India had landed in Durban. Their status was just one step above slavery. Most of them were dark skinned members of the lowest castes from the south of the colony, who had been 'imported', like a commodity, to work the sugar plantations of Natal.

Later members of the lighter skinned higher castes arrived here, who often were Muslims, and who were mostly merchants or artisans. The descendants of both groups are still easily distinguished from each other, even now.

Under Apartheid all Asians in South Africa were usually referred to as Indians, even though many were Muslims. These should later more correctly have been called Pakistanis, but this name never took hold in South Africa. Both these groups, of course, had been in this country for generations, long before the separation of colonial India into the present three modern states.

Originally, they lived almost exclusively in Natal, and consequently they spoke English, but many had kept to the present day their Indian languages, as well as their native religions. One could encounter their mosques and shrines or temples in many places in Natal, even in unexpected out-of-the-way places.

Another small group of Asians were the Chinese, who mostly originally had settled in and around Port Elizabeth in the Eastern Cape Province. But today they have also established substantial minorities elsewhere, particularly in Johannesburg und Cape Town.

That finally brings us to the early White minority racial grouping, other than the one of the Cape of Good Hope. They all referred to themselves as Europeans, even though some of them, especially the Afrikaners, had been here for centuries. As mentioned, their ancestors had predominantly come from the Netherlands, but also from France, and to a lesser extent from Germany.

The arrivals during the years from the 1830s to the 1860s from England and Wales, from Scotland and Ireland, played a dominant role in the strengthening and securing of the new colony of Natal. They were generally landless farmers, who had been allocated farms by the colonial administration. Up to this period there had only existed military posts, as well as trading and mission stations. Durban, the main city here, was only founded in the 1830s.

During the early nineteenth century several groups of German immigrants arrived in Natal. My wild guess would be that they consisted of about one or two dozen families each, based on the number of German family names still in existence in Natal.

On the South Coast, more or less close to Marburg and Port Shepstone, we have a substantial number of farming families, who at the moment are threatened with the confiscation of their lands. They are closely structured around their church near Shelly Beach.

In and around Wartburg and Hermannsburg in the interior of the province exists a similar, but much more populous colony of descendants of German immigrants. They maintain German boarding primary and high schools, which are renowned all-over South Africa.

A further large German colony exists in New Germany near Pinetown, which provides today, same as the others, scientists, teachers, judges, politicians and many other professions for this country, in addition to the original farmers.

All these immigrant groups of German extraction in Natal have maintained their home language over the centuries. An oddity, which we spotted immediately after we had arrived here, was their habit of addressing each other by their first names, but newcomers like us were also included in this relaxed atmosphere.

In contrast, as I have observed elsewhere in this story, in Germany colleagues could sit in the same office for ten years and would still address each other by their surnames. A different world!

German churches could be found in many other places in South Africa. Usually, they had developed out of mission stations staffed by Germans. Also to be found in many cities of this country was a German Club. Only during our early years here did we ever enter two of those, in Johannesburg and in Durban. Both were for our taste too nationalistically orientated. They appeared to us to be Nazi or Neo-Nazi enclaves.

On April 20, the birthday of Adolf Hitler, these clubs saw important beer-swilling festivities with the singing of the infamous Nazi songs. The Johannesburg club had a former high-ranking SS officer as a cherished member, who was proud of his past. I met him, back in the 1960s, as an employee of INEFEN, the management consultancy company I was then working for.

This was not at all our glass of beer! We preferred a more relaxed South African 'braai', something similar to a barbecue. Originally, this was a specialty of the Afrikaner community, but it was by now generally considered as a national heritage, much cherished by all South Africans, including many Non-Europeans.

The other major component of early Europeans in South Africa were the later arrivals of immigrants from England, Scotland and Ireland after 1870, but also officials, missionaries, soldiers and sailors, who had chosen to settle here after termination of their deployment.

Another quite substantial wave of immigrants to South Africa in the decades prior to the first World War were Jews fleeing the pogroms of czarist Russia. They came mostly from the Russian provinces of Poland and Lithuania, almost exclusively maintaining their religion and culture, as they did in most of the other countries they emigrated to.

Finally, after World War II, there were the numerous more recent immigrants from Europe, like us, who had been fleeing the devastations and deprivations of the war. After the collapse of communism, there was a further wave of immigrants from Eastern Europe, who were also enticed by the Apartheid government to come here.

They usually attached themselves rather quickly to one of the two dominant sectors within the White communities. But some also kept their ties to local national churches and clubs, particularly those who stayed outside the Afrikaans and English language communities. Portuguese and Greek clubs, for instance, existed in many places, just as German or Norwegian and Swedish mission stations and churches.

When we arrived in this country almost fifty years ago, we encountered virtually neither racial hatred, nor open social upheaval. The most obvious friction, if not to say hatred, was the attitude of many of the Afrikaners against the English-speakers of the country.

A substantial percentage of the Boers had still not overcome the defeat of the Anglo-Boer War at the start of the last century. In particular, because of the concentration camps, where thousands of their women and children had hungered or died. It was therefore astonishing for us that most Afrikaners did not understand the suffering of the Blacks under the Apartheid rules.

The two main sectors of the population, Whites and Non-Whites, lived then side by side, but with almost no contact between them. Thus, the one side knew almost nothing about the other one. The result was that we knew about the discrimination of the Non-Europeans, but we never consciously gave this any serious thought.

Partially, because there was this rather convincing-looking 'Separate but Equal Development' concept. And partially, because of our status as guests in the country who should, in our opinion, not get involved in internal 'family' disputes. And finally, because of the chasm between the two cultures, which we did not understand properly at the time. Did we also close our eyes for selfish reasons? Yes, probably this happened as well.

The Apartheid regime has sometimes been compared to the Nazi rule in Germany, but this comparison is invalid and misleading. Hitler had in the beginning of his rule the support, or at least the toleration, of the vast majority of the German people. The Apartheid concept, on the other hand, was based on the oppression of the majority of the people of South Africa, to suit the ruling minority.

The only two things both had in common was the stupidity and arrogance to cast their respective racist doctrines into laws, and to alienate the majority of the world's peoples by their insistence on racial prejudices. The failure of both systems was of their own making, was pre-programmed, and the collapse was inevitable in the not-so-long run.

Any similarity of the collapse of either of these systems with the failure of the Soviet rule is purely coincidental and not justified, because the Soviet Empire was based on a socio-political doctrine and not on race. Russian nationalism surely also played a role, but this is not the same as the racism of the Nazis and of Apartheid.

It was interesting for me to observe the strong influence of the communists over the ANC during the decades of developments in South Africa. However, the communist doctrine had very little to do with that. It was their White leadership, which was responsible for the strong influence of the party. From early on they had quite correctly understood that the overwhelming numbers of the poor African laborers, and therefore of the eventual voters, would after the collapse of the Apartheid regime automatically guarantee a strong influence for the Communist Party.

A telling example of how business was done by the Whites with the Non-Whites I encountered when I was working as a management consultant in a car dealership in Kimberley. This client had a surprisingly large turnover in secondhand cars with Africans. Surprisingly, because at this time almost all employed Africans were unqualified or semi-qualified laborers who were paid the low wages for these lowly categories of the South African workforce.

I was shocked to see how this company handled credit sales to these customers. They first of all demanded a large deposit, which already covered a substantial part of their credit risks. This looked at first glance like good business practice, but it was simply an expression of the racial prejudices of the time, since this practice was generally restricted to Africans and the other Non-Whites.

If this deposit was not available, and this was the usual position, they first inflated the list price by fifty percent and then gave the credit customer a receipt for twenty-five percent of the inflated selling price, which then served as the deposit.

Thus, they had met the legal requirements for the banks and for themselves, which stipulated such a deposit. This law was well-intentioned to prevent reckless lending but was subverted by the dealer and the bank in the name of doing business, namely of making a profit.

In the real world this example of creative financing looked like this: at this time the price of a second-hand VW Beatle was about six hundred Rand. If this was the list price, the inflated price then became nine hundred Rand. The legally required deposit of twenty-five percent of this inflated price would have amounted to two hundred and twenty-five Rand.

The poor African now had to repay nine hundred Rand, minus the fictitious deposit of two hundred and twenty-five Rand, totaling six hundred and seventy-five Rand, plus interest at the prevailing rate, obviously. Thus, the dealer landed up with an extra seventy-five Rand in his back-pocket, tax-free of course.

Theoretically, all three parties were happy, the African buyer, the dealer and the bank. But I never thought to ask any of the Africans what their feelings were. In those days Europeans did not talk to Non-Europeans, other than to ask for information, or to give orders.

9

WHAT WAS IT LIKE?

Now that I have concluded my working life it is probably the appropriate time and place to talk about my reactions to, and my impressions of, the Apartheid era in South Africa. In this Part of the book I should excessively have made use of the 'inverted comma' quotation marks. This would have been necessitated by the fact that I have constantly quoted Apartheid and Afrikaans terms, which I decided not to translate, in order to preserve the 'whiff' of this odious period. But to avoid a 'graveyard' of these marks I decided to generally avoid their use.

The word Apartheid translates as separate-ness, and this was supposed to mean "Separate but Equal Development for Whites and Non-Whites alike". This was how it was explained in a guidebook on South Africa which we had bought before emigrating here. At face value this definition appeared reasonable enough to us, not knowing much else about this country, apart from the basics regarding climate, history and geography.

During our first few years here, we were discouraged to have any social contact with the Africans, Coloreds (mixed blood of any kind) or Asians, otherwise lumped together as the Non-Whites. By the way, in this country the term Blacks equally referred to only the Africans, as also to the wider definition of Non-Whites. They were all discriminated against, politically as well as economically and in the workplace. And even in education, maybe the worst example of them all. Their human rights and dignities were trampled-on intentionally by the ruling class.

One of our first memorable experiences with Apartheid was some-what unsettling for us. Our large new property in Kloof needed a lot of work to bring it into some sort of acceptable shape. We hired a so-called garden boy for one day to get this started.

At lunchtime we invited him to sit down at our table to have his lunch, but we could see that he was very uncomfortable. We under-stood only later that we had made a serious *faux-pas* and that his behavior was normal under the circumstances, because no African would have expected to be treated in such a way by White people and to be asked to sit at the table of a European family. We actually unknowingly had embarrassed the young man.

Because he spoke perfect English (better than we did) I later asked him why he did such low-paid work. His reply was: "I had to leave Johannesburg in a hurry to escape my creditors". The use of a sophis-ticated word like creditor by an African laborer was practically unheard of. But maybe he was no simple laborer? I did not enquire any further, to avoid possibly embarrassing him even more.

It took us quite a while to understand, at least to a certain extent, the substantial cultural gap between Africans and Europeans. This manifested itself in many ways, from polygamy to social and group behavior. The way our State President Zuma was elected and subse-quently kept in office, may serve as a good, or rather, as a bad exam-ple. In spite of his obvious corrupt past and his criminal actions or omissions the ANC, and therefore the majority of the Africans, shielded him and kept him in office, long past his sell-by date.

In Europe such a tainted person would never have succeeded in becoming leader of his party, and eventually of his country. But even if he surprisingly would have managed to do this, he would not have lasted long. Yes, I know, Signore Berlusconi in Italy, but he had a media empire behind him, and I would have assumed that helped substantially in his case.

One of the worst economic aspects of Apartheid was for the Non-White majority the doctrine of job reservation. The government had ordered that practically all jobs above the level of laborers and clerks were reserved for Whites, except in cases where Non-Whites were working for or with other Non-Whites. This would really have been for Parliament to decide, but this distinction was theoretical because the majority of seats were anyway occupied by the governing party.

It was therefore decreed that, for instance, a Black medical doctor could only treat Black patients. Rebellious as always, I asked myself at the time whether he would have been allowed to help a White patient in a live-threatening situation. If so, such a patient would presumably have had to be thoroughly decontaminated after-wards.

My own experiences with this doctrine were quite extensive. As explained in a previous part, our builder's yards were regularly invaded and controlled by the Black Jacks. This was a government or municipal organization of Africans in their black uniforms, specialized in checking construction sites to ensure that no persons were employed illegally. I asked myself whether they also controlled factories and workshops, and I suspected that they did.

The Black Jacks were not the only example of the employment of Africans by the government. Police and the prisons administration employed many thousands of them, and the army had formed special units, which had been nick-named "Askaris", to fight the Anti-Apartheid 'terrorists'. This name originated during the Great War in German-East-Africa for those local Africans, who had loyally fought under General Paul von Lettow-Vorbeck against the British troops which had been sent from South Africa.

Every time the State had raided one of our contract sites and caught us employing Africans illegally, as the sole director of our group of firms I had to appear in court. The usual crime was the employment and remuneration of Blacks as artisans, instead of as laborers.

Sometimes our lawyers managed to get the case to be withdrawn, but often enough hefty fines had to be paid. These expenses had already been allowed for in their tenders by all the builders, since we were all forced to work like that because of the scarcity of White artisans in the builder's trades and the prohibition of utilizing Non-White artisans.

The Magistrates and Judges in Natal and the Cape provinces were generally more understanding and less dogmatic than those in the Transvaal and the Free State, the hotbeds of the Apartheid doctrine. But they also had to apply the laws, whether they liked it or not, and their hands were tied. But as recalled earlier, a one-hundred fifty percent Apartheid prosecutor of Natal had threatened to have me deported back to the cold German winter, if in future our firm would not better respect the holy Apartheid laws.

At all three levels of the State, and in the state-owned enterprises, in addition to all levels of management, only Whites were employed as clerks or, for instance, as stewardesses by the state-owned South African Airways, the SAA.

The companies owned or controlled by Afrikaners also employed

Non-White office workers only as a rare exception. On the other hand, in every office in the country there was to be found the ubiquitous African tea boy. As an aside: I do not remember any tea girls.

The white clerks of the Railways and Harbors Administration were effectively in sheltered employment. Many of them had practically no education, and we often wondered how the railways were able to function with such personnel. Maybe all the lower positions were occupied by two clerks! Money meant very little in this case, as the railways had a monopoly. Even the use of long-distance trucks was restricted by government to help them. After all, this was where the government hid the Afrikaners who would otherwise have been unemployed.

The above did, however, not apply to the Post Office, the other huge state-owned enterprise. This also employed almost exclusively thousands of Afrikaans employees, but they generally appeared to be more competent.

Here in Natal practically all firms apparently employed exclusively Indians in all clerical positions. Our group companies would not even have considered to hire an African for such a job. This is an example of how deeply these rules and regulations had become engrained in this country. I am not even sure if such an unusual action would not have resulted in another court appearance for me.

10

'GRAND' APARTHEID

Up to the end of the Second World War the segregation of the races had worked more or less smoothly in this country, in line with what happened worldwide in all the other colonized countries at that time.

Things changed drastically in South Africa in 1948. The National Party (under a slightly different name), the main political party of the Afrikaners headed by General Malan, had won this year's parliamentary election against the United Party lead by General Smuts.

The erstwhile Boer republics had produced a large number of generals, measured against the moderate size of their populations. Most, if not all of them, had retired after having temporarily served during one of the many skirmishes with the Africans or the British during the Anglo-Boer War. Some, like the two just mentioned, had served with the British forces during World War II. Now they were usually farmers or lawyers or politicians.

The new government placed now the hitherto quietly under-stood race relations for the first time into the law books. This was enthusiastically supported by the Dutch Reformed Church, the predominant confession of the Afrikaners. They even had formed a secret society, the *Broederbond*, to cement their hold on the State and on society, and also to establish the ideological and 'philosophic' foundation for the Apartheid doctrine.

While typing these lines (dictating would sound much more impressive, but would unfortunately not be true), I was immediately reminded of a parallel memory in respect of Nazi Germany, regarding the treatment of the Jews. The existing informal Anti-semitism in that country was shortly after Hitler's 1933 election win transformed into the Anti-Jewish race laws, which finally led to the extermination camps during the war, and the resulting global condemnation of Germany.

The first thing these "Neo-Nazis" did was to officially and legally recognize four racial groups, based on appearances and ancestry: Whites or Europeans, Africans, Coloreds (mixed races) and Indians or Asians/Asiatics. Later the local Chinese were added to the Indian group. The latter three were collectively classified as the Non-Whites or Non-Europeans. The implications of these negative terms must have been particularly galling for those concerned.

But visiting Japanese businessmen were promoted to Honorary Whites, after they had invested billions of dollars in their Toyota car plant at Isipingo south of Durban. Business is business, after all! The international diplomats of color accredited to South Africa were also awarded this status, obviously to side-step diplomatic frictions and problems.

To avoid some to-be-expected misunderstandings: the term Coloreds related in South Africa from times immemorial to people of mixed blood, while internationally the meaning was rather referring to all Non-Whites, and therefore included the Africans.

After the end of Apartheid another classification problem arose. The term Blacks, which was also utilized in legislation about the new meaning of job reservation, would sometimes refer to Africans only, or to all Non-Whites.

Act after discriminatory act was churned out by the government 'law factory', to cement the White minority rule, their preferential economic position, the privileges of the Whites for the future and the discrimination of all the Non-Whites. I won't bother neither with exact titles, nor with a complete list. Examples of their diligent work were:

- The Prohibition of Mixed Marriages Act of 1949 started the legal frenzy. It was highly unlikely that many such marriages would have existed at the time.
- The Population Registration Act of 1950, which of course did not apply to Europeans. That would presumably have been a 'black' mark (pun intended) against the personal freedom values of the Boers!
- The Immorality Act, also of 1950, forbidding sex over the color lines. All the time during Apartheid there were

prosecutions of white men, usually Afrikaners, who had sinned across the racial lines.

The scope of this legislation was clear enough: one did not want to create additional Coloreds, because the ones already existing could unfortunately not be made to disappear. The situation was slightly different regarding the Indians. The government offered a lot of money to those of them who were prepared to go back to India. But there were not many takers! Our Indians preferred racist South Africa over free India, something I always found difficult to understand, even after taking into account the equally inhuman caste conditions in that country.

In the Apartheid era, after all the racial mixing for centuries, there existed tens of thousands of people, particularly in the Cape province, who were difficult to classify according to the legal prescription. The poor overworked Apartheid officials had a tough life! One could actually feel sorry for them, just for a moment, that is.

As mentioned earlier, we had often witnessed during these years in the English newspapers heated arguments amongst the Afrikaners, who of their group were tainted by this 'bad blood', and quite a few proud members were technically actually Coloreds, including a cabinet minister.

This kind of information was of course not found on the state-run radio, nor on the later *ditto* television. It was only available through the English-language newspapers, which for this and other reasons were vigorously persecuted by the police and the prosecutors as perceived "enemies of the state".

The race classification officials were permanently busy with re-classifying people, but I do not recall any case where an Afrikaner was 'degraded' to the racial level of a Colored. Typically, I also do not recall any instance, where an Afrikaner female was subjected to this kind of traumatic and inhuman treatment.

There followed a plethora of other laws, all designed to protect for all time the identity of the superior White race and their political and economic dominance and interests. The most important and hurtful one of these for the Non-Whites was the Group Areas Act.

This act was setting aside exclusive localities for each racial group, for habitation and even for business! Regardless, whether for ownership or rental. Naturally favoring the interests of the Europeans, who were allocated the best areas of land and the most profitable parts of the business districts. This was possibly the most vicious and far-reaching of all the Apartheid laws. To keep things clear: Africans were not allowed to own any piece of land, but this provision did not apply to Coloreds and Indians.

On the average commercial farm was usually living a White family of six to eight persons, with several African or Colored families of servants and laborers, with maybe thirty to forty heads, staying in a separate compound nearby. These Non-Europeans were naturally not affected by this law, because that would have created insurmountable problems for the White farmers.

Because they had been staying, or because their businesses were located in the "wrong" Group Area, millions of Non-Europeans were forced to abandon their abode, land or business, which in most cases they had possessed or occupied for long times, sometimes for centuries. Because often they had refused to move, they were subjected to the infamous "forced removals", without any or only scant compensation. A brutal form of internal deportation (any mental connection seen to the behavior of a certain Mr. Stalin?).

In addition to the economic hardships for the Non-Whites in connection with these deportations, they had to cope with the further psychological and cultural trauma of having been forced to abandon their ancestral burial grounds. It must be remembered that the majority of the Africans, and particularly the rural populations, have held on to their atavistic beliefs, where the close relationship with their deceased elders played a decisive role. Their membership of Christian churches and sects was often only superficial.

The Cape Malays and the Indians suffered the same hardships in this regard. These ancestral beliefs were not only deeply rooted in the African psyche but as well in the beliefs of the Muslims. All these considerations were completely ignored by the Afrikaners, because these heathen believes were disregarded as Non-Christian.

Hundreds of such Group Areas had been established all over the country. It is impossible for me to go into much detailed descriptions of the hardships suffered by the people who were expelled and resettled. I will use just one of these narratives as an example to illustrate what was done to the displaced people in the name of Grand Apartheid.

In Cape Town existed the infamous "District 6", close to the historical center of the city. For centuries this area had been the home of thousands of families of the Cape Malays, with their mosques, cemeteries, community centers, markets and all the other structures which usually develop over a long time in any established community.

When they first started to settle in this district in the seventeenth century, this area was well outside of the nascent town and was not considered as particularly desirable by the Europeans. That is the primary reason, why they were then allowed to build there. Everybody knew everybody in this district, and the community spirit was exemplary.

Unfortunately for them, centuries later the small town had grown into a world metropolis and this quarter had become part of the inner city. Now it had become the ideal area to develop upper-middle-class residential properties. If one could only get rid of the present occupants of this choice piece of land! But what for did one have the Group Areas Act?

Quickly, the necessary legislation was prepared, and Parliament was instructed to pass it *pronto*. Remember, apart from the ineffective Official Opposition of the United Party, which was almost as racist as the National Party, there was only one single genuine opposition Member of Parliament, Mrs. Suzman. She was an unflappable fighter, but apart from pointing out and protesting the brutal and inhuman ways of Apartheid, she obviously was powerless to stop this onslaught by the ruling National Party.

There exploded, however, a completely unexpected and very strong protest movement by the white Capetonians against this sacrilege. They vigorously opposed this move, but I am not sure whether this happened because of the racist background of this action, or because the district was a cherished architectural landmark and tourist attraction of the city.

But all was in vain; the Apartheid juggernaut could not be stopped by decency and logic! Without undue delay, these thousands of families were brutally uprooted and banished to the wilderness of the Cape Flats, a desolate former salt marsh and extensive sand area, twenty kilometers away and well out of the way of the eyes of the Europeans. Thus, this problem was solved; elegantly, quickly and legally, of course. And some of the 'right' people were able to make a few millions in the process.

All over the country some poorer Whites had at all times in the past been living amongst the members of other racial groups in some of the less affluent and desirable neighborhoods. Such suburbs were subsequently declared Non-European group areas. Amazingly, but quite in conformity with the Apartheid doctrine, these Whites also had later to leave their abodes and move to a White area.

This happened, regardless of whether they were able to afford the higher prices of properties and rentals in these more upmarket areas, or not. Their forced moves brought still other hardships for them as well. To start with, the cost of living was always somewhat higher in a posh European quarter than in the more primitive surroundings of a less desirable suburb.

Another negative aspect was the fact that these 'poor Whites', a group which is even to-day still discernible, had got along with their Non-White neighbors much better than they did now with the more affluent Europeans. This latter strange fact caused the eternal consternation of the Apartheid High Priests!

The Johannesburg suburb of Hillbrow displayed in the 1960s almost the character of a continental European town, because it was mostly populated by recent immigrants from Europe. This whole densely populated part of the city also possessed the typical characteristics of a huge transit camp for recent immigrants.

Most of the newly arrived Europeans (there were no others, naturally) were very soon sucked up by this huge country, but new arrivals always replenished the vacuum very quickly again. The immense population density, and the fast turnover of the inhabitants, created a very special European culture in the middle of this black country.

In those days it was perfectly safe to go for a walk in the evening after dark; to have a late dinner in one of the numerous ethnic restaurants, or to rummage at this time in the huge international Hillbrow bookstore. All the shops and restaurants in this suburb were owned and managed by Whites, and the employees were almost exclusively Europeans or Indians.

One could hear many European languages in this polyglot quarter, but surprisingly very seldom any Afrikaans, the language of the dominant White population group of this country, which controlled this African state with an iron fist.

The relatively small number of Africans at this time in the city mostly spoke enough English to be able to survive in this unAfrican metropolis. They were only allowed to perform menial tasks, because everything else was reserved for the Whites. Any jobs having fallen somehow through the cracks of this system of job reservation were quickly snatched up by the agile Indians in town.

Durban was a city of about one and a half million people, give or take a million. In those days, the numbers of inhabitants were recorded as accurately as in Europe, but only in regard to the minority group of the Europeans. The others; Africans, Coloreds, Indians and

Pakistani, were not considered important enough to count and record properly.

The official population figures for South Africa, as I remember very well, shot up by more than five million shortly after the demise of Apartheid when, for the first time, proper census figures became available, even if these were in the beginning rather sketchy in some of the details.

Most of the Non-White residential areas in the country were well outside of the cities and towns and, most importantly, they were therefore out of sight of the Whites. This touchy subject covered on the one hand the Afrikaner's perceived mission to look after the 'savages', but it was simultaneously deeply rooted in the racial bigotry of the dominant group of the Europeans. My guess is that at this time ninety-nine percent of the Whites had never entered one of these dormitory townships.

The vast majority of the inhabitants of Durban were Indians, and that was what unfortunately the place looked like. Very much like what we later had encountered on Mauritius, with its likewise large Indian majority. Rubbish and detritus every-where. These Asians were naturally also subject to the Group Areas Act, but they were somewhat better-off than the Coloreds in Cape Town.

Their residential areas near the center of the city were so vast that to remove these people, and to offer the land to the Whites, would have been practically impossible. Furthermore, these quarters were not the most desirable ones of the city, and most of the Europeans would have balked at moving there. In any case, there was for them no shortage of accommodation in nice neighborhoods.

Only a few juicy bits of land were declared a White Group Area and were thus reserved for the benefit of the superior European race, or rather, for the benefit of a few well-connected individuals. One of these special areas was a relatively small complex very near the town hall, but in the wrong direction from it, as far as property values went.

This area was cleared of its original inhabitants but lay then fallow for decades. Either none of the Whites wanted this land, or the displaced wily Indian families had tied-up the State for many years in the courts. As far as I know the land is still partially undeveloped.

In addition to the traditional Indian residential and business areas near the center of Durban, two further huge dormitory suburbs, relatively close to town, have been developed for them by the government, because their numbers seemed to mushroom exponentially. Both of these Indian townships were almost completely built by the group of companies I worked with for sixteen years.

South of Durban we built the Chatsworth Township, a huge sprawl of single- and double-story dwellings, with schools, many apartment blocks, police stations, community and medical centers as well as a huge hospital complex thrown in for a bit of variety. I do not recall the total number of dwelling units built by us over the years, but they amounted to several thousands.

Just now I have recalled in my memory, what this huge area looked like from an elevated point; exactly like the view out of the window of a plane landing at the Las Vegas airport. The same picture of rows after rows of tiny houses on winding and apparently narrow streets.

Afterwards the identical drill was repeated in the north of Durban, where we built the Phoenix Township for the use of the Indian community. This was rather a political cliff-hanger, because right next to this development was unfortunately situated the suburb of Durban-North, probably the most prestigious, and therefore most expensive, European quarter of all of Durban.

But this attack on the racial prejudices and interests of the White inhabitants was considered by government as accept-able, because at least ninety percent of the inhabitants of this exclusive suburb were English-speakers, who did not really count, because they did not vote for the National Party in any case, and it was only a handful of blue-blooded Afrikaners who were subjected to these unseemly neighbors.

The Coloreds of Durban also had, somewhat reluctantly, a number of their own small townships built for them by the government. Here our company only constructed about fifty percent of the total of about one thousand dwelling units, all in the form of three-story apartment blocks.

The other half of the work went to another company. As we found out later, this firm had spent a lot of money to buy some city councilors and senior officials. I will come back to the subject "just now". This phrase is a typical South African usage and can mean, for instance, right now, or very soon, or maybe soon, or. . . .

All of these usually very large building contracts were, on the side of the contract owners, administered in a rather confusing decentralized way by the Department of Community Development. But most of these construction contracts were for all practical purposes administered on behalf of this Department by the City Engineer of the Durban Corporation. This applied particularly in regard to the certification, evaluation and the disbursement of the monthly progress payments for the con-tractors.

There remains now to talk about the townships for the Africans. But as far as Durban is concerned, there were, to the best of my knowledge, none built for them during my time. Yes, two huge African townships existed here; Umlazi south of Durban and Kwa Mashu to the north of the city. These were laid out in such a way that each of them had only one combined entrance and exit road, which in case of riots could easily be controlled or closed by the police or the army.

It appeared to me that he majority of the mostly single-story houses were built, or had been contracted to be built, by their inhabitants. I remember that these areas generally lacked the uniformity of design and appearance of the dwellings in the townships we had built for the Indian community. But I also remember other parts of these townships, which did look like having been built in one fell swoop by some contractor.

However, for my time with our construction group, I do not recall any building contracts for any African townships in Natal. But by now it is obvious that in addition to private houses also shops, office blocks, petrol stations and super-markets have been built privately and commercially there.

My lack of knowledge about any government building activities for Africans is not coincidental; same as the majority of the Whites I did not frequent these areas. Their shebeens (illegal pubs, sometimes with a rustic restaurant attached) were sometimes visited by a certain type of young Europeans, but this was against the law and dangerous, and could have serious consequences.

During my time in Durban the only building work in conjunction with Africans and connected to government, and therefore to Apartheid, were the construction of the hostels for African migrant laborers. These massive multi-story clinker blocks housed single African workers, employed mainly by the SARH, the South African Railway and Harbor Administration, in dormitory-like complexes. To the best of my recollection, this work was never put out to public tenders. I wondered who has built these barracks?

These hostels quickly became hotbeds of criminality. To start with, gang-related activities prospered around the illegal housing of people who were not at all supposed to live in these structures, which resulted in heavy overcrowding and all the automatic consequences of such an unhealthy situation. It must be explained here that living quarters for Africans were almost nonexistent in Durban. If available at all, maybe as a garage or an outbuilding, they were expensive because of the permanent African migration pressure from the countryside into the cities.

The sanitary conditions in these cramped quarters quickly became atrocious. Combined with an almost complete lack of building maintenance, and the deterioration of the facilities, such as toilets and washing installations, the quality of this accommodation rapidly turned them into slums. One of the many reasons for the lack of maintenance were the frequent attacks on maintenance personnel by fellow Africans. In addition, there also was an element of senseless vandalism and theft of sanitary equipment items.

Additionally, political rivalries soon started to play-out in these overcrowded quarters, primarily between members of the ANC and the IFP, the party of the Zulu traditionalists. They considered the members of any other tribes as unwanted interlopers, competing with them for their jobs. Over the years hundreds of men have been killed in the Durban hostels alone. Even more were murdered in the much larger complexes in the mining areas of the Transvaal province around Johannesburg and the mining towns.

Since the official inhabitants of these hostels were all single-living African men, it is not surprising that women also soon found their way into these quarters. This naturally caused more conflicts and, regrettably, conflict amongst Africans often equated to manslaughter and murder.

Another aspect of this situation was the fact that most of these single-living men were married, or at least in a relationship with a woman back in the homelands. In most cases these women were also the mothers of their children. The men were supposed to send a large part of their wages back to their wives and children in the rural districts, instead of spending it on the hostel women, on drink and often on assorted drugs.

There is an interesting but slightly subversive thought coming up here: if all these men had done the right thing by their dependents in the homelands, what would have happened to these hostel women? But I better stick to my job of writing this very important book, and not digress into my usual critical analysis of "what if's". But I also have to record that very many, and probably the majority of these laborers, regularly sent home part of their modest wages. A large part of the rural population was completely dependent on these transfers by the itinerant workers, since as far as I know there were no social payments for Africans during Apartheid.

Now let me return to the corruption incidences relating to the tendering processes for the construction of the dwellings for the Non-Whites in Durban. This was one of a number of times that I had personal knowledge and involvement in tendering corruption during the Apartheid era.

Previous to this point in my story, and before my time, there had been some massive rumors of wide-spread corruption in the Durban City Council. The government had subsequently established the James Commission, which had discovered endemic corruption in this city administration. Durban was then politically controlled by the opposition United Party, just like the Province of Natal. Thus, the unusual interest of the National Party government in this local situation.

The James Commission had found many cases of massive fraud and corruption. But, as is so common in this type of investigations, in many cases the Commission could not find the necessary proof acceptable in the criminal courts. As a result, a number of shady politicians and officials were still sitting in their power seats and well-paid positions of the City Council and its departments.

There has been another incident of corruption of which I had personal experience, and this was a particularly nasty one. The Deputy Mayor of the Durban Corporation had told my boss that our companies would have to look after him if we intended to get any more work from the Durban Corporation, even if our tenders were the lowest and of the best quality and highest reliability.

I know that he was a number of times allowed to use my boss's motorboat and trailer for free, but what else had transpired I do not know for sure. This incident was especially galling, because the company desperately needed and was dependent on this specialized kind of work to survive. This was therefore not just corruption, but a form of blackmail as well. The timing of this event fell between the findings of the James Commission and the subsequent work of a further government investigation. This motorboat user was one of the city councilors who decided to prematurely retire after the second investigation had been announced.

This new investigation had now started, and I had to spend a lot of my time under interrogation by the investigators, because subsequent to having received some anonymous tips we, that is our group of construction companies, had been able to point the investigation of the police in the right direction. By the way, in South Africa the SAP, the South African Police were an organ of central government, and not functions of provinces or municipalities, as was the case in many other countries. They had the country-wide monopoly on criminal investigations.

The authorities now discovered that a certain company listed on the Johannesburg Stock Exchange had given bundles of their shares for free to a number of Durban City councilors and senior city officials, mostly those who had already been under suspicion by the James Commission. I do not know what exactly transpired in the end, but some councilors and officials resigned shortly afterwards, just as the Deputy Mayor, which probably was just a coincidence.

In another case of corruption, we were puzzled for quite some time when our concrete, and particularly our concrete building blocks, inexplicably failed so often in the laboratory tests of the Durban City Engineer's department, after our own laboratory had shown positive results.

To skim on the cement content of concrete and concrete products has always been a favorite means of 'cost cutting' on building sites anywhere, but we always had made sure that we did not 'economize' on the cement content of our concrete mixtures.

Per chance we discovered at one point the cause of our troubles. Our fiercest competitor building company had bribed the Clerk of Works of the Durban Corporation on our major contract to falsify the test results of our concrete and concrete products, causing us a lot of worries, delays and unnecessary expenses.

This corrupt activity had far-reaching cost implications for us, particularly in the context of the concrete for the foundations of the houses we were building. These tests took several days to complete, and when the negative results were eventually announced, the in the meantime largely completed houses had to be demolished and to be rebuilt.

Corruption during the Apartheid years appeared in many different guises. During these years corruption, influence peddling and other shady activities were always only a stone-throw away. And of course, it was not only in government circles and on the municipal level where these things happened. As a matter of fact, the situation was not much better in the private sector.

If an employee wanted to chisel a short-time paid holiday out of his employer, all he had to do was to visit certain Indian doctors in Durban to obtain a sick note, without any consultation necessarily taking place. I knew that this sort of thing can occasionally happen anywhere, but in our case the situation was so prevalent that our company had compiled a list of general practitioners, whose sick certificates landed unattended in the waste-paper basket.

This I know because I was the author of this list. Our action was probably illegal, but none of the gentlemen concerned has ever complained.

This was not an isolated situation. A friend of ours owned a company which imported chemicals through Durban harbor, and which supplied these to factories all over the country. He regularly had the designated buyer of one of his major customers come down to Durban for his "all expenses paid" holiday and stay with our friend. He naturally was also forced 'to look after' the customs officials who inspected his chemical imports, to avoid having his supplies blockaded. A lucrative arrangement for them.

Another friend had a very elevated position in one of the major South African groups as a Customer Relations Officer, or something similar. Every year he spent hundreds of thousands of Rand of his employer's money on the so-called 'Entertainment of Customers'. This activity was, and probably still is, a major South African 'industry' in its own right!

This entertainment consisted, for instance, of costly visits to prestige restaurants and night clubs. I won't mention rumored visits to brothels and strip clubs in this context. Stays at up-market game reserves or posh casino complexes, and expensive admissions to major sports events, such as rugby and cricket, the 'religions' of South African sports enthusiasts, were other perks for discerning and 'deserving' customers. And all financed by the taxman, via the allowable deductions from the taxable income.

Because we live (very happily) in South Africa, I had to battle with the US-configured keyboard of my laptop computer. This is generally fine, but I am also writing these books of mine in German, and very occasionally I make a typing mistake. Accordingly, I have installed a German spell-checker in addition to the English one.

Microsoft has unfortunately firmly connected this app with a German virtual keyboard. As a result, more than thirty keys of my laptop produce something different on the screen than what is shown on the keys. Very frustrating, but back to the treadmill.

Now let us now have a closer look at the various aspects of Grand Apartheid, as they affected the political rights of the Non-White majority. These rights were easy to describe; there weren't any! The discrimination was achieved by the simple and efficient expedient that they did not have the vote, and consequently they had no political rights.

Racially based parties were illegal in this country. Rather a poor joke, really. All parties in Parliament were by definition racially based, namely in favor of the Whites, since no other race was allowed into those sacred halls. Non-Europeans were also not allowed to join any white political party, as far as I remember.

During our times in the Apartheid era there were only three parties in Parliament: the ruling National Party of the Afrikaners, the Official Opposition in the form of the United Party, which had mostly English-speaking voters, but was almost as racist as the ruling one, and the Progressive Party, which over the years changed its name more than once. Most of the time this party had only Helen Suzman as the single representative, the Member of Parliament for Houghton, Johannesburg. She was on her own a more effective and decisive opposition than all the MPs of the United Party.

All Africans who were allowed to enter the White areas had to carry at all times the much-hated 'Dom Pass', if they did not want to risk arrest. This legal requirement caused wide-spread opposition and unrest, particularly from the African women, for whom this annoying rule apparently was particularly cumbersome.

A revolt against this racist prescription led to the infamous Sharpeville Massacre of 1960, which was organized by the PAC, the Pan Africanist Congress. Thousands of Africans, mostly women, were marching to the local police station to demonstrate against this law and to voice their protest against the hated 'Dom Pass'.

The originally peaceful demonstration later turned violent. The police were probably fearing for their lives, panicked and opened fire on the marchers and killed sixty-nine Africans and wounded one hundred and sixty-eight further victims (Wikipedia).

This brutal event, even though it was unintended and not planned by the authorities, ignited for the first time wide-spread protests in the overseas public opinion and newspapers. It galvanized activists everywhere against Apartheid and South Africa. But the overseas governments did not react to any substantial extent. South Africa was, after all, an important and loyal bastion against world communism, in addition to be the source of important minerals!

In the 1970s the Apartheid government had cut out large swaths of the country, those which were overwhelmingly populated by Africans, to create the so-called Homelands, which in South Africa were colloquially called Bantustans. This word was a derivate of

Bantu, the generic term for all the southern African tribes of the Nguni language group. The government's intention was to later proclaim these structures as independent states. The basic idea of this sleight-of-hand political *vabanque* play was to be able to officially reduce the apparent number of Africans in South Africa.

A further 'positive' side-effect was the fact that in the process these Africans lost their South African citizenship. Therefore, they could not obtain anymore a passport from the country of their birth, which came in handy because now they could not travel anymore overseas to agitate against the Apartheid system. Machiavelli would have been proud!

In the period from 1960 to 1983 three and a half million Africans (Wikipedia) were forcefully removed from the white South African heartland, their original home, into these Bantustans. I have not been able to find out how many were altogether during the full duration of the forty-six years of Apartheid removed and lost their homes by the creation of these so-called homelands.

These claimed "sovereign states" were only created to further the Apartheid ideology and were never recognized by any countries, except by South Africa, of course. They were not really meant to be fiscally viable. The South African government had made sure of that, to keep them down and in line through their control over them.

One way of finding some revenue for these artificially created 'states' was to arrange for them to issue tenders for licenses to build and operate gambling casino complexes near the South African borders. To be close to the borders was imperative, because only the hoped-for tourists and the Euro-peans out of 'White' South Africa had the necessary money to feed the one-armed bandits and the roulette and blackjack tables of these 'immoral' enterprises. Any perceived similarities to the reservations for the AmerIndians in the States are purely coincidental.

An important consideration in this connection was the fact that 'games of luck' of any kind were strictly forbidden in South Africa. This made it very likely that large numbers of Whites and Indians would cave in to the temptation to try their luck in these sin-temples in the homelands.

This whole plan was a typical example of political and religious bigotry. At home, for religious reasons South Africans were not allowed to gamble, but as soon as the pious Afrikaners were beyond the internal borders in one of the homelands, the government and the

Afrikaans churches could wash their dirty hands of this 'devilish' behavior of their flock.

A behavior which they claimed to abhor as much as the dreaded television. This two-faced attitude was defended with the shady excuse that there was nothing they could do about what their people did outside of South Africa.

The first and the largest of these homelands was the Transkei, which was intended to be the Bantustan of the Xhosa tribe. It had been excised from the Eastern Cape province of South Africa. Its nearest border from us was just about thirty kilometers south from Margate, where we now lived.

The tender sums for these casino complexes were intended to initially fill the coffers of these so-called states, but most of these monetary flows were reported to have landed in the pockets of the local tribal strongmen, as also happened so often in other countries in Africa. In the case of the Transkei, these were the ample pockets of the Xhosa Paramount Chief Kaiser Mathanzima.

One of these casino complexes opened near us on the Wild Coast, just over the interior border between the province of Natal and the Transkei. Gambling was only part of the attraction, however. There was also a medium-sized cinema, with three or four shows every night, which were always well patronized, even though nobody admitted to ever having entered these premises.

This peculiarity reminded me immediately of the frugal Aldi chain-stores in Germany, with a similar trading concept as Walmart in the States. In the beginning, nobody ever admitted shopping there. It was one of those inexplicable coincidences that this cinema showed exclusively pornographic films, which were of course strictly forbidden in South Africa. This was a veritable money fountain.

On a more conventional plane, there was also a huge Five-Star hotel as part of the casino. The complex also had its own small airfield, water sport facilities and a golf course designed by the world-renowned South African golf star Gary Player. There was as well a very nice horse-riding establishment. One could hire a horse and go for an extensive outride along the beach, and then ride inland for many kilometers, galloping or moving more sedately.

One could also walk a few kilometers along the beach or through the African bush, in almost complete isolation. Additionally, there was the short walk to a large lagoon, where fossils of petrified trees and ammonites could be admired. Unfortunately, the local Africans have developed a home industry of chiseling these unique fossils out of the coastal rocks.

And there was the beautiful typical African scenery of the renowned Wild Coast, which had earned this name by the wild storms and seas which had caused probably hundreds of shipwrecks along its practically uninhabited rocky coast. From times immemorial, sailors had lost their ships, and more often than not, their lives here.

The local history goes back probably more than two thousand years. These wrecks started with the boats of reported (or speculated) Phoenician explorers from the Western Mediterranean Sea to those of the Chinese trading and exploratory flotillas of the Ming dynasty. One can find even today shards of fractured Ming porcelain pottery along this coast.

They were followed by dozens of ships of the East India Companies of Holland, France and England to the more recent ones of the colonial powers. Numerous passenger and freight ships are buried here, and even the wreck of the odd German submarine of the last war has been reported.

A special aspect of this past is the fact that there were survivors from many of these wrecks who had been able to cross the surging surf and to reach the beach. We are aware now that during the centuries many had been able to reach Port Elizabeth in the south, or the distant Mozambique in the north.

But we also know of hundreds of these survivors, who have been taken care of by the local population, who usually had their huts some kilometers inland. Many light-skinned Africans live near this coast. Some years ago, I read here that our hero Nelson Mandela probably had one or more of these survivors amongst his ancestors.

Ironically, this would mean that Mr. Mandela was under the Apartheid rules technically a Colored. But this was just speculation on my part, since I do not know how exactly the Apartheid administration classified the Non-Whites. The Nguni are generally not quite black, but rather black-brown. Fact is that a large percentage of the Africans in South Africa have a skin color varying from deep black-brown, through all the intermittent shades, to light brown.

But I would suggest another possible explanation. When the Nguni tribes came south from East Africa, they met the light-skinned Khoi-San people in their future homeland. We do not know what happened there at the time, but it is not unreasonable to assume that most of the Khoi-San men would have been killed in the inevitable skirmishes, and that the victorious Xhosa warriors would have taken care of the widowed women, which would also easily explain the appearance of so many light-skinned offspring along this coast.

Another ploy of the Apartheid regime was, to allow the homelands to issue their own postage stamps. This was supposed to provide the necessary cashflow and simultaneously to support the fictitious claim of their sovereignty. Behind the scenes it was, of course, the South African postal administration, which arranged on their behalf the design and which printed all their philatelic products and sold them worldwide. An entirely separate question remains, whether the various homeland administrations ever saw any of this "manna from heaven".

It was an easy way to make money, because in the homelands existed practically no postal services. Due to the catastrophic results of the infamous Bantu administration, most of the inhabitants could neither write nor read, and there existed neither industrial nor commercial undertakings of any real importance.

How fictitious the whole exercise was is best illustrated by the fact that genuinely used Homeland postage stamps were virtually unobtainable for the stamp collectors, except for those of the normal letter rate, and even these were difficult to find. Collectors who wanted to have genuinely used specimen were forced to manufacture their own postal items and to send them under cover to a postmaster in the respective homeland to get them posted. Apparently, they had been instructed to accede to these demands by collectors.

The South African stamp dealers and collectors, and to a large extent also local speculators, bought these stamps by the sheets, for which the posts had virtually no services to provide, because most of the stamps disappeared immediately into stock books and collections.

The homelands issued not only stamps, but additionally manufactured and sold, like on a production line, full sheets, Control Blocks, First Day Covers, Miniature Sheets, special postmarks, commemorative and plain postal stationary postcards, and all sorts of other philatelic junk. Large quantities of these spurious products were also exported, mainly to the USA, Germany and the Netherlands, notwithstanding their questionable pedigrees.

In my later established stamp auctions I made a substantial part of our turnover in the stamp issues and all the related products of these 'reservations for Africans'. And this applied at the time as well to all of the many stamp dealers and auctioneers then operating in South Africa.

Not surprisingly, after the demise of Apartheid, and of these so-called 'Independent States', the market in these pro-ducts, and consequently their value, had completely collapsed overnight. It was a bit like the end of the tulip craze in Holland, a few hundred years ago. These sheets of the Bantustan/Homeland stamps were since then only good to decorate the walls of the kids' playroom. Luckily, I had disposed of most of my stock of these products well before this collapse happened.

Sun City, locally better known as Sin City, was another such casino complex, this one was located in the Bophuthatswana Bantustan, near Johannesburg and Pretoria, which was very similar but much larger than the Wild Coast resort in the Transkei homeland. It became world famous for its fantastic architecture and its golf course, which was also designed by Gary Player.

This huge compound was utilized as the location for some world-class golf tournaments and also provided the setting for a number of international films. Numerous international VIP personalities visited (free of charge, probably) the facilities and provided some fictitious respectability to this setup.

At the time it was often said here: "the Dutch Reformed Church is the National Party in prayer". But in my opinion it would have been more appropriate to state: "the National Party is the Dutch Reformed Church in executive mode". The Afrikaans churches, there were two or three of them, were as committed to the Apartheid ideology, at least until shortly before the very end, as were the National Party and its even more radical off-shoots themselves.

The racist attitudes of these Christian churches of 'Love thy Neighbor' origin were particularly despicable because they had insisted that their places of worship must especially be preserved in their pure Whiteness. They were the true seedbeds of Apartheid.

One other population group has not been mentioned at all so far, namely the Albinos, who were missing the dark pigmentation and consequently had a white skin. Racially, they were of course Africans, and the Apartheid era classified them as such. It was tragic that most Africans were deeply suspicious of these poor people, just because they were different. Based on a lack of knowledge and understanding, they were discriminated against by their own people, and sometimes even killed.

Finally, we are coming back to the group of building companies I was involved with. We had established a separate division, consisting of our specialized building material companies. This had resulted in us having stepped on the toes of the established building material wholesalers, who in turn created difficulties for us to obtain our supplies of certain materials, mainly of structural timber.

To solve this problem, we bought a large sawmill in Mount Ayliff, a small rural town in the Transkei homeland near the border of Natal. A German specialized engineer from Hamburg was in charge of the technical aspects of this undertaking.

He told me one day that he had come to South Africa because as a half-Jew (the Nazi terminology for a Jew of mixed parentage) he did not enjoy staying in Germany anymore. He did not dwell on details about what had happened there. We were not close friends, just colleagues. Later I found out that he had told this episode only to me and to nobody else. But why only to me?

Once a month I drove up there to see that the administrative part of the operation went correctly and smoothly. This side presented few problems, but there were always strident demands from the representatives of the local African population of Mount Ayliff.

Making demands was, and still is, unfortunately the usual way of the Africans of this country, particularly if they were in a group (I am not allowed to use the word "mob" here), to ask for or to complain about something. And most of the time they added a threat or two, in case their demands were not met in full and by the time or day stipulated by them.

My guess was that this confrontational and often violent attitude stemmed from the underlying tendency to violence by many of our Africans, and especially the Zulus, but of course I was not a psychologist and therefore I had it probably all wrong.

To deal with these volatile situations, and to diffuse any possible political repercussions by the local politicians who suffered from understandable insecurity, I had to fly almost every month to Umtata, the capital of this Bantustan. This presented for me a pleasant interruption from riding my office desk.

Some of these flights in a small single-engine plane were rather hair raising. In the beginning I often felt queasy during these stomach-churning flights, until I had discovered that sitting next to the pilot solved this particular problem for me. The sole pilots of these small planes always happily acceded to my wish to take the empty seat of the non-existing copilot.

Additionally, due to this arrangement, I could have at a push almost qualified as a copilot myself. The relatively straightforward dashboard and communications, far removed from those of an intercontinental jumbo-jet plane, were more or less understandable even for a non-flyer like me. Flying one would maybe have been possible, but how to land such a beast would have been an entirely different matter. But such a necessity luckily never developed.

From Durban International we flew south along the Wild Coast, which on some days greeted us with high speed bumpy winds. On reaching the mouth of the Umtata River, we took a ninety degree turn to the right and followed this medium sized river up to the Umtata airport. Following our flight path was dead easy for the pilot, because these small planes flew at a very low altitude, probably about three-hundred meters high. Since we most of the times had a clear blue sky, it was easy for me to follow our course.

Now I have probably shot myself in the foot again! I should all along have written about Mthata instead of Umtata, which was the spelling at the Apartheid and Transkei homeland time, and which is therefore now not 'politically correct' anymore. Sorry! But I did not correct this since I was recording here events in the Apartheid era, and for this reason I have retained the contemporaneous spelling, to preserve the ambience of this time.

In Umtata I regularly met with Minister Booi of the Transkei cabinet. In my dealings with him I was never quite sure whether this African gentleman was actually running his department, or whether the director general was in charge, a White public servant seconded by the South African government.

It was made very clear by Minister Booi when he wanted something out of these meetings. He confided in me that his niece was battling, as a poor victim of the inadequate Apartheid education regime for the Bantu, at some higher education facility in South Africa, and that she would have very much appreciated some financial assistance. He gave me her contact details and I remember that the young lady somehow for a short while appeared on our payroll.

I suppose this could possibly qualify as another case of corruption, but only as a minor one, as we helped a 'poor' individual, and furthermore, at least officially, in a foreign country. Again, there was here again a whiff of blackmail, as is so often the case in conjunction with corruption.

During one of my numerous visits I would have loved to have met Bantu Holomisa, who later became the leader of this home-land, but that unfortunately never happened. He had joined the Transkei Army in 1976 and was already in 1986 promoted to Brigadier General. In 1987 he deposed the thoroughly corrupt Chief Minister George Matanzima, the Paramount Chief of the Xhosa tribe (Wikipedia). Of all the Bantustan leaders, Holomisa was the one with the best reputation.

The careful reader has of course spotted that the name of the previously mentioned Paramount Chief Kaiser Mathanzima was spelled differently from that of his brother and successor George Matanzima. This was not a mistake of the team working on this book, of course not! The reason was that the spelling of the languages of the African tribes were never recorded by them in the precolonial times, for the simple reason that they could generally neither write nor read.

These languages were for the first time recorded in writing by later White missionaries. The Germans and Scandinavians with their phonetic languages had no particular problems with that. But the French, and particularly their British colleagues, were battling with the transcriptions because of their aphonetic ones.

Each of them had to decide individually how to transform these foreign-sounding words into the spelling of their own language. That obviously had to result in numerous deviating forms. Only now have the African experts started to standardize the spelling. Consequently, many place names, for instance, had to be changed, and sometimes more than once.

Since I was talking about a minister a little while ago, albeit one of a 'foreign' country, it seems like the right time to talk about my personal experiences with the two then surviving High Priests of the Apartheid doctrine, after Prime Minister Verwoerd had been assassinated. They were the Prime Minister and the President, respectively, of South Africa.

First, I met Prime Minister B.J. Vorster during a fund raising 'do' for the National Party in Durban, which my wife and I had attended with my boss and his wife. As already explained, my boss, or rather his company, was moderately contributing to their coffers (another example of corruption?), and I was not sure whether he was at this time a member of this party.

But I suspect so, because much later he was under consideration to stand for, and therefore automatically to become, a Member of Parliament for Pinetown. But he was pipped at the post by Jan Marais, the founder, main shareholder and chief executive of the innovative Trust Bank. He was definitely a more substantial contributor to the petty cash box of the Party than my boss.

The cocktail party was boring to tears, as was common for such events. Vorster delivered his usual public performance; an unsmiling wordless sourpuss. He stood there like a cardboard cutout of himself. For determination a star, for public charisma a thumbs-down!

There was an illustrative joke at this time doing the rounds (not there, of course) that one of his ministers had publicly been called a liar, after he had reported that he had seen the Prime Minister smiling. This minister was almost dismissed from the cabinet as a pathological liar when he added that he thought the Prime Minister might actually have laughed a little.

That reminded me immediately of the political jokes which had circulated during the Nazi rule in Germany about the Party and its leaders, naturally only very secretly. The same thing had happened after the war in the East German communist dictatorship of the GDR, known as the "workers' paradise". Very popular was the one about a laborer's son, who had his bum warmed when he proudly reported to his father that he had saved Walter Ulbricht, the strongman of this state, from almost drowning.

The National Party had altered the South African constitution in parliament, replacing the non-executive President and the Prime Minister with the institution of an Executive President. When I later met President P.W. Botha at another of these fundraising gatherings, my experience was in sharp contrast with my previous meeting of B.J. Vorster. Botha was a bundle of volatile energy and an extrovert politician. He talked loudly in a strident voice and he used both his arms to underline any of his outrageously racist arguments.

He habitually pointed his finger like a handgun at the person he was talking with, or should I more correctly say, he was talking to. He behaved as if he was permanently on the speaker's rostrum during an election campaign, when he launched his polemics against communists and the Black Peril, even in a private discourse.

11

'PETTY' APARTHEID

This term, naturally enough, did not emanate from the architects of the Grand Apartheid scheme. I do not know who invented this in South Africa very popular terminology. It was 'petty' in the sense, that it was meant to consist of thousands of pinpricks by the system against the Non-Whites, because they had to be kept in their place. But many of these petty restrictions and prohibitions were rather knuckledusters than pinpricks!

Now we have a look at the various aspects of the Petty Apartheid, as it affected the Non-White majority, and I am using the terminology of the Apartheid times on purpose, to convey a realistic impression of this time.

Human Dignity: Adult men and women, particularly of the Africans, were routinely addressed as 'boys' and 'girls', irrespective of their age or social standing. This was intended to establish how underdeveloped and useless they all were considered to be by the Afrikaners.

Any semi-literate White railways clerk was considered to be racially superior to a Black university professor.

Completely contradictory to this attitude was the belief of the Afrikaners that they loved their black 'brothers and sisters', but obviously only to a certain point!

Land: This had to be kept in the hands of the Whites, because the

Blacks would not know how to work the land and would just be laying in the shade, since they were known to be notoriously lazy.

The Europeans had to ensure that the country produced enough food to feed everybody, and the Africans had to render a helping hand on the farms, since the White farmers could not seriously be expected to sweat in order to produce enough food for the Non-Whites.

Health Services: The Non-Europeans had to have their own health facilities, inferior to those of the Whites, of course, since their presence in the European hospitals would have been unreasonable and would have resulted in dirt, deceases and vermin brought in. They would also steal and create general disorder.

As the Afrikaner lawyer of our company once formulated it so succinctly: "Why build hospitals for the Africans? Let them die in the bush as they have done forever before".

Education: The discrimination in the education sector was based on the Afrikaner doctrine that the 'Natives' should work exclusively as unskilled workers for the Europeans, except when dealing with their own.

Therefore, they did not need any but the most basic education. As a matter of fact, most of them did not receive any schooling at all, which was just as well.

In any case, their intellect was sub-prime, and therefore not suited to any higher education by the state.

The few African University Colleges were located in distant districts where they would not be seen by the Europeans and were, of course, second class and under-resourced.

Public Transport: Obviously, Europeans could not be expected to sit in the bus or on the train next to an unwashed and smelly 'Non-European'.

An English-speaking Durban City councilor of the United Party transported his 'garden boy' in the boot of his car to avoid being contaminated by him. He was very surprised when questioned about this civilized form of transport. After all, due to this generous arrangement, his 'boy' was spared to have to walk!

. . .

<u>Sport</u>: This had to be separate *par force*, otherwise there was the horrible vision of the Europeans being forced to getting into physical contact with the Blacks, with all the health and psychological risks involved.

What a revulsive thought! Just think of rugby, the holy sport of the Afrikaners, and the subsequent communal shower! Utterly unthinkable!

Furthermore, there was the unacceptable possibility that Blacks would possibly prove to be the better athletes.

<u>Public Amenities</u>: Anything, from National Parks to play-grounds to park benches, had to be segregated by necessity, to avoid contamination by the dirty and mostly undisciplined Non-Whites.

In any case, they would not go to the National Parks anyway, because they did not have the slightest interest in the fauna and flora of the country.

Segregation of the beaches was obligatory since otherwise the Whites would suffer infections from the polluted ocean, and the Non-Whites would just laze around and usurp the best places, therefore depriving the Europeans of their God-given rights.

<u>Housing</u>: The sensible and reasonable Group Areas were clearly needed to prevent Whites from suffering the ignominy of having Non-White neighbors.

Quite apart from the culture shock, this would immediately have devalued their properties.

When our company was building private houses, a Pinetown lady town councilor of the National Party complained bitterly about the layout of our show house, because the servant quarters were under the same roof as the "master" bedrooms.

<u>Job Reservation</u>: This was codified in laws and regulations which quite correctly reserved all qualified and better-paid jobs for the Europeans.

There had to be strict discrimination in the work place in favor of the Whites, to prevent them being swamped by the Black masses, and to protect them from their cheap and therefore unfair competition.

The Non-Whites were severely restricted to inferior and menial jobs, because this was all they were capable of, anyway.

It was strictly forbidden that a white employee would work under the supervision of any Non-White, since this would have been insulting and below his well-deserved status.

Imagine such a poor Afrikaans fellow being ridiculed about such a ridiculous situation by his colleagues, but an English-speaker would not have been much better off.

It was expressly forbidden that a White artisan would train a member of any other group in his trade. This rule was easily enforced, because most of the White tradesmen would of course have refused to do this, anyway.

Many employers tried to circumvent these rules, not because of anti-Apartheid sentiments, but out of economic necessities, because many positions could be filled legally correctly only with great difficulties, if at all.

Economy: Non-White businesses were prohibited in the Euro-pean group areas. After all, 'dirty' competition must not be allowed, and nobody should have been subjected to have to look at Non-White firms, who might have, (unfairly, of course) out-performed their White counterparts.

It is hoped the reader has noted my sometimes heavy-handed attempts at irony. But it must also be clearly stated that the vast majority of the Afrikaners, and also a large proportion of the English-speakers, were actually thinking along the lines I have intentionally utilized here.

PART IV

THE ANTI-APARTHEID STRUGGLE

INSIDE AND OUTSIDE THE COUNTRY (1948 TO 1994)

12

THE OPENING

1948 TO 1961

The United Party, which ruled South Africa from 1910 to 1948, was opportunistic and racist, but without any ideological or specific religious background. The National Party, which took over and ruled until the end of Apartheid in 1994, cemented the racist-religious attitudes of the majority of the Afrikaners in the shape of the Apartheid doctrine.

The ANC, the African National Congress, is today globally recognized as the spearhead of the fight against Apartheid. It was founded by Langabalele Dube in Bloemfontein in 1912, two years after the formation of the Union of South Africa. For more than eighty years the Congress attempted to improve the lot of the Africans, but without any results.

The Africans, Coloreds and Asians had no vote and were not allowed to have or to join any political parties. The ANC was a resistance and freedom-fighter organization, but not a political party. Only after the demise of Apartheid in 1994 they reluctantly started to transform their organization, and not without problems.

Towards the end of the 1940s, after the National Party of the Afrikaners had taken over the government, the ANC decided to oppose the newly proclaimed discriminatory Apartheid system, originally with non-violent methods.

The means towards this goal required to abandon the hitherto clearly understood concentration towards exclusively operating in the interests of the Africans. This re-orientation of the ANC as a non-racial mass-movement, including the also disenfranchised minorities of the Indians and the Coloreds of the country represented a sea-change.

In South Africa the term 'Colored' had always been reserved exclusively to people of mixed blood, usually of a European father and a mother which was Colored, African, Indian, Malay or Khoi-San, whereas in the rest of the world this term generally referred to all Non-Whites.

Additionally to this change in direction, a close but informal coalition was formed with the non-racial South African Communist Party, the SACP. A peculiarity of this arrangement was the possibility for the members of one of these organizations to also be a member of the other, if they desired to do so. I remember, for instance, that Thabo Mbeki, our second ANC State President, had one day returned his membership card of the SACP. Jacob Zuma, his successor, later made the identical choice.

The Communist Party in those days had many White members and was under the leadership of European Jews. It was rather strong amongst the miners of the Witwatersrand, particularly in the gold mines. The party and its leaders had excelled them-selves in the mineworker's strike of 1922.

Following this new direction, the ANC organized in 1955 the Congress of the People, which included the Indian and Colored minorities. This non-racial assembly adopted the Freedom Charter, a highly emotional document which was very close to the hearts of the freedom fighters. Some of the far-reaching demands of this Congress are still being hotly debated within the ANC.

An ANC faction under the leadership of Robert Sobukwe refused to countenance the inclusion of the communists and of the Non-African minorities into the movement. They insisted on a purely African organization. In 1959 they broke away and formed in Soweto, the sprawling African township outside of Johannesburg, the PAC, the Pan Africanist Congress of Azania. This imaginative Greek word was their preferred name for their hoped-for "New South Africa".

In 1960, as an opening gambit, so to speak, the newly formed racial freedom-fighter PAC organized in the large African township of Sharpeville, in the mining area of the Witwatersrand, a mass protest against the hated pass laws. A huge group of Africans marched towards the local police station and the frightened policemen lost their nerve and started shooting. A large number of the protesters was killed or wounded, as has already been described.

This tragic bloodbath triggered the ANC's and the PAC's decisions to abandon the peaceful protests and to escalate the fight to an all-out 'armed struggle'. Subsequently, the ANC formed their armed wing, the Umkhonto we Sizwe or MK, while the PAC organized their Azanian People's Liberation Army or APLA. Both adopted their specific war cries, "Get me my Machine Gun" and "Kill the Boer", respectively.

The government in turn replied by banning (prohibiting) both organizations. The result was that the ANC and the PAC both joined the already outlawed Communist Party and went under-ground within the country. Additionally, they both started to establish representative offices in a number of foreign countries.

The ANC sought primarily the support of the communists of the Soviet Union. The coalition with the South African Communist Party was obviously the deciding point for this choice. The PAC, on the other hand, tended more towards the Chinese Communists, as I seem to remember. The communist parties of Russia and China were bitter enemies at that time.

Likewise, the ANC and PAC fought a very hateful battle about who should lead the fight against the Apartheid system, and for the support of the global public opinion, particularly of Africa, the US and of the European countries. The ANC had its nose in front in this conflict, with their insistent demands of "Free Mandela".

They soon had established bridge-heads in several African countries. In most cases their local offices were afforded the status of 'diplomatic observers', similar to that of a low-level diplomatic mission. From these bases they were able to liaise with the newly established post-colonial African governments and their counterpart organizations of local former freedom fighters.

Simultaneously, the ANC was setting up offices in the capitals of the most important overseas states, and even at the United Nations in New York, to spread the Anti-Apartheid demands. Their call to "Free Mandela" was heard all over the world. The fact that they were able to finance all this is a strong indication of how much support they received at this time from abroad.

In the battle against Apartheid within South Africa there was also a small but dedicated group of Europeans at work. The 'Black Sash' activists kept up the internal fight. These were mainly White women, who stood silently and indefatigably with their black sashes and placards at busy street corners of cities and towns. They were often insulted and ridiculed by some of the Europeans, usually Afrikaners.

They were also regularly harassed by the police, but they did not budge, nor they did give up.

At first glance, it appeared that they had not achieved anything with their silent protests. But I am firmly convinced that their steadfast and peaceful actions formed a sort of 'Chinese Torture', slowly undermining the righteous racist attitudes of many of the Europeans, at least those of the English-speaking sector of the population.

The English-speakers themselves were seen to be divided in their attitude towards Apartheid. One large sector supported the Afrikaners in their racist behavior, mostly for purely egotistical reasons, and they voted for the United Party. Some of these people were as bad, if not worse, than the Afrikaners. In previous chapters I have illustrated some typical examples.

A much smaller number of more liberally inclined Europeans of both language groups was more sympathetic towards the suppressed Non-Europeans. They suggested certain rights for them, but even they did not go so far as to demand the vote for the Non-Whites.

Their dithering attitudes are best illustrated by a proposal floated by Harry Oppenheimer, the archetypical South African establishment figure of the Anglo-American conglomerate, who suggested to give the vote to those Non-Europeans who owned real estate.

A typical liberal's idea: as previously explained, under the Apartheid laws, Africans were not allowed land ownership! I suppose he was a very busy man and may have overlooked such a minor point.

When we arrived in this country in 1965, it became apparent to us that at that time there was an eerie quiet in South Africa. No apparent major racial conflicts since Sharpeville, no overt racial hatred by the Non-Whites. But an unspecified feeling of uncertainty and queasiness regarding the future of this country and its people was omnipresent.

It was rather obvious to us that the oppressed masses were then reluctantly willing to try to seek an accommodation with the dominant Europeans. If it had not been for the pig-headed and intransigent majority of the Afrikaners, the violent insurgencies by the freedom fighters after 1970 would not have been necessary, and all the killings and mayhem on both sides were a pitiful waste of human lives, which surely could have been avoided by a more flexible and humane government.

13

WITH BRACHIAL VIOLENCE

1961 - 1985

The Sharpeville Massacre of 1961 did not only lead to the wasteful armed struggle, but it also contributed to the country leaving the British Commonwealth of Nations. This latter epochal event was, officially, the consequence of a spat involving a Non-White player in a Rugby team from New Zealand which was to tour South Africa. The Prime Minister put down his foot: utterly unacceptable!

The chain reaction following this affront was spectacular. Up to this point the Union of South Africa had been a respected member of the world's community of nations, and not only in sport. Now, that it also had converted to the Republic of South Africa, the country was known worldwide as 'The Apartheid State'.

This change, from a Commonwealth Dominion, nominally headed by the British monarch and locally represented by a South African High Commissioner, to a Republic headed by a non-executive President and a Prime Minister elected by Parliament, was profound and far-reaching.

In addition to these political developments the country also had to digest a number of practical and economic changes, such as the introduction of the systems of the International Standards Organization ISO. The numerous European immigrants like us were able to profit from this, because they were already familiar with the metric system. This facilitated their future integration into the economy of the country. As an immigrant, one had to be thankful for even the smallest benefits, since this integration was not always easy!

The British currency had been replaced by the Rand, in the relation of one Pound Sterling equal to two Rand, but the old coins and banknotes continued for some time to circulate in parallel with the new South African currency.

The simultaneous adoption of both these systems, maybe as a kind of 'showing the finger' to the former colonial power, had positive side-effects. The Imperial system of measurements, as well as the Sterling currency, were both clearly outdated and inefficient, and therefore costly to the economy and for the population. In the long run this introduction has definitely turned out to be very beneficial for South Africa.

Another, often overlooked, point in this regard was the previous disadvantage for millions of school kids who had for years to battle unnecessarily with the complicated and antiquated Imperial system and the British currency, instead of being able to concentrate upon more important subjects of their loaded curriculum.

Beginning in the early 1960s, the United Nations started to take a more active stand in the fight against Apartheid. In addition to India (there were over a million Indians living in South Africa!), this push came mainly from the Soviet Block and the smaller UNO members, the more than one hundred Third World countries.

In sympathy with their fellow Whites living in South Africa, who were fearful about their future, Great Britain and the White Common-wealth members were at this time always trying, most of the time successfully, to block these efforts of the developing countries and their Soviet Block allies in the United Nations forum. They were, naturally enough, simultaneously mindful of their very substantial economic investments in South Africa, and of the importance of the country regarding the threat of the communist world.

The similar attitude of the Americans was naturally also influenced by their substantial investments in this country, and by the strong bi-lateral trade, particularly in strategic raw materials. Additionally, there was the stead-fast anti-communist position of this government. It is more than understandable that they were worried about the possibility of South Africa landing under the Soviet umbrella.

Europe and Japan, on the other hand, were 'sitting on the fence' and maintained a constraint attitude towards this country. The European countries found themselves in a cleft stick. On the one hand, they sympathized with their emigrated European brothers, and they obviously also had to consider their substantial commercial interests, but on the other hand there were also the rather strong Anti-Apartheid feelings of parts of their populations and voters.

These overseas attitudes towards Apartheid reactivated the internal resistance as well as the financial support of the ANC from overseas Anti-Apartheid organizations. But nothing much had internally changed here, yet. The grip by the dreaded State, and especially the hated Security Police, on the country was still all-powerful.

However, there was another facet to this picture. Sometime in the late 1980s I remember to have received, shortly after midnight, a phone call from a Texas customer of our stamp auctions, strongly admonishing the White South Africans "to keep the bloody Negroes in their place". Apparently, the overseas public opinion was still not unanimous in condemning Apartheid and South Africa.

The motivation for the support of the Anti-Apartheid movement had various, and sometimes competing reasons:

- India acted primarily in consideration and defense of their brethren living in this country.
- The Soviet Empire was supporting the ANC and the South African Communist Party because they clearly hoped to eventually add this country with its immense mineral riches to their "sphere of influence", which would automatically also have had the beneficial side effect for them of weakening the position of the Western Allies.
- The smaller UN members of the Third World acted in understandable solidarity with the suppressed millions of fellow Non-Europeans in this country. While they did not represent much power or trade volume, their sheer number of votes turned out to be a major support for the Anti-Apartheid movement in the United Nations assembly.

Parallel to the incremental changes in global attitudes, in particular against racial discrimination generally, and against Apartheid and South Africa in particular, there were now also some tentative changes in South Africa to be recorded:

- The English-language newspapers started to strongly attack the government.
- The Whites, other than most of the Afrikaners, became more and more critical of Apartheid. Now, for the first time, doubts began to be raised about things which had up to now been considered as entirely normal in this country. And it began to sink in what had been going on

in this state, and what was all wrong with this Apartheid system.

- During these years, some judges (they were all Europeans, of course) began to use their rulings to undermine the Apartheid ideology, particularly in Natal in the field of the job reservation for Europeans.

- Some religious leaders, except those of the Afrikaners, started to speak out and preach more and more strongly against the Apartheid ideology.

- Eventually, the venerable Afrikaner cleric Beyers Naudé had declared Apartheid to be a sin against humanity. This was the decisive attack against the pseudo-religious basis of the Afrikaners for the Apartheid doctrine. Finally, the beginning of the end appeared to be coming in sight.

Even the pathetically dragged-out, reluctant and bumbling attempts by the government, to try to somehow relieve the external pressure on the country, were sufficient to have led over the years to various splinter groups of the Far Right of the Afrikaners to have left the National Party. They formed their own parties, because they were not prepared to allow even the tiniest steps back from the 'holy' Apartheid doctrine of the assassinated former Prime Minister Dr. Hendrik Verwoerd.

One such right wing group, under the leadership of Andries Treurnicht, created in 1962 the even more racist Conservative Party, the CP. He had been the leader of the National Party in the Transvaal, the most conservative and also the most populous of the four South African provinces.

Dr. Albert Hertzog had attacked his party leader and Prime Minister John Vorster for trying to deviate from the Apartheid ideology. He subsequently left the National Party with some like-minded racists and arch-conservatives and formed in 1969 under his leadership the HNP, the Herstigte Nasionale Party (the True National Party).

This was the same politician, who had earlier, as the Minister in charge of the Post Office, refused to introduce television in South Africa, because he saw this as dangerous 'work of the devil'. And he was clearly not alone in the party with his 'progressive' frame of mind.

The development of these extreme splinter groups illustrates quite clearly in what a difficult position the government found itself in relation to its members and its voters, when it was considering , even only vaguely, of modifying or modernizing Apartheid. It was not surprising, therefore, when even the more moderate and enlightened leaders did not dare to touch the Apartheid edifice. They clearly realized that the first small steps to 'improve' the system would without fail lead to an irreparable breach of the dyke.

But dealing with the Non-Europeans and the communists did not create such headaches. The Suppression of Communism Act of 1950 had already allowed:

- Banning of individuals and organizations.
- Prohibition of labor unions and strikes.
- Criminalizing the painting of political slogans or signs. "Graffiti" was either too foreign a word, and no Afrikaans translation was yet available, or maybe they did not even know the word.

The just mentioned term of banning warrants an explanation. The conventional well-known definition is the one of sending a person to a prescribed and usually remote locality, which such person is not allowed to leave. But under Apartheid the term also had much wider-reaching meanings. It could include the prohibition of certain types of professional work, public speeches, publications of any kind, member-ship of specified organizations and many more such restrictive prescriptions.

The General Law Amendment Act of 1962 added substantially to the already ample arsenal of B.J. Vorster, the Minister of Justice, for the defense of Apartheid:

- The reversal of the proof of guilt (= guilty until proven innocent!).
- A minimum conviction of five years in jail and a maximum one of hanging, for any breach of the laws regarding State Security.
- A fine of twenty thousand Rand, then about as many US Dollar for any publication attacking the government.

A special position in this country was taken up by a White political party which had already been founded back in 1958, the Progressive Party. It was created by a break-away faction from the stodgy United Party. After many changes it morphed to the DA, the Democratic Alliance, which is the present-day official opposition to the ANC.

They only managed, in election after election, to get Helen

Suzman elected into Parliament, a single but formidable opponent. She was for many years a determined fighter against Apartheid and the only genuine parliamentary opposition to the ruling National Party.

She was the MP, the Member of Parliament, for the Houghton constituency of Johannesburg. It was a European Group Area, of course. This was one of the most select residential areas, and therefore also one of the most expensive ones in South Africa. This ensured that none of the Non-Whites could afford to live there, even if the Group Areas Act had not existed.

A standing joke amongst Europeans at election time read: "We are voting for the Progressive Party, and we hope that the National Party wins". This illustrates quite clearly the two-faced attitude of the majority of English-speaking voters towards the Apartheid situation.

As a sign of the very slowly changing times, Harry Oppenheimer, the mining magnate who controlled the Anglo-American gold-mining conglomerate and the global diamond monopoly of De Beers, was an early supporter of this party, while the majority of White business people continued to support the National Party, the 'Nats'.

In 1966 the Prime Minister Dr. Hendrik Verwoerd was killed in Parliament by a parliamentary employee, who was promptly declared being mentally ill. No sane White South African could possibly have contemplated such a horrible deed. Now the Minister of Justice B.J. Vorster took over the government as the new Prime Minister.

As was usual, this rumpus saw the Rand fall precipitously and shook the whole nation. The White part of the nation, I mean. As was usual, the Europeans did neither record nor bother about the reaction of the Non-European majority. However, some did realize already then that the Apartheid system's foundations had been irreparably damaged and weakened. Verwoerd had not only 'invented' Apartheid, but he had also provided the ideological fundaments and the infrastructure for all the subsequent sorry 'enhancements' by the National Party.

Another important political organization of this period needs to be mentioned here, but this time it was again an African one: the Inkhata Liberation Movement, founded in 1972 by Mangosuthu Buthelezi, the traditional First Minister of the Zulu king, which was strongly supported by the monarch. This was a nationalistic and conservative tribal protest movement, but of course not a political party, due to the respective prohibition of such and the absence of the vote for Africans.

It was important to his followers that the ANC was perceived by the majority of the Zulus to be under the control of the Xhosa tribe. The rivalry among the many African nations was and still is very much alive all-over Black Africa, and not only in this country.

Buthelezi also did not trust the ANC to protect the status of the king and of the other traditional leaders of the tribe, as well as the whole tribal structure of the Zulu nation, after their expected taking over the power in South Africa in the near future. As a former leader of the ANC Youth League, he was well versed with the thinking of the ANC leadership. Further-more, his religious leanings did not sit well with the atheist communist allies of the ANC. He was a rather prickly adversary for both the National Party and the ANC.

In 1981 the government had excised Zululand from the Province of Natal and had created a claimed autonomous homeland there for the Zulus, with the final political aim of turning it into another independent Bantustan state. But Buthelezi has always successfully out-maneuvered this plan. All the South African government could achieve was to persuade him to 'rule' this part of the province of Natal with his Inkhata movement. Zululand had effectively become a cross between a South African province and the usual Bantustans.

He saw his resistance to the plans to create a Zulu Homeland, like the Republic of Transkei for the Xhosa tribe, as his participation in the struggle against Apartheid. However, I have always had the suspicion that his conservative, tribal and religious attitudes had also much to do with his political posturing and activities.

His opposition was a very effective blockade of the grand designs of the government, because the Zulu tribe was not only by far the largest in South Africa, but the other South African tribes were still fearing the fighting mentality and prowess of the Zulu warriors. Just less than two hundred years ago the Zulus under King Shaka had subjugated most of Southern Africa under their bloody rule.

His movement differed, however, with the other Anti-Apartheid organizations about certain subjects. He opposed, for instance, the ANC's call for economic sanctions against South Africa, which he saw as damaging to the interests of the poor. The armed struggle was another point where he disagreed with the freedom fighters, person-ally preferring other options with-out violence.

His main all-conquering demand of government was this: If the Zululand territory would ever become a Bantustan, then the whole of the province of Natal would have to be incorporated, under his lead-ership, needless to say. This demand, politically utterly unacceptable for the National Party, was effectively killing the Grand Apartheid scheme of clandestinely and surreptitiously excising the majority of Africans out of the remaining then lily-white South Africa.

Interestingly, the original enthusiastic endorsement of Inkhata by the Zulu king evaporated later. I suspect that the king, or his advisors, had perceived that the support of this organization by his subjects had waned, and that many had joined the ANC instead. It seemed to me that he was as good a politician as his experienced traditional First Minister.

In 1965, the year of our arrival in South Africa, the British colony of Southern Rhodesia had pronounced their UDI, the Unilateral Declaration of Independence from Great Britain, under the new name of the Republic of Rhodesia. The South African government had actively supported this insurrection by our northern neighbor.

South African troops were sent there to help fight the African insurgents/terrorists/freedom fighters - take your pick! Furthermore, urgently needed liquid fuel was supplied by South Africa to the rebel colony, in breach of the hastily arranged UN sanctions.

In the past there had already been a few attempts to persuade the (White) population of this colony to agree to the incorporation with its relatively strong European population and vast mineral wealth into the Union of South Africa. Nobody had bothered to even consider what the African majority thought of this splendid idea. But these early efforts had all come to nothing.

Rhodesia was now seen by South Africa as the last bulwark against the flood of African nationalism, which was called in this country the "Swart Gevaar", or the "Black Peril". Despite protracted and vicious fighting for several years, and after the loss of probably thousands of lives of South African soldiers, the Republic of Rhodesia succumbed, not on the battle fields, but under the pressure of international sanctions and public opinion. The freedom fighters had won, and the country eventually became in 1980 the Republic of Zimbabwe.

After this defeat the South African troops were deployed in the mandated territory of South West Africa to fight the incoming 'terrorists'. This South African Mandate, awarded by the League of Nations after the Great War, had earlier been rescinded by the United Nations. South Africa ignored this minor set-back and administered the country almost like a fifth province. For all practical purposes, the African Liberation War had finally, after many years of protracted fighting, crossed the borders into South Africa.

Internationally, the cries of "Free Mandela" had become more and more strident and forceful. Streets in cities and towns in many parts of the world were named after him and after his wife Winnie, herself a formidable Anti-Apartheid fighter. Simultaneously, now there could be observed a marked stiffening also in the international resistance to Apartheid in the form of cultural and sports boycotts.

In 1970 the government had allowed, for the first time, the participation of Non-White members of foreign sports teams to play and compete in South Africa. The fact that a Maori had been able to play very successfully for the New Zealand rugby team had enraged the right wing of the party.

Particularly so, as the government had also quietly and unannounced allowed the Non-European diplomats stationed in South Africa to live in European residential areas of Pretoria, the Holy Grail of the Afrikaners. They saw this, quite correctly as it turned out, as the first holes in the dam holding back "The Flood" of the African 'hordes'.

1973 was the year of Muldergate, or the Info Scandal, the most momentous political scandal of the Apartheid years. The Information (read: Propaganda) Minister Dr. Connie Mulder and his Director-General Dr. Eschel Rhoodie had persuaded Prime Minister B.J. Vorster to authorize a planned propaganda counter-offensive to defend the Apartheid ideology and the Apartheid State against the stinging international attacks of the recent past.

These two politicians intended to buy an American newspaper, the Washington Star, and to help financing the founding of the Citizen, the only English-language newspaper in South Africa which would be supportive of the government policies. The intention was for these two newspapers to actively carry the propaganda fight into the opposing camps. All this was to be financed via a slush fund of sixty-four million Rand (Wikipedia), which had been illegally diverted from the military budget of the country.

Such creative accounting required, of course, the assistance of Senator Horwood, the Minister of Finance. The same minister, whom I had earlier convinced to change the Income Tax Act, not only because the Act had been an ass, but to save our group of companies. He was the only Non-Afrikaner and English-speaker in government, and he found himself therefore in a vulnerable and precarious position.

When he was later asked about his involvement in this affair, he declared that he had signed the relevant secret documents without being allowed to look at details, because he had not been made privy of this undertaking, but also, because he lacked the necessary level of security clearance.

Later, when these shenanigans had been revealed by the Sunday Times, Vorster denied in Parliament any knowledge of these plans, but he was proven to have lied and was forced to resign, and his two co-conspirators as well. After his resignation he was 'elevated' to the position of non-executive State President. Hear, hear!

Two things in connection with this saga have always puzzled me:

- At the time I was surprised that the democratic spirit was still strong enough in this country, and especially in the National Party, to force such a spectacular bunch of resignations.
- And why had Vorster, instead of lying to Parliament, not simply declared "I have done what had to be done, to protect the national interests of our country".

My feeling was that he would have gotten away with that position, because the local (White) public opinion would surely have supported him. And the international public opinion he could have easily ignored, because practically the whole world was by then anyway actively determined against the Apartheid regime and its leaders.

In 1974 the Mahlabatini Declaration of Faith was signed by Mangosuthu Buthelezi, the leader of Inkhata, and Harry Schwarz, the chairman of the Progressive Party. This poorly publicized document was the first time that the leaders of White and Non-White political bodies had, so to speak, stood on the same platform. And why was it not widely publicized? I thought that the media supporting Schwarz preferred to still ignore Mr. Buthelezi, and the ones in support of Inkhata did not like the Progressive Party.

Neither of these two politicians was powerful, in the literal sense of the word, but their declaration positively incubated a positive change in the general thinking of the political elites in this country and abroad.

In 1975 the regime in the neighboring Portuguese colonies of Angola and Mozambique had collapsed under the relentless attacks of the liberation movements of Unita and Frelimo, respectively. This left until 1980 only Rhodesia as a country ruled by Europeans and a bulwark beyond the South African borders. The practical consequence was that South Africa for the first time had now direct borders with Black Africa, in the form of Angola and Mozambique. With the for our government tragic concomitant result that the infiltration of 'terrorists' had now become much easier.

The 1976 Soweto Uprising of school children shook the country and triggered a chain reaction of events. The root cause was the revolt of the African school-going generation against a Department of Education decree. The government, in their blinkered and stubborn ideological and shortsighted attitude had dictated that henceforth all African pupils would be taught in Afrikaans, the hated language of the hated Afrikaners and the hated Apartheid state.

These pupils lived by the impressive-sounding slogan Liberation before Education. Whether this political statement was their own idea, or whether this was handed down from the leaders of the external or the underground ANC is not clear to me. When violence erupted, which was unfortunately the standard reaction to differences of opinion in all of Black Africa, at least one schoolboy, Hector Pieterson, was shot and killed by the police in the ensuing confrontations.

This fatality served all over the country as the catalyst for the stubborn resistance by young Africans towards anything the government did or said. The underground ANC now tried to make the country ungovernable, and particularly so the Black townships. Some marches of Africans into White areas were also organized by them. They were bent on disrupting the quiet routine of the Europeans, to unsettle them and to generally cause as much mayhem as possible.

On the one hand, this resistance was politically very powerful, but on the other hand it created the so-called Lost Generation of under-educated or even un-educated millions of African youth. I am in no position to judge whether this tragic outcome was worth it or not, but I do know that the members of this generation represent a disproportionately large percentage of our unemployed and also of the prison population. These youngsters paid a very high price for their freedom!

In 1977 Steve Biko, the founder and leader of the Black Conscience Movement, was murdered by the Security Police. More accurately speaking, he died in the back of a police vehicle while in transit from the Eastern Cape to Johannesburg or Pretoria, due to the utter negligence and callousness of the police officers involved.

The then Minister of Police 'Jimmy' Kruger declared in a television broadcast "This leaves me cold!", illustrating the prevalent attitude of the Afrikaner Master Race. This public display of the 'caring disposition of a butcher's bulldog' further fired up the Anti-Apartheid resentment, both here and beyond our borders.

This tragic event was originally not revealed by the government, and it only became known to the local and overseas public by the investigative work of Helen Zille, a fearless female European journalist, who later became the leader of the opposition Democratic Alliance, the DA.

She had always been a fierce opponent of Apartheid, but after 1994 she had begun to sharply criticize the shenanigans of the ANC and to unveil the shortcomings of their government. She lambasted the present Black reverse racism and claimed that colonialism had not all been bad and negative. This factual statement was seen as White racism by the Black members of her party, and despite her proven anti-racial credentials she was squeezed out of her leadership positions as head of the party and Prime Minister of the Cape province.

In order to be able to keep borrowing money on the global financial markets, the country was in 1979 forced to create the Financial Rand currency. This was an artificial construct, without neither banknotes nor coins, and with its separate but lower international exchange rate. By 1983 this measure had been rescinded, but it had to be re-introduced again in 1985, when recurring hefty capital flight again endangered the South African currency.

The most effective opposition against the Apartheid regime was probably provided by Cosatu, the original umbrella fede-ration of labor unions. Their leaders continuously organized strikes and political demonstrations. The South African labor unions saw themselves at this stage primarily not as a body to defend the interests of the workers, but as a political organization opposing Apartheid. Accordingly, after 1994 they formed with the ANC and the SACP the Tri-Partite Alliance, to underline their claim to be entitled to equally participate with the ANC in the government of South Africa.

Already in 1981, when I was still the Finance Manager of our group of building companies, a large number of labor unions were openly active in South Africa. I am not sure whether they were by then operating legally. Their activities were possibly simply tolerated by the in the meantime much weakened Apartheid State.

Our building companies were in those years often hit by strikes with, for instance, all of our two thousand African laborers walking off our Durban building sites. When we inter-viewed some of our long-time employees about the reasons for the walkout, we could never get a straight answer, other than "We were told to go on strike - or else!". Everybody in the African townships knew perfectly well what "- or else!" entailed, after quite a few, who had not listened, had been beaten-up or killed by union activists.

One should keep in mind that all the African laborers were only allowed to live in their townships, where it was easy to intimidate or kill any dissidents. In situations like these, the police did not receive any assistance at all from the people, because they were seen as "the enemy". For that reason, the police were completely ignored and blocked out, even in the cases of non-political crimes, for instance in the frequent occurrences of murder, rape or theft committed against fellow Africans.

If one wonders about how the White laborers were affected by these things: no construction firm in South Africa employed any such persons. Yes, there were quite a few Whites who would have worked as such in Europe, but here these people were classified as operators. As such, they were clearly elevated above the level of laborers. It was always a hassle for the managers to find an opening for these un- or under-qualified people. Usually they just operated some basic piece of equipment.

In the beginning, as I have previously mentioned, the tactics and demands of the unions were somewhat ham-handed and unrealistic, due to their lack of relevant experience in these matters. These African union bosses were at that time rather naïve in their proper union work. If we wanted to negotiate with one of them about their demands, we would either get no sensible reply at all, or a wage demand for a two-hundred or three-hundred percent increase, or some other unrealistic claim.

After the initial unsatisfactory efforts, the upshot in every single case was the same: all two thousand Durban strikers were paid-off immediately, without us bothering to negotiate again with anybody. By then our personnel office was well organized to have the pay packets ready for all the dismissed strikers within two hours of their walk-out. Next morning, we started re-hiring, and most of the time the same laborers, at the same old hourly rates, and work continued as before.

Wage levels in the South African building industry were in those days not set per building contract or per company, but for all construction sites and companies in a large area. The union bosses either did not know better, or they simply ignored an inconvenient fact like this and, instead, hurled their demands against the managers of individual companies, or more often than not, against a site agent or a foreman at an individual contract site, who had absolutely no authority to agree anything with anybody.

But later the leaders of the labor unions were among those who, in my opinion, were most successful in bringing down Apartheid. Their actions were more effective than the armed struggle, and as efficient as the international sanctions and the arms embargo, which both also had a major impact on overcoming Apartheid.

About 1982 our boss was talked into 'employing' the notorious Apartheid-supporting journalist Gordon Winter, one of the few English-speakers in this category. He was supposed to research something or other for the government. I forgot or never knew what his employment by our group was intended to achieve. Maybe it was just a "thank you" by the boss to the National Party.

In 1983 the government adopted a new or changed constitution and created the Tricameral Parliament, which provided separate assemblies for the Indian and for the Colored communities, in addition to the existing parliament reserved for the Europeans. There was no mention of a similar body for the African majority of this country!

The representatives who moved into these two Apartheid structures were typical politicians, and this was also how they behaved! Corruption, nepotism, faction fighting, back-stabbing and all the other unsavory activities one has seen in many parliaments, particularly of developing countries in various parts of the world.

In the same year the United Democratic Front, the UDF, was formed by the underground ANC and their sympathizers, specifically to fight this divisive Tricameral Parliament construction. This organization was of course not a political party, because its members had no vote. It rather saw itself as the internal wing of the banned ANC and was particularly strong in the Cape Province, where it enjoyed the enthusiastic support of Archbishop Desmond Tutu of the Anglican Church of South Africa. Interestingly, he never became a member of the ANC! Why was that, I wondered?

In the eyes of the "Nats", the National Party members, and also of the majority of the Europeans, the term 'Democratic' was almost as devilish as 'communist', because it was perceived by them to be code for "Votes for the Non-Europeans". Such demands created, as a knee-jerk reaction, the determined opposition of the majority of the (White) voters, and also of large swathes within the South African economy.

The UDF continuously organized all kinds of political protests and they were therefore permanently under the observation of the feared Security Police. I remember vividly a television reportage, where Desmond Tutu had courageously protected a member of the Security Police, who had clandestinely joined the UDF mourners at an emotionally charged burial ceremony for one of their members.

This policeman had been recognized and was under immediate

threat to be 'necklaced'. The "Arch" (short for Archbishop) had saved him from certain death. Desmond Tutu was one of the most outstanding moral beacons of the freedom fight. He would have been my first choice as the Non-executive President of this country! In 1984 Desmond Tutu was given the Nobel Peace Prize, which award was also widely seen as an international protest gesture against the Apartheid regime. He had preached and protested against violence by either side.

A brand-new invention had seen the light of day a few months earlier in the African townships everywhere: the 'necklace'. This new development, ingenious in its simplicity, but devilish in its application, consisted of an old car tire draped around the neck of an "enemy of the people". It was filled with petrol and ignited. Hundreds were killed that way all over the country. It is likely that some of the victims were really police informers, but how many were dying this terrible death, innocent and wrongly accused?

This was also the year when, at the demand of Prime Minister P.W. Botha, the office of the Prime Minister was abolished by Parliament, and an Executive Presidency was created in its place. This action was clearly inspired by the very doubtful precedents of the USA and France and the even worse examples established by scores of dictators in Africa as well as in many other developing countries.

In the same year the newly established President announced with great fanfare that he would shortly make a speech in Durban which would shake up everybody and everything in the country. It would be his "crossing of the Rubicon", as he formulated it. The country and the whole world expected accordingly that he would announce the release of Nelson Mandela and the unbanning of both, the ANC and the PAC, as well as the early end of Apartheid.

Instead, his speech turned out to be a damp squib. Everybody was deeply disappointed, and the people of South Africa had to realize that no major relaxation of Apartheid could be expected under his leadership. The overseas reaction, particularly in the financial markets, immediately was devastating. The most shocking aspect of this debacle was probably the fact that he could not even understand, or did not want to, why this negative local and global reaction had happened!

As a result, the government was now forced to introduce the strict foreign currency controls of the Blocked Rand, a further variation on the earlier theme of the Financial Rand, to stem the rising tide of capital flight from South Africa. These measures of financial desperation resulted in a renewed and automatic international collapse of the exchange rate of the local currency.

However, these desperate measures were not sufficiently successful, because the country was forced to declare a default in servicing the interest payments on our foreign debt Instruments as they became due, and the repayment of the international foreign currency debts as these matured. This was a strong indication of how successful the international Anti-Apartheid fight on the financial battlefield had turned-out to be.

In an effort to appease the African majority, in the following year the Pass Laws and a few other 'Petty Apartheid' measures were rescinded by government. But at this late point this was of no avail. Too little – too late, to prop up the crumbling edifice of the Apartheid ideology.

14

THE BEGINNING OF THE END

1985 - 1994

Since 1983 I was finally spared, as the sole director of our construction group, the constant battles with the COSATU labor unions. From then on, my wife and I were running the Durban Stamp Auctions business. As such, we were now largely isolated from the Apartheid nightmare and the continuing Anti-Apartheid struggle.

A further development was the South African invasion of Angola, as a counter-offensive measure against the incursions by the African freedom fighters. This in turn brought the 'volunteers' from Cuba into the game. South Africa became subsequently involved in a war against a substantial Cuban Expeditionary Corps.

The Arms Embargo had now been already in force for quite some time. Each downed plane, for instance, had become irreplaceable. South Africa was involved here in a war of attrition, which this country had no chance of winning, and which, for this simple reason, should never have been started. But the threat of the freedom fighters was probably simply too over-whelming for the leaders of the National Party!

Eventually, the government was forced to realized that they were running against a brick wall. They had to abandon this war in Angola unconditionally, and had to withdraw their troops to South West Africa, where they continued to fight Swapo, the South West African People's Organization. In due course, the final result of this fighting was the appearance of the independent Republic of Namibia.

The United Nations had, after dithering for a long time, finally agreed to the imposition of general economic sanctions against South

Africa. Very quickly these were beginning to bite. It had previously been the accepted wisdom that international sanctions did not work. But these ones against Apartheid most definitely did work effectively and efficiently!

Of equal seriousness as the Arms Embargo was the Oil Embargo for this country. As long as the Shah of Iran was in power, his country had been a reliable supplier of oil to South Africa. In his youth, during the Great War, he had lived in exile in South Africa, and ever since he had maintained close connections with this country. But by now he had lost his throne, and the Mullahs thought it best to sell their valuable Black Gold to other customers.

One of the consequences of these successful international sanctions was the fact that many essential goods and services were now not available anymore in South Africa. More and more of the usually imported numerous articles had disappeared from the shelves of the supermarkets and shops. In addition, the South African economy was now cut off from the international services it desperately needed in order to be able to function properly.

In addition, South Africa now had begun to experience the even more serious threat of being unable to export as hitherto. Sure, the gold production and some other mineral exports still flourished, but our agricultural and horticultural exports to Europe, the United States and East Asia and Australia suffered badly.

Additionally, there were even rumors at this time that the postal and telephone services with the rest of the world would soon be closed down. The SMS and e-mail of the electronic age had not been invented yet, and the vast majority of newly immigrated people in South African still maintained close contacts with family and friends overseas, particularly in Great Britain and Europe, which they naturally had been keen to preserve.

Now there were even threats (or rumors?) that the airlines serving South Africa would be forced to terminate their flights to and from this country. Up to now the planes connecting Europe and Africa had refueled in Kenia at the Nairobi airport, until President Kenyatta refused them landing rights there.

As a result, they later had to fill up at the airport at Kano in Nigeria. When this country also blocked these services, the airlines were obliged to use the facilities of the Portuguese island of Sal, part of the Cape Verde Islands, for this purpose. All this necessitated longer flight paths, extra travel times and additional fuel costs. Every little pin-prick helped in this battle against the hated Apartheid!

Now one of the famous 'unintended consequences' manifested itself in South Africa, in the form of sanction busting. The more they started to bite, the more grew the determination to counteract them. A lot of money was made that way by a select few, and even more was wasted in the efforts to import around three corners scarce commodities, equipment items and some spare parts, in addition to the military goods which had already been imported clandestinely for quite some time.

Busting the arms and oil embargoes was an exhilarating past-time for some 'late-teenagers' in government and in the economy, but these mostly futile shenanigans depleted the country's foreign currency reserves and devalued the Rand internationally ever more. I suppose that these deals were also a little bit illegal in international law. In any case, these attempts helped to undermine and to ruin the South African economy and bankrupted the State even further.

A point to record here is the fact that large sums of taxpayer's money have not only been wasted, but have been 'misappropriated', in other words, they were stolen and laundered and finally landed in some personal numbered account in Zürich or Nassau/Bermuda.

It is only natural that some enterprising people started to fill this void by trying to provide the embargoed goods locally by the so-called import replacement endeavors. These obviously had some positive economic effect, but this program was insufficient to balance the catastrophic consequences which the wide-spread economic sanctions have had by then on the national economy and the country's finances, because these replacement products and services were in most cases too expensive.

I remember vividly the situation at this time in the industrial estates of our province. More and more industrial and commercial properties had been abandoned by their owners or tenants and had remained vacant. It was a picture, reminiscent of what we had seen in many American films about the aftermaths of the 1929 crash in the US. Many American industrial complexes apparently presented in the early 1930s a similar picture: smashed-in windows, ruined and graffiti-covered walls, damaged roofs and weed-infested factory grounds.

Many of these vacancies were the result of over-seas companies having left this country because of the sanctions. Also, particularly US companies had been under ever increasing pressure from home and were forced to leave the Apartheid State. Names like General Motors, Ford and IBM come to mind.

But many of the British firms were no better off. Here we saw mostly financial companies leave, such as the leading banks of the country, Barclays and Standard Bank, who were forced to dispose of their companies in fire-sales to wide-awake local investors.

Again, golden opportunities for a select few, but at a tremendous cost to the national economy and the country's foreign exchange position. There were also very serious consequences for the labor market, when thousands of laborers lost their jobs and could not find alternate employment.

Parallel to these developments, another serious consequence of the international squeeze affecting this country became now apparent. More and more of the Europeans, particularly amongst the rich and well-to-do, had by now come to the conclusion that the Apartheid regime would not last much longer. They were naturally worried of how the changeover would exactly materialize and how all this would affect them personally and financially in their bank accounts.

The result was predictable; they started to transfer as much of their funds as possible into overseas safe-haven accounts, to protect them against further foreign exchange losses and against the not improbable possibility of expropriation and confiscation in the "New South Africa".

Already in the decade prior to this time these people had started to salt away substantial amounts of their money by buying stamps, coins and small art valuables, all easily taken overseas if and when it became necessary. The easy portability was the most important aspect for such transactions by these customers.

In the final years of our stamp auction business up to 1994 we sold more and more valuable stamps and coins to general practitioners and medical specialists, to company directors and successful businesspeople generally. Other auction houses in the country experienced the same developments. The exponentially increased demand against a diminishing local supply level naturally resulted in inflated prices, and most of these assets had therefore been bought at unrealistically high local valuations.

One of the most telling incidents of this nature happened to me, when the Mayor of Durban, a former subcontractor of our group of building companies, came to see me to buy valuable stamps of Great Britain. He showed me the type of philatelic material he was interested in. These were high value stamps of the reign of Edward VII, which he told me he had bought at Stanley Gibbons in London. This was the leading stamp dealer in England and publisher of the standard Commonwealth stamp catalog.

These particular stamps had been printed in fugitive ink to prevent the removal of their postmarks, in order to fraudulently use them again. Every one of his stamps had lost their gum (a large part of their value) and had been re-gummed, and their fugitive ink had run terribly. They were all without much value! This showed clearly that this gentleman did not know the first thing about stamp collecting. So, why did he buy them, if not for the purpose of 'transferring' some money.

Naturally, I did not know whether he really had bought them at this reputable firm, which appeared highly unlikely to me. Anyway, I definitely was shocked for a moment, because there were all kinds of possibilities:

- a shady middleman offered to sell stamps below their market value which he claimed had originated there.
- a dishonest employee suggested to meet at the 'Pig and Thistle', to sell stock cheaply under the table.
- or my customer just used this illustrious name to impress me with his status of a substantial collector.

Simultaneously with these precautionary actions by the well-off, the tendency to emigrate escalated with ever increasing speed and volume. In many cases rich Whites started by initially sending their children overseas, to reduce the risk of the consequences of a possible violent take-over, but many families packed up entirely and left the country at this point. A number of travel agencies specialized in this lucrative type of one-way travel and actively advertised in newspapers and magazines their services as "emigration specialists".

Interestingly, a handful of rich Non-Europeans also joined this exodus. One wondered, why did this happen? Or maybe one does not, because some of them had been profitably cooperating for many years with the Apartheid government and were now justifiably worried about their assets and their future.

As a consequence of the tightening noose, the values plummeted of those assets which were not easily portable. Real estate prices in the select suburbs of the wealthy and along the coasts dropped strongly, and it took at least a decade to get resuscitated. Even the prices of luxury cars and yachts took many years to overcome their precipitous reduction in value. And even most of the share values at the Johannesburg stock exchange were affected negatively.

Now we were also experiencing an escalation of the armed struggle. More and more Africans chose to become freedom fighters to escape the ever more vicious suppression by the Apartheid State. They first made themselves scarce and then most of them were channeled by the underground ANC across the borders and joined their structures in foreign countries.

Most entered the ANC military training camps in various African countries. Not too surprisingly, conditions in these camps were sometimes atrocious. Often political or tribal factions developed there, which landed quite a few of the 'comrades' in the isolation cells. Or they were executed, if they were suspected to be spies of the Apartheid regime. As a matter of fact, quite a few crimes were committed there against these recruits, which only became known many years after the abolition of these camps.

The ANC in these African countries was paranoid in their worries about Apartheid spies being infiltrated into their ranks. I suspect that the South African government did not even consider such action, because I believe that they did not recognize these camps as a real threat to their rule, just as a nuisance.

Other freedom fighters went for their military training to Russia and the satellite states of the Soviet Empire. This applied particularly to the ones which had early been selected for future leadership and command positions in the New South Africa. These included positions of leadership in the still-to-be-formed future ANC Party, the government and state administration, the Defense Force in particular, but also the SOEs, the State-Owned-Enterprises and, of course, the economy in general.

Many of these exiles sought to further their education in these foreign countries, including those, who were able to obtain entry into a foreign university. If I remember correctly, our second President Thabo Mbeki studied economics in the United States. After the fall of Apartheid in 1994 these cadres brought desperately needed knowledge and skills back to their country of birth, but unfortunately there were not enough of them. In any case, I personally think that *summa summarum* they achieved more for their country than the armed struggle managed to do.

The members of Umkhonto we Sizwe, the MK, who constituted the ANC's military wing, had not been able to achieve the hoped-for results, in spite of their dedication, their high numbers due to our porous borders, and the local support they enjoyed. Yes, their various activities had a psychological impact on the Europeans, because some ran scared and were worried to go shopping in a super-market, or to go out at night to have a beer or three, but overall their impact was, in my opinion, not decisive.

On the other hand, the defensive actions by the government, like having checked the shoppers at the entrances of the shopping centers, were also not much more effective. They were, I would think, mainly designed to assuage the worries of the White public. But this kind of action at least prevented an MK cadre to walk with his AK47 into a Woolworth shop or OK supermarket which, I am sure, would definitively have raised a few eyebrows.

The infamous AK47 was the unmistakable symbol of this armed struggle. As is well known, Gospodin Kalashnikov invented this fabulous assault rifle for the Russian Army in the aftermath of the last war and this weapon has served in all trouble spots of the planet and was more often than not in the hands of the bad guys.

Now these fighters are being celebrated as heroes in the shebeens of the townships, and why not! By the way, these illegal but usually tolerated drinking establishments served as meeting places, where politics, sport, women and other urgent subjects were discussed. During the Apartheid years the townships were the only places were Africans were able to meet and conduct any business.

One of the leading figures in the efforts to make the country ungovernable was Nelson Mandela's wife Winnie Mandela. Through the underground ANC structures, she actively instigated mayhem in the townships and ensured that the calls for her husband's release from prison had never a chance to stop.

Because she was one of the most radical leaders, General van den Bergh, the Apartheid Boss of the State Security organization Stratcom initiated the 'Romulus' action. He had vowed "We will destroy this woman" (Wikipedia), and he fully succeeded. His campaign of misinformation led to her enduring isolation and damnation within the Black communities and organizations, right up to her passing-away more than twenty years later.

In Soweto, the huge African township outside Johannesburg, a group of young freedom fighters, the 'Winnie's United Football Club', had killed, allegedly on her instructions, the fifteen-year-old activist Stompie Seipel. Jerry Richardson, the trainer of the club, was after his confession to this murder sent to prison for this crime, but Winnie Mandela herself was never accused in court. He confided years later that he had been an informant of the Security Police. Her 'right hand' Xoliswa Falati was also later reported to have informed on Winnie Mandela (Wikipedia).

Her own ANC government had cited her in 1997 to appear in front of the Truth and Reconciliation Commission, where she was accused by the two Security Police informants that she had personally stabbed the teenager. As a result, the national and international media tagged her as a terrorist. The true facts only became public knowledge after her passing-away in 2018. This has now finally rehabilitated her life during the Apartheid years.

Quite another story was, however, her behavior after 1994, when she was appointed a Deputy Minister in the first cabinet of her husband. She was rumored to have committed certain dishonest and doubtful acts, which led to her loosing her appointment. Apparently, she was also only human.

If one considers the terrible conditions under which this poor women had to live while she had to campaign for twenty-seven years for the release of her incarcerated husband, then it is maybe understandable why she, as so many other freedom fighters, succumbed after the 1994 events to the temptation to consider herself to be above the law and to be entitled to enrich herself.

Another activity of the underground ANC was the fabrication of bombs and placing them in places where Apartheid personnel gathered or where acts of sabotage were possible. One such target was the Pretoria headquarters of the South African Police, the SAP. As far as I remember this action was not successful.

Magoo's Bar in Durban, where Defense Force personnel congregated to have some after-hours drinks or meetings, was bombed successfully. The bomber later became the head of the police unit in charge of IA, or Internal Affairs. Naturally, a new designation had to be created for this function: Independent Police Investigative Directorate, the IPID. Otherwise one could have been under suspicion of having watched too many of the decadent American police shows on television!

Other popular targets were the small suburban electrical transformer stations, because the bombs could be placed there quite easily, the bomber could retreat safely, and the explosions were spectacular. But some of the bombers were rather less daring and preferred to plant their bombs in waste-paper baskets or on telephone poles.

There is one more weapon to be mentioned here which the freedom fighters used to good effect. These were the already described strike actions instigated by the nascent labor unions. Originally these activities were just 'dry-runs' to gain some experience for the unions in the field of labor relations.

To start with, these organizations were mostly bumbling along, not really knowing what to do, because they simply had no experience with this kind of actions. Up to now this type of activity had been prohibited for Africans, and now it appeared that it was condoned, forced by necessity.

These strikes had later become powerful weapons in the fight to overcome Apartheid. The economy was again and again disrupted by wildcat strikes in one company after the other. There were not yet any well-organized general strikes covering the whole country, or at least whole industries. The necessary experience to organize such major activities was simply missing. But the damage inflicted on the economy was real enough, as was the political pressure created by these labor union activists.

In the end all these various actions and activities came together and succeeded to topple the Apartheid regime:

- weapons embargo,
- oil embargo,
- financial restrictions,
- international general economic sanctions,
- wild-cat strikes,
- armed struggle,
- international condemnation,
- internal criticism by the English-language media,
- the Black Sash activists,
- persistent complaints by some English-speaking politicians,
- protests by religious leaders of all denominations.

In the end, the decisive factor turned out to be, at least in my opinion, that the Afrikaners realized slowly but surely that their beloved Apartheid was not only un-workable, but that it was morally wrong and religiously indefensible.

And that realization crystallized most decisively in their minds after Beyers Naudé, one of the most revered of the Afrikaner clerics, had declared the Apartheid doctrine and practice to have been a sin against Christ.

Near the end of the 1980s the Soviet Empire imploded (nothing to do with me, honest!). This had implications for South Africa in so far as the Soviet Union had for decades strongly supported the ANC in many ways. This development led to a weakening of the ANC's position in their dealings with government.

A monumental shift was taking place at this time. As the result of the previously mentioned negotiations between the government and the ANC, South Africa was now emerging from the Apartheid past into a democratic presence and, hopefully, an alike future.

All this was keenly looked forward to by the African majority, but was awaited with much trepidation by the European minority, and partially also by the Colored and the Asian sectors of the population, and even some small groups of Africans, who were not particularly pleased with the prospect of being ruled by fellow Africans of other tribes.

Everybody among the Whites was worried about the future, mainly because we did not know what would happen during the preparations for the referendum and the elections. I suspected that even the top people on both sides of the negotiations were not sure what to expect.

Repeatedly, I have mentioned the worries and fears of the members of the racial minorities of South Africa at this time. How realistic were these sentiments? Unfortunately, based on past experience of genocides in Black Africa, they were extremely justified!

- tens of thousands of Blacks had been killed by warriors of one tribe in Zimbabwe, only because they belonged to 'another' tribe!
- up to a million fellow Africans were claimed to have been murdered by Blacks, after a violent revolutionary take-over in Ruanda, because they were members of the 'wrong' nation!

This latter slaughter had largely been committed by means of pangas, because firearms had been in short supply. These handy bush knives usually did not kill at a first attempt, but they caused horrific wounds. It needed many strikes, and it took some time, until the victims had bled to death. Welcome to Black Africa! Our Zulus in Natal were also very handy with these traditional weapons.

At this critical time rumors were flying about thick and fast. One of the stories, which made the rounds amongst the African male and female household employees, claimed that they would be entitled to take over the properties of their employers. Not exactly the type of thing we wanted to hear at that time!

South Africa had a number of newly founded Non-European political parties, and the voters had no experience with democratic elections. Additionally, there was the real danger that some super-conservative Afrikaners, who had just lost their 'God-given' privileges, might try a putsch.

New laws were promulgated now, giving voting rights in the forth-coming referendum of April 1992 not only to the former Non-Euro-peans but also to the Permanent Residents, like us. As members of this group, we had not been allowed to vote during the Apartheid era, but now for the first time we could cast our vote in this plebiscite.

In Germany, as explained in my earlier book "For All It Was Worth" we had, due to my disenchantment and bitterness with the Nazis, never voted in any election. But this new beginning in South Africa was deemed appropriate by us for a new start in this regard as well. We now were able to do something very satisfying; we went to cast our vote in the referendum, thereby approving the long-awaited introduction of real democracy in South Africa.

Prior to the first free elections of June 1994 in the New South Africa, the electoral law was changed again, and the Permanent Residents of the country lost again their only just acquired (passive) voting rights. As apparent compensation (?), the voting rights were now extended to all the prison inmates. Maybe somebody in the ANC leadership had the bright idea that this change would shift huge numbers of votes from the opposition to the ANC?

The political opponents had arrived in their negotiations at a realistic and smart decision. Considering the tensions, the high-flying expectations, but also the wide-spread distrust amongst the political opponents, the leaders had agreed to form after the elections a coalition government, as a temporary arrangement.

This would operate under the leadership of the ANC, with Nelson Mandela as executive State President. In addition, there would be two Deputy Presidents; F.W. de Klerk, the leader of the National Party, and Mangosuthu Buthelezi, the leader of the newly formed Inkhata Freedom Party, the IFP.

One could ask, where our family had stood in this Apartheid conundrum. As citizens of Germany we were, according to the German constitution, not allowed to hold dual citizenships. Since we never had any intention of abandoning our German nationality, it followed that we could never become South African citizens, and thus achieve voting rights in this country. Our legal status here, as already explained, was that of Permanent Residents, without voting rights.

We therefore had always considered ourselves as guests in this wonderful country. This, to my mind, dictated to stay out of 'family squabbles'. In other words, to refrain from getting involved in the internal politics of our host country, whether we agreed with them or not. For these reasons it could be said that dictated by circumstances, we have been 'sitting on the fence' in this regard. This worked both ways; we neither behaved as racists, nor did we participate in Anti-Apartheid protest actions.

PART V

FREEDOM

POST-APARTHEID SOUTH AFRICA (1994 TO 2014)

15

THE AFTERMATH OF APARTHEID

Index of Sections

- Apartheid Legacy
- African Middle Class
- White Minority
- African Politics/Political Parties
- Truth & Reconciliation Commission
- Feeling of Entitlement
- Corruption
- Arms Deal Scandal
- President Zuma
- ZUPTA/Zuma & Gupta Families Scandal
- Guptagate/State Capture
- Race Relations/Racism and Reverse Racism
- Affirmative Action/Quotas/Cadres
- Public Service
- Cultural Differences
- Environment
- Crime/Violence
- Xenophobia
- Tribalism/Tribal Violence/Traditional Leaders
- Languages Policies
- Gender Equality
- Labor Relations/Strikes/Unions
- Skills Shortage/Training

- Secondary and Tertiary Education
- Economy/Finance/Banks
- Positive Observations

Now that we have reached the year 2014, it was time to have a look at the post-Apartheid picture, twenty years after the end of this era in 1994. On the positive side was the fact that the Non-Europeans had now, after a century of struggle, finally won complete political and personal freedom. All racial restrictions within the legal framework had by now been removed.

But there remained some economical and job-related aspects to be considered, as well as a number of other problems. The transition from the oppressive but well organized and orderly Apartheid system to the post-Apartheid stage was fraught with problems, as was only to be expected. Dramatic shifts like this take some time and throw-up all kinds of expected and unexpected challenges.

The reasons for the shortcomings were obvious. Any new state in the Third World has always been faced with a myriad of problems, some inherited and some self-inflicted. Lack of political, administrative and economic as well as financial experience were usually the cause. Other reasons were lack of intellectual capacity, personal defects of the leading politicians, inflated expectations of their followers, and many others.

Apartheid Legacy

The country started in 1994 to change from the bitter Past to a free and democratic Present, and hopefully to a likewise Future. This development had clearly been longed for by the Africans. The Indians were also hopeful, because the majority of them had fought together with the Africans. But future events were expected with substantial misgivings and fear by the White and the Colored communities.

The old Apartheid laws and regulations were now slowly and orderly rescinded and the new democratic laws replacing the Apartheid legacy were subsequently debated and promulgated. One of these gave finally the right to vote to the former Non-Whites.

The freedom fighters returning to the country of their birth from abroad brought their knowledge and experience back, but not to the extent necessary for the ANC to be able to smoothly take over the running of the public service and the economy, as their leadership had hoped.

The structure of the new government had been inherited from the Apartheid era. As recorded previously, the National Party had changed shortly before the end of Apartheid the system of government from a Non-Executive State President, plus a Prime Minister in charge of the government, to an Executive President with a Deputy President to conduct the government business under his instructions.

South Africa and the newly independent African nations, or rather their leaders, had opted for the US system, because it gave them almost absolute powers. In many cases this motivation was proven when they refused to vacate their office at the end of their tenure, or when they installed, or tried to do so, a family member or a tame friend as successor. Any existing constitutional obstacles to such shenanigans were blithely ignored by them, or the constitution was quickly changed by their allies or cronies to achieve the desired outcome.

This whole basic idea of an executive presidency was clearly copied from the USA, and in particular from France, and in both countries the shortcomings of such a structure had become obvious.

The Americans, when institutionalizing their executive presidency in the eighteenth century, more or less copied the almost absolute monarchy of Great Britain of the time, but simultaneously they created some counterbalances against the far-reaching powers of their President. Over the centuries there have been numerous incidents of costly battles between the Presidents and Congress.

The French governments, also with an executive president, but also with a prime minister, often battled with conflicting ideas and demands of the sitting Executive President and his Prime Minister, especially if they belonged to different political parties.

Another heritage from the previous regime was the local currency. The Rand was the only free-floating one amongst the developing countries. Because of this unique position, the global financial professionals used the Rand as the representative currency for the developing world.

The Rand therefore fluctuated violently every time when bad news came out of this country, or out of any of the other developing states. If caused by South Africa, this situation was neither the fault of the Rand, nor of the Treasury or the Reserve Bank, but was caused by the mistakes of the respective South African governments of the day.

The global rating agencies always kept an eye peeled on this country, due to its past history and notoriety, but also because of the advance accolades garnered by our first president Nelson Mandela.

After a honeymoon period they downgraded the country's currency and debt repeatedly. The typical African government reaction to such misfortune: forget about them and let us establish our very own (tame) rating agency.

The armed struggle was now fondly remembered by the African majority as the decisive blow in bringing down Apartheid. This was, in my opinion, wishful and selective thinking, because this was only one of many elements which lead to the demise of Apartheid. Other major factors were as important, if not more so;

- the changes in the attitudes of the Afrikaners,
- the very successful work of the ANC overseas,
- and finally, the international condemnations and sanctions as a result thereof.

One of the most popular hobbies of our African politicians has always been their references to the consequences of Apartheid. Now some of the Black intellectuals have started to decry this habit. Naturally, these arguments were in many cases fully justified, particularly regarding the terrible Bantu education and the enforced lack of job experiences, due to job reservation in favor of the Europeans. But in most cases, these were only excuses to whitewash the shortcomings of the ANC government twenty years after attaining freedom.

As a genuine Apartheid inheritance, tens of thousands of the African laborers were still living in compounds for single men. Obviously, this type of accommodation has created a number of problems for these men, but also for society in general. Apart from the trauma of separation for the men, their women and their children, there were the sexual implications and more specifically, the inherent criminality in connection with this type of involuntary separate living.

African Middle Class

This sociological class started from almost nothing in 1994 and has made some mighty progress since then. To start with, the political rearrangement created immediately a huge number of well-paid politicians, such as Members of Parliament and of the nine provincial assemblies, ministers and municipal councilors. These were counted in their thousands.

Additionally, there were also the public service appointments in all three layers of government. Here we easily dealt with tens of thousands of new members of this class within the African community.

The next wave of newly created members of the emerging African middle class came from the board appointments and the executives of the SOEs, the State-Owned Enterprises, and there were plenty of those in a socialist/communist country like South Africa. These boards often had twenty or more members, when half a dozen of competent persons would have sufficed and would in addition have delivered better results. But there were so many loyal party members to be looked after!

A further addition to this rising sociological class was provided by the now legally required participation of the Non-Whites, and by Africans in particular, in the management and at the board level in the companies of the private economy.

And those, who still had not obtained a well-paid job, they would have been moved into one of the numerous newly created (and claimed to be independent) agencies, which were intended to guide and to supervise various aspects of policy and within the economy. I would guess that we had about a dozen of those, with about twenty highly paid members each.

It is surely no exaggeration to say that ninety-nine percent of all of these positions were awarded to trusted members of the ANC and the SACP. Competence and experience were of no particular importance, and the question of ethics was not even raised. It was generally a case of "don't bother us with uncomfortable facts". And if such questions actually were raised, they were brushed aside by the ANC as racist obfuscation by the Apartheid benefactors.

Additionally, there was now a legal requirement to 'sell' a certain percentage of the shares in European-owned companies to Black empowerment bodies. This presented the government with a tiny problem: how to sell anything to somebody, who had neither money nor other assets, and who often did not even have any intention to pay for anything. Imaginative mental acrobatics were employed to achieve this goal, sometimes successfully, and sometimes not.

Companies were established for this sole purpose, their shares nominally belonging to Blacks, but remaining under the control of the selling companies concerned. The dividends were credited to their African owners, but not paid out, until they covered the full purchase price of the shares, if and when the transaction was successfully completed.

This created the next large group of millionaires or middle-class

Africans. Naturally, there was wailing and hysterics if there were no dividends, or if the whole procedure took forever (more than two years!) or if the get-rich-quick (also called empowerment) scheme had failed completely.

The laws about the economic empowerment of the Blacks was a bonanza for the legal profession. More and more acronyms popped up in conjunction with this legalese framework. Companies had to obtain a minimum number of 'points' to be able to do business with the three tiers of government. Black ownership was closely intertwined with this subject, which created many successful and wealthy African businesspeople.

During the next twenty years a number of Black-owned firms were established, which usually were prosperous because of the government policy to give such companies extra points when comparing prices and tender sums. This amounted to about an extra ten percent margin below the offers of European firms.

Inevitably, these provisions created a strong temptation to fraudulently claim these BEE, Black Economic Empowerment bene-fits. This policy had well-meaning intentions but opened the door wide for corruption as well. Many cases of 'fronting' were reported, where a few Blacks were engaged (who thereby got rich quickly) to provide a Black smokescreen for a White-owned company. Another unintended consequence was that it tended to inflate the internal price levels and pushed-up inflation.

White Minority

For people, who have not lived in South Africa during the years immediately before and after the collapse of Apartheid, it must be difficult to imagine what the attitudes, expectations, fears and experiences of the less than five million Europeans were, when they were confronted with a majority of about fifty million Africans and another few millions of Indians and Coloreds, all with equal rights.

It was not unreasonable for the Whites to expect and to fear a violent backlash after the atrocities, particularly during the final years of Apartheid, when numerous crimes were committed by the security and defense forces in a final attempt to shore up this moribund system.

It came as a great surprise for us when we noticed that in particular many of the Coloreds, but also some of the Indians, and even certain sectors of the Africans, were as worried as we were. Fortunately for all of us, the whole exercise of the handover of power ran generally very smoothly. No wonder that it was globally declared the "Miracle of South Africa".

In general, we all were positively surprised how well the takeover of power in this country had functioned. In particular the absence of violence and revenge towards the European minority was rightly hailed as a miracle.

First, we had in 1992 the referendum about the adoption of the CODESA (Convention for a Democratic South Africa) agreements between the ANC and the National Party government of the country, including the new democratic constitution. Then followed in 1994 the first free elections.

Naturally, there were the odd incidents of violence before, during and after the referendum, and also some relating to the first democratic election. We experienced some shenanigans by politicians trying to influence or to change the voting numbers. This had to be expected, since all involved were African politicians, and these things had been par for the course all along in Black Africa.

Bantu Holomisa, the strongman of the Transkei Homeland, for instance, illegally infiltrated in quickly requisitioned busses hundreds, or possibly thousands, of his Africans into southern Natal to boost the ANC votes here. The homeland citizens were not yet allowed to vote, as far as I remember, in these first free elections. Or maybe this happened in conjunction with the referendum.

The Independent Election Commission under Judge Kriegler (an Afrikaner!) adjusted the results in Natal to neutralize these tricks, and all parties accepted this Solomonic decision. This saved the situation for this country, because a political and racial confrontation at this point would surely have been catastrophic.

Generally, all concerned were positively surprised how well the whole process of taking over the power by the ANC had been handled. The absence of revenge and violence in dealing with the Europeans was the other part of the "South African Miracle". This was largely due to the moderating influence of Nelson Mandela, who managed to neutralize the hot-headed amongst his followers. And also due to his statesmanship. He had acted as a true statesman and neither as a freedom fighter nor as a petty party politician.

After fifty years of basically ignoring the Non-Europeans, one saw now, for instance, for the first time an African traffic policeman on his motorbike in town or in a European suburb. What would happen when he stopped a dyed-in-the-wool Afrikaner racist? It was only logical to expect at least the occasional confrontation. But astonishingly, nothing much happened, at least generally, and as far as we in Natal were aware.

Similar worries referred to the first encounters with Non-White clerks behind the counters at the municipality or at state offices. Would they be vindictive and racists-in-reverse? We did not come personally across any such feared attitudes. But would they be competent to do their jobs? Many of the newly installed clerks floundered to start within uncharted waters, but some took to their new environment like the proverbial ducks take to water.

And what would happen if one found oneself in the in any case awkward position of having to face a court of law? There again, most judges, prosecutors and lawyers just continued with their work as before. I suppose that some outright white racists had lost their positions, but this did not play out in public. The same had to be said in respect to the police.

A particularly tricky worry existed regarding public toilets. Imagine that now hordes of Africans would use these facilities! Horror and horror again! And what about venereal diseases and AIDS? And what about cleanliness, or rather the absence thereof? But again, the "roof did not cave in" and we all survived this imagined catastrophe.

Despite all the privileges and the pampering of the Europeans during the Apartheid era, there obviously must have been at all times some Whites who were poor, or at least who were struggling to make ends meet. These situations usually arose then only if people were unemployed because they were alcoholics or drug addicts. The latter problem was rarely encountered in South Africa at that time. Unemployment among Europeans did practically not exist. We had the railways for that, after all!

Now however, there emerged a new class of 'Poor Whites', who had lost their jobs, usually without their fault. Valiant efforts, particularly by religious communities, were being made to help these people. In many cases, however, the previously emphasized 'superiority of the European race' was shown to be fictitious and only skin-deep.

Some of these people regressed now into a primitive slum mentality, even beyond the restrictions imposed by their new-found poverty. Quite a few moved into one of the African townships, where life was much cheaper (in every sense of the word, unfortunately!), and where they came for the first time in close contact with members of the majority of the South African people.

The worries about feared putsch attempts by fanatical Afrikaners at the time of the first elections, but also shortly afterwards, did fortunately not materialize. But many years later the Security Police discovered an attempted conspiracy to overthrow the government. It was conducted amateurishly and was easily snuffed out by the authorities. As far as we could understand, there were only a handful of Afrikaner conspirators involved.

African Politics/Political Parties

In 1994, one of the first definitive steps taken by the new government was to launch the application for South Africa to rejoin the British Commonwealth of Nations. This was particularly important for economic and political reasons, but also psychologically, especially for the Whites, the Coloreds and the Indians. It reassured them that they would not be completely swamped by the huge majority of Africans in the country. It also meant that they had not been simply abandoned in Black Africa.

The premature end of the negotiated coalition government in 1996, which had been agreed upon at CODESA, had to be expected. It was supposed to last for five years, until 1999, but the internal conflicts and tensions were just too basic and strong for this sensible arrangement to survive any longer.

This development did not do too much damage internally. Overseas, however, it was seen as the beginning of the incessant slide of the country from an 'African Miracle' to another typical 'African Banana Republic'.

One of the peculiarities within the South African political landscape was the tendency for a faction to leave the movement and to form at the drop of a hat a new party, if a difference of opinion, or just a clash of personalities, had developed. This had happened to the ANC more than once. But other parties were occasionally not spared this situation either. The PAC and IFP also had such problems, but not as often as the ANC. But the Apartheid political parties of the Europeans had not fared any better.

The main reason for such calamities was the general tendency of African politicians to quickly form factions within their parties. This happened occasionally in other countries, too. But here the crucial point was that the individual politicians appeared to have placed their personal interests, or those of their faction, above the interests of their party. These factions were usually based on mutual support and patronage considerations, but not necessarily on political differences of opinion.

At the Polokwane party congress in 2008 the ANC delegates dismissed the sitting Party and State President Thabo Mbeki and elected Jacob Zuma as President of the ANC, and also an interim incumbent for the remainder of Mbeki's tenure as elected State President. Despite the well-known facts of Zuma's corrupt involvements, the ANC members of parliament elected in 2009 the dismissed previous Deputy President, and their sitting ANC president, as the new State President.

After Mbeki was recalled, many of his supporters left the ANC. Under the leadership of Mosiuoa 'Terror' Lekota they formed the Congress of the People, the Cope party. His nickname did not refer to his activities during the armed struggle, but to his former prowess as a soccer player. The name of this new political party was the identical one of the Freedom Congress which in 1955 had adopted the Freedom Charter, one of the most powerful and emotional documents of the ANC.

The deposed rulers of two of the four Bantustans were another source of new parties.

- Bantu Holomisa, the former strongman of the Transkei homeland, had formed the United Democratic Movement, the UDM when, after a clash (of personalities?) with the party leadership, he had been kicked out of the ANC. No convincing reasons for this action could be found on the internet.
- Lucas Mangope, the former ruler of the Bophuthatswana homeland, had founded the United Christian Democratic Party, the UCDP, after he had lost his lucrative former sinecure.

The former dictators of the Venda und Ciskei homelands sulked and did not want to play in this sandpit with their previous colleagues. Presumably, they did not find sufficient support among their former disciples to engage in this profitable game.

Mangosuthu Buthelezi, a former leader of the ANC Youth League, and later the de-facto ruler of Zululand, had already formed much earlier the Inkhata Liberation Movement, after he had disagreed with the ANC leadership's approach to the fight against Apartheid.

As its leader he had strongly opposed the ANC's call for economic sanctions against South Africa, because he believed that these would hurt the people more than the Apartheid government. But he also had steadfastly refused to have his tribal Zululand turned into another one of the Apartheid Home-lands.

This name of this conservative tribal movement, based on the Zulu nation's traditions, had been changed in 1994 into the Inkhata Freedom Party, the IFP, in order to be able to participate in the first free election.

In 2013 Julius Malema, the then leader of the ANC Youth League, was expelled with his faction from the party, because of his clashes with President Zuma. The same Zuma, whom he was "prepared to die for" a few years earlier, when he was fighting for Zuma to become President of the ANC and the country. Later, he was accused of tax fraud of fourteen million Rand, and of corruption in connection with some road building contracts in his home province. Apparently, these serious matters have somehow simply evaporated. Had they possibly been fabricated out of political motivation?

After his spectacular one hundred-eighty degrees turn, from fervent supporter of Jacob Zuma to his most virulent accuser, he founded with his faction the Economic Freedom Fighter party, the EFF. He appointed himself as the 'Supreme Commander' of his cohorts and used overt military terminology extensively to name structures within his 'very own' party.

He invented a uniform for his followers, which they also wore sitting in Parliament; red overalls, black rubber boots and red berets. This was something completely new for South Africa, and heavily reminiscent of Germany of the 1920s and '30s. In my earlier book "For All it Was Worth" I have described the similar behavior of the Nazis in Germany during these years. Surprisingly, there was no reaction from the Speaker to this provocation. She was most likely completely ignorant of the Nazi parallel.

This new party introduced into our Parliament also a substantial level of primitive violence, with physical threats, fisticuffs and hustling, after ANC and IFP members had earlier behaved in similar ways in the Natal provincial legislature, in addition to numerous political murders, mostly in the rural districts.

In the parliamentary elections of 2014, the main political parties obtained the following results:

- the ANC garnered about 62%,
- the DA, as the official opposition, about 22%,
- the EFF, the new party on the block, about 6,5% (Wikipedia).

Truth & Reconciliation Commission

This commission started in 1996 under the chairmanship of Archbishop Emeritus Desmond Tutu. He had been an outstanding icon in the fight against Apartheid, but he had never been a member of any political party or grouping. He also continued with his balanced views to protest against injustices and wrongs under the new dispensation. He was a fair, prudent and outstandingly caring man.

The "Arch" was, together with Nelson Mandela, one of the few Non-Whites which were trusted by many amongst the Whites. During the previous period, both of these men had been depicted as 'devils' by the propaganda of the National Party. But now their true character became obvious. They both strove to unite all the people of South Africa, and they were prepared to forgive many of the sins committed on both sides of the struggle.

The commission's main purpose was to provide closure to the families of the murdered victims of Apartheid. This was very important for the descendants of those who had been killed by the police and the army during the struggle, and who in many cases had been buried in foreign countries. It was the main purpose of this commission that these families should be given the true facts about the fate of their loved ones.

The Commission promised judicial forgiveness for voluntary full and honest disclosure of actions against Anti-Apartheid activists. This was the only realistic way to discover the truth about all the clandestine activities of the Security Police, the 'Boss' organization and the Defense Force inside and outside the country.

Nelson Mandela personally had made heroic efforts to heal the former chasms and to fill-in the concomitant chasms of mistrust between the races. He even went so far as visiting the widow of Hendrik Verwoerd, the infamous architect of Apartheid. He also paid a courtesy visit to P.W. Botha, a real 'fossil' with his rigid racist attitudes, and the final Apartheid President, who was dedicated to defending this system to the last breath.

His reconciliation efforts have established him as a true statesman.

Here I have regrettably to report that these efforts by Nelson Mandela were originally vehemently opposed by certain factions within the ANC, and more particularly by their Youth League.

Only a few of the former prominent acolytes of the Apartheid era have publicly swore off their former beliefs by now. Prominent among them was Pik Botha (no relation to P.W. Botha), the former Minister of Foreign Affairs, who after 1994 demonstratively had joined the ANC as a simple member.

Feeling of Entitlement

Since 1994 existed this perception by the average Africans of being entitled to all sorts of things and services. The basis for this attitude was their feeling of entitlement to compensation, preferably in cash, for past sufferings, discrimination and the missed opportunities to acquire riches. This in addition to the truly justified expectations of personal and political freedom and of the recognition of their human dignity and rights.

With this wide-spread African attitude of entitlement it was therefore not surprising that the masses demanded housing, education and health services, electrical power and water, even if they could not pay for them or they refused to do so. Nobody gave any serious attention to the question of whether the State could afford to provide these things free of charge. Alter-natively, where the money was supposed to come from, which would then unfortunately be missing somewhere else.

By now, this tricky situation has been greatly simplified. The ANC voters are now simply demanding all these things for free. This bypassed the difficult problem of how to finance these bonanzas. This also solved the further problem of most of the African households owing huge debts for power and water to the municipalities (which they would never be able to honor), who in turn were bankrupting Eskom by not paying for the electricity supplied by this SOE.

The South African's ingrained socialist/communist belief in the State's obligation to solve all the problems of the people, instead of urging them to make an effort to solve those themselves, provided a further inducement for this unrealistic expectation.

There is a minor but telling historic example available about the provision of free services. During the early 1920s the Postmaster General of the Soviet Union provided the postal services free of charge. The postage stamps were therefore abolished as unnecessary.

Until eventually it dawned on the authorities that this sort of thing was financially ruinous, because this revenue was now missing and had to be replaced by the state and was then missing somewhere else. They quickly had to reintroduce the postal charges and the stamps, to the great relief of the stamp collectors!

Corruption

Many of the problems of this country were undoubtedly rooted in the Apartheid past. One of the most serious one was the corruption in South Africa. After 1994 this was apparently condoned by the majority of Africans, as is evidenced by their acceptance of many of their leaders who were mired in corruption. One popular explanation for this attitude was the belief that they would have committed the same acts if they were given half a chance to do so. But this opinion may very well have been sour grapes by the other racial groups.

Fact was that after the ANC takeover corruption became endemic at all levels of government, but also in the economy. We had now created a brand-new class of businesspeople, the 'tenderpreneurs'. Overnight they have become millionaires, and a few of them maybe billionaires, by fictitious or criminal tendering for roads, housing or any other activity of the public service, aided and abetted by equally corrupt politicians and public 'servants'.

Cheating in construction contracts was normally not all that easy, as I can confirm as a former finance director of a group of such companies. But our 'tenderpreneurs' found an easy solution to the problem; they submitted a tender for ten million Rand, handed-in their monthly progress payment documentation, and banked the relevant payments.

But where is the catch? Simple, they spent no money and performed no work at all! All they had to do was to share a small part of their ten million with some officials or politicians. Sometimes, and only sometimes, these corrupt people were caught, they were (maybe) subjected to a disciplinary hearing, and subsequently they were suspended for two or three years, with full pay and benefits, naturally. There-after the matter was buried in some filing cabinet and conveniently forgotten.

There is one important point I would like to make here. Protecting a corrupt individual or government departmental staff, because they belonged to the same political party, or to the same racial group, or to the same tribe, was also a form of corruption. The same applied to private enterprise, if it shielded directors or executives who had committed crimes, in order to protect the image (and the share price!) of the company.

We had, for instance, the sad example of the Judge President of the Cape Province, who in spite of certain misdeeds was protected by the African majority in the Judicial Service Commission from being censored, obviously because of the color of his skin.

Arms Deal Scandal

1999 was an *'annus horribilis'* for the new country. Stocks of weapons and equipment of the Apartheid era Defense Force had been largely exhausted in the years of border wars and invasions into neighboring countries. The new government, therefore, considered it necessary to urgently rectify this situation. For several reasons this assessment was a huge mistake by the authorities, because the situation had not been analyzed properly and holistically by them.

To start with, there was no urgency since there was no imminent threat against the country in sight. And where was any later threat supposed to come from? The neighboring countries were militarily and economically too weak (even more so than the bled-out South Africa) to start an invasion. Any major power could of course easily have managed to invade South Africa, but in that case our rearmament efforts would have made no difference.

This wasted money was more urgently needed for social purposes, such as the amelioration of the worst forms of the endemic poverty and suffering, and for the provision of edu-cation, housing, employment, policing to fight criminality, as well as sound health services for the masses.

The Arms Deal proved to have become the biggest and worst case of early corruption in the 'New South Africa'. This 'deal' started the by now endemic corruption in the country. The total amount involved in this affair was claimed to have been about five billion US dollars (Wikipedia).

It took several government and parliamentary commissions to whitewash all the culprits, after lengthy and costly proceedings. It appeared to me that the commissioners were either incompetent, or that they themselves were corrupt, maybe? The fact that bribes were paid by overseas arms manufacturers (or even governments?) was easily established.

But these various commissions did not find a single recipient of these millions of dollars in this country. Nobody has been able to discover the individual amounts and the identities of the recipients of all the numerous bribes which changed hands in this context, even though some European governments had offered their assistance to help answer these queries!

The Deputy President, the *de-facto* Prime Minister and future President Thabo Mbeki was believed to have collected forty million (Rand or dollar?) for the ANC, and was said to have claimed, with a certain justification, that the newly constituted party needed some money to finance the coming first free parliamentary election.

The same *rationale* was used by the ANC to justify a number of bank heists by their *cadres* shortly before the 1994 election. But if any such illegal behavior was rationalized as acceptable, because it was necessary, then the floodgates will be wide open in future.

Tragically, some of the leading ANC figures, like the Defense Minister Joe Modise and the Shaik brothers, were seen to fill their large pockets this way. Modise had been for twenty-five years the Commander in Chief of Umkhonto we Sizwe, or MK, the armed forces of the ANC. It was disheartening to see so many former freedom fighters to succumb so easily to temptation like this. Other tranches of multiple millions of dollars, dished out by arms manufacturers from Europe and the USA, apparently landed in several other private pockets, and thereby producing quite a number of newly coined Black multi-millionaires.

President Zuma

In 2005, while we were overseas, we learned there that President Mbeki had fired his Deputy President Jacob Zuma because of allegations of corruption in conjunction with the Arms Deal. Zuma had reportedly been 'financially supported' by Shabir Shaik, one of the influential Shaik brothers. Shaik acted on behalf of Thales or Thompson-CSF, the French weapons manufacturers, and he had procured some 'minor' annual payments of five hundred thousand Rand each for his *protégé*.

We were very happy to hear such positive news, and the overseas friends we discussed this with voiced the same positive sentiments. There was at this time some hope that this pigsty would be cleaned out pronto.

The judge in the Shaik trial found the accused guilty on two counts and to have been in a 'corrupt relationship' with Zuma and sentenced the former to ten years in prison. Why the court did not pronounce further on Zuma himself became never clear to us and puzzled the public for years. There was some talk that the prosecution had indicated that the case against Zuma was not winnable. How was that possible, if money had been paid to him, which was proven in the Shaik trial to have come from the French?

Nobody was particularly surprised when Shaik after his jailing was found by three medical doctors to be terminally ill. He promptly received from Zuma a medical pardon, despite the obvious conflict of interest. Since then he frequented hotels, spas and sports arenas in obvious best health! As far as we know, no questions were ever raised about the background to this medical certificate and the miracle cure. In my opinion, this scandal was, in a way, as terrible and contagious as the Arms Deal corruption itself!

Later, the Prosecution Service opened an investigation into Zuma's role and went to court with this. His lawyer opposed the indictment on the grounds that the prosecution was politically motivated. Judge Nicholson ruled that President Mbeki had illegally influenced the prosecution and he squashed the legal proceedings on this ground.

Why this peculiar judgement in Natal, the Zuma and Zulu home province? Fear of the many violent and fanatical Zuma supporters? Blackmail? Bribery? Well, we will probably never know. In my humble opinion as a simple-minded unqualified person, I would have said that this looked very much like a seriously flawed verdict.

If President Mbeki was found to have illegally influenced the Prosecution Service, and it rather looked like it, the court should then have ordered his prosecution. There was no logical reason to squash the proceedings against Zuma, since the *prima facie* facts of the case clearly justified prosecution, regard-less of any alleged interference.

Subsequently, for a long time there was total silence, except for the praise of the judge by the ANC, of course. But four months later the Supreme Court of Appeal annulled Judge Nicholson's verdict in sharp terms. Subsequently, the judge had somehow faded into the woodwork and he was later active in thespian productions.

This whole saga about the corruption charges against President Zuma has not been resolved even to the present day. Originally, there were hundreds of corruption accusations leveled against him, but for all these years his lawyer has been able to keep him out of the court-rooms, apparently quite legally, by using the infamous Stalingrad Defense.

According to a Google quote, this is a strategy of wearing down the plaintiff by tenaciously fighting anything he presents by whatever means possible and appealing every ruling favorable to the plaintiff. Here, the defendant does not present a meritorious case. This tactic or strategy is named for the Russian city besieged by the Germans in World War II.

Maybe there existed some justification for a look at some other South African laws, just as this was necessary for the Income Tax Act some years ago? We were all deemed to be equal before the law, but it seems some were rather more equal than the rest of us.

I know that Zuma has not been found guilty by any court, as he repeatedly and with deep hurt assured everybody, but this was only because his lawyer had manipulated the law and the legal procedures so efficiently and effectively, which kept him out of the courts for so many years. To add insult to injury, Zuma has consistently demanded "his day in court" in order to proof his innocence! Yes, he knew how to pick the correct lawyer!

It had soon become clear to everybody in the country that Zuma had been involved in corrupt dealings in conjunction with the Arms Deal and other suspect transactions. Most of the Africans were aware of his corrupt involvement, even those who could not read or had no access to the radio or TV news. The word-of-mouth communication by the bush-telegraph amongst Africans has everywhere in Black Africa always been exceptionally efficient.

To my mind the worst aspect of this whole drama was the fact that the ANC members, the mass of the Africans in South Africa, kept supporting and protecting Zuma, despite all the obvious damning facts against his character and conduct. Prominent amongst the political supporters of Zuma at this time was Julius Malema, the then leader of the ANC Youth League. He dramatically declared: "Our members are willing to die for Zuma".

Apparently, this emotional outburst was caused by his wish to get rid of President Mbeki. We were not aware of his real reasons for this, other than that he accused him of having failed the HIV/AIDS sufferers, and to have been arrogant and aloof. These points, I thought, were taken correctly. But to be prepared to die for a man with such character flaws as Zuma appeared to be going overboard. Had Mbeki possibly committed the unforgivable crime of not taking Malema seriously?

Already some years ago, our excellent Public Protector had accused Zuma to have privately profited by something like more than a hundred million Rand from the refurbishing of his extensive estate and kraals in Zululand. She was very likely the most influential force which started the process of vigorous investigations which later led to his ousting as president of the ANC, and subsequently as the State President.

ZUPTA/the Zuma & Gupta Families Scandal

Now we come to the Gupta family, possibly the worst of all the horrible corruption subjects. Atul Gupta, his two brothers and a nephew arrived here in 1993 from India. They met and befriended the then Deputy President Jacob Zuma in 2003 (Wikipedia). A look at the timeline indicates the cunning of these people: they came in 1993, still under Apartheid rule, but at the cusp of the ANC takeover.

They early on selected to financially support him and his family in his lavish lifestyle, naturally without any ulterior motive, since he was living well beyond his means with his small harem. But they also helped him in his challenge against Thabo Mbeki for the presidency of the ANC, and later of the State, even though they had previously given some money to Mbeki as well.

Their selfless political generosity extended even to Helen Zille of the Democratic Alliance. I wondered, how much they gave to Julius Malema of the Economic Freedom Fighters, the EFF? Or were his chances to win influence and power not considered realistic enough? In other words, they heavily invested in wholesale political influence peddling across the board! This was a classic example of far-seeing criminal planning and execution.

In no time at all had they obtained South African citizenships and had established their luxury compound in the leafy upmarket suburb of Saxonwold in Johannesburg. In a suspiciously short time, they had mysteriously become overnight multi-billionaires, and equally so the Zuma family.

Their holding company Oakbay Investments Ltd. controlled the Gupta Empire of more than a dozen companies in several different fields. These included the computer, the mining and the media industries, amongst other holdings. This company employed Zuma's son Duduzane in a prominent position.

Guptagate/State Capture

By 2014 it had become clear that the Gupta family, with the enthusiastic help of President Zuma, had their hot little hands in numerous pies in the politics and the economy of this country. In addition to their more or less legal involvement in many different industries in South Africa, they were particularly involved with the SOEs, the huge State-Owned-Enterprises.

Here the Guptas appeared to have found their Eldorado! The pickings were immensely rich. All they had to do was to transfer their loot to Dubai. Board members and executives of these companies were bought wholesale and ordered or influenced to award the most profitable contracts at inflated prices to Gupta companies. All this enabled and tolerated by Zuma and many high-ranking ANC luminaries. Without their corrupt help none of this would have been possible!

Because of their sheer size, these entities repeatedly had to award contracts worth billions of Rand. This area of economic and financial management has always been notoriously shady, even in well run states. But much more so in a developing country like South Africa.

Due to the cadre deployment of politically worthy but inexperienced and often incompetent and/or corrupt ANC appoint-tees in all of these firms at board level and in the executive management, there were rich pickings available for them. Loaded tenders and huge unauthorized disbursements, were welcome gifts for unscrupulous but influential and well-connected crooks and businesspeople.

These entities were, almost without exception, badly and/or corruptly managed and catastrophically unprofitable because of that. As a consequence, they needed repeated bailouts by the Treasury (meaning by the taxpayer). In other words: they were typical state-run enterprises in a socialist/communist country. Of course, nobody in South Africa would have publicly considered to privatize these 'bottomless buckets'. This would have been seen as a sacrilege, and as not PC, politically correct.

The specifically coined term 'Guptagate' referred originally only to their criminal activities in the economic field, including the appointment of board members and executives of the State-Owned-Enterprises. Later, this term also covered their dealings in influence-peddling within government as well, such as the hiring and firing of ministers and Members of Parliament. Their dealings in this field created another new expression in the South African dictionary, that of 'State Capture'. The Guptas have stolen billions of Rand from this country, but in compensation they have at least helped to enrich our language by these two terms!

Quite a few ministers and very senior public servants had lost their jobs this way, and their replacements had been appointed at the Gupta's behest by President Gupta, sorry, by President Zuma. One of their most prominent victims was Pravin Gordhan, the then Minister of Finance, an apparently honest, competent and courageous politician.

Minister Nene, another finance minister, was replaced by a Gupta shoe-in for only three days, when the financial markets forced Zuma to recall this unsuitable replacement. Nene had refused to sanction the Gupta-sponsored spending of trillions of Rand on a slew of Russian nuclear power plants, which South Africa would never have been able to afford.

One of the most telling indications of the deep penetration of government business by this family manifested itself at a wedding cere-mony they celebrated here. They 'instructed' that a private plane, bringing over a hundred guests from India, was allowed to illegally land at a South African Air Force base near their home.

The popular perception, widely publicized by the media, was the existence of a Gupta shadow government. South Africa was called by the media "a colonized country, with President Zuma as the Governor appointed by the Guptas".

Parallel to their other activities the Gupta family also heavily invested (their South African illegal loot, apparently) in Dubai. They were accused by the media to have moved huge sums of money out of this country, probably also illegally. Amongst many other peculiar actions, they had, over some time, invited Zuma, several ministers and many executives of the SOEs to Dubai. Our President was claimed to be now the proud owner of a luxury apartment there, which he presumably had paid for out of his saved pay as a Freedom Fighter during the Apartheid era.

But eventually, the Guptas were neutralized. Early in 2018, after Zuma was ousted, the Prosecution Service finally got around to look into their machinations, after the new President Ramaphosa had replaced the head of this organization. But, surprise, surprise, they had already fled the country. Because their home country India was also looking for them, for tax offenses and money laundering, they now have to suffer their impoverished existence as billionaires in Dubai. Shame, as South Africans are used to say, ironically.

Two judicial commissions are at present working feverishly, looking into this whole state capture and SOE saga, with new disclosures and new culprits among the top ranks of the ANC every week. If this carries on a while longer, the ANC will have more members in prison than on the streets. Just kidding, of course.

It was now apparent that the Gupta brothers single-handedly managed to bring the major State-Owned-Enterprises close to financial collapse, with the complicity of President Zuma, by stealing billions out of their coffers through manipulating their boards, such as

- Eskom, the electricity monopoly,
- SAA, the South African Airways,
- Transnet, the South African Railways and Harbors behemoth.

Race Relations/Racism and Reverse Racism

Let us start this subject with an observation, which is neither earth-shattering nor particularly important, namely the appearance of mixed couples in South Africa. During Apartheid one obviously did not see any such thing in public, because a jail term would have ensued immediately. Straight after the end of Apartheid, one could observe a number of such couples in public places, usually of a White male and an African or Asian female. Less often, of a European female and an African or Asian male.

Apparently, it was the lure of the novelty or, in some instances, maybe a coming-out of the closet. Now, twenty years later, such couples seem to have again all but disappeared in public. I have neither an explanation nor any comment to offer for this conundrum.

This thought opened of course the door to think about gay couples as well. During Apartheid, such sinful behavior was not seen in public. This would have violated the staunch Christian tenets of the Afrikaners, maybe even more so than in the case of the mixed couples. After all, there was rather a bit of racial mixing going on amongst the male Afrikaners, while 'spoofs' were the bottom of the pit!

But now one could observe quite often such couples, openly opting to show their sexual orientation. Even the local TV producers have jumped onto the band wagon. A dicey business in Africa, where homophobia is still strongly and widely established. In some African countries they may even today risk execution!

Racial integration at the workplace appeared to work reasonably well by now. The relationship among colleagues seemed generally to be relaxed and free of racial stress, at least here in KwaZulu-Natal. My perception could, however, be tainted because I watched local films and state television, which both obviously strove to present a politically correct relaxed image for the people of this country.

One point of friction, however, was the occasional accusation of racist behavior by a superior towards an employee. In such cases it was impossible for outsiders to determine whether the manager was a racist and whether he really had made racist remarks. Or were the accusations merely a pretext to get rid of an innocent but unpopular superior?

A telling example of what I would call invisible and unintentional racism we had experienced some years ago in our own home. My wife alerted me to what had happened, which I had not even noticed. We had a company's White representative here, to measure up for the installation of some fly screens for our windows and doors.

We were chatting with him, asking questions and enquiring about the exact working of the suggested installation. He had an African helper with him, whose presence we, for all practical purposes, had completely ignored. And this twenty years after Apartheid had been abolished, and we definitely did not consider ourselves to be racists!

This thought opened another window into this situation. How many African friends did we have among our acquaintances? The simple answer was, none. What about Indian and Colored friends? Same reply. And why was this so? Where we really such engrained racists?

Only my wife had met some interesting people during her botanical excursions, and all of them Europeans. So far, the Blacks by and large showed no interest in ecological subjects. My experience with our chess players was exactly the same. African players are still the big exception, even though some of them are very good at the game.

An honest and comprehensive answer to these question, complicated and controversial as usual, could only be found if one took a holistic approach. How many European friends did we have? For quite a few years now, just one. A few others we had been friends with had passed away over the years. After all, we were living in a retirement village, where we had few contacts with outsiders and there were only Whites living here, even though it was open to all races, of course.

On the one hand, in our advanced years we had not been particularly social people, and we had generally preferred to stay on our own. No new friends had been made by us inside the village (I'm not allowed by the boss to talk about an old-age home). We had never experienced the strong wish to make new friends. I myself hated to waste time on small talk, something essential for social intercourse, and what the Non-Whites generally loved very much.

On the other hand, there existed a cultural barrier, admit-ted or not. We felt that we simply had nothing, or at least not much, in common with the local Non-Europeans, and sometimes we did not feel comfortable in the company of members of the other racial groups. Particularly, since we rightly or wrongly had the impression that the feeling was mutual.

On the third hand . . . .

With all this involvement with race in South Africa (rather like in Nazi Germany!) I could not help noticing that a very large percentage of our Africans were actually technically of 'Mixed Blood', or Coloreds in South African parlance. Their light-brown skin color, as opposed to the black-brown of the Nguni tribes, indicated such.

When we saw on television our luminaries standing next to the leaders of West or Central African countries, the fact became obvious that most were not as black as these our northern neighbors. But this was probably just my nasty and suspicious mind, so forget about it. Anyway, our new President does not have any problems there. Nobody is going to doubt that he is a dyed in the wool genuine African!

We recently learned of some vicious verbal attacks by some super-Blacks against some of their fellow Africans who were accused of being "not Black enough", referring obviously also to their mind set and attitudes, and not only to the color of their skin.

Affirmative Action/Quotas/Cadres

During the Apartheid years, the National Party had strictly enforced job reservation in favor of the Europeans. In con-sequence of the historical discrimination, there was now in the New South Africa a counter reaction in place, the affirmative action. Understand-able as this clearly was, up to a point, it sometimes produced unin-tended consequences (that seems to be the fashionable catchphrase nowadays) in the economy as well as in the public service.

To nobody's surprise we now experienced a strong drive by the ANC, using the same methods of legal preferences as their predecess-sors had done, but this time of course in favor of the Non-Whites. They refused, however, to acknowledge that this attitude represented reverse racism, as claimed by some of the Europeans, rather labelling it, quite correctly in my opinion, as a correction of past injustices.

Both, the public service and the economy, had suffered badly since

1994 by reserving key jobs for Non-Europeans, based only on racial quotas. This favored the Africans, not only over the Whites, but to a large extent also over Indians and Coloreds. And the fifty percent quotas reserved for women were also just as harmful in both areas.

In many cases qualified persons from the prescribed racial or gender group were simply not available, and in such cases, positions were either left vacant or were filled by unsuitable members of the 'correct' quota group. The very negative results for the economy, and particularly for the municipal service delivery, quickly became obvious.

Things were getting even more skewered by the ANC insistence on cadre deployment, meaning to place faithful and loyal, but often intellectually and/or ethically challenged party hacks in elevated positions, which would have required competence and high ethical standards.

Unfortunately, two aspects of competence, training and experience, had been denied to the Non-Whites during the Apartheid years. This was clearly a complex and difficult situation for government, with no elegant and politically acceptable quick-fix available.

Things were lately beginning to look even more grim. Some prominent ANC politicians were now stridently calling for and demanding what they termed "radical economic transformation" of the country. This sounded suspiciously like the battle-cry of the EFF, the Economic Freedom Fighters.

As far as I was able to decode this populist cry, it would mean to place Africans into all positions of any gravity in the public service as well as in the economy, regardless of their competence and ethics, or lack thereof.

Public Service

Right from the start in 1994 the ANC committed the same sin as the National Party did in 1948, when they took over the government of the country. In both cases the Public Service should have been above party politics, because only this stance would have guaranteed the best results for the State and the people. This would have been a feather in the cap for either party, but the temptation was unfortunately irresistible to both of them!

Let me cite here just one typical example out of hundreds of similar incidents reported by the media, including the state-owned television. This incident clearly illustrated the very common confused thinking in our government circles regarding the proper function of the Public Service and its place in the scheme of things.

The position of the Police Commissioner of South Africa had during Apartheid times always been filled by a career police officer, working under the Minister of Police, who as a politician was appointed by the State President. After 1994, these public officials, who had to deal with many problems inside and outside of the SAPS, the South African Police Service, should also have been selected, as before, from the ranks of this organization. Instead, they were installed by the President as political appointees, without any relevant police background. As a result, they did neither act nor feel like a public servant and police officer, but rather like another politician.

A female political appointee had been chosen by President Zuma. Her two predecessors, also presidential appointments, had been fired for misconduct. This now called-up lady had no police experience at all and was therefore from the outset not a competent candidate for this vital public service posting. She had consequently no chance to do her job properly.

A few weeks later in 2012, the infamous Marikana Massacre took place, when thirty-four striking miners were killed by the police, under highly questionable and suspicious circumstances. A number of mine security personnel were killed by the striking miners. A judicial commission was established to investigate the background of these tragic events and found the Police Commissioner was lacking the relevant experience and her handling of this incident to have been incompetent.

Similar situations could be observed all over the country. Just about the worst picture was provided by the almost three-hundred local authority administrations. One of their main function was supposed to be the delivery of services to their inhabitants. The newspapers and television channels reported an endless stream of complaints about inefficiencies, corruption, nepotism and plain incompetence. When one of the reporters dug deeper to find the root-cause of such problems in a specific case, it turned out that there were a number of possibilities, singly or in combination, for this sad state of affairs:

- missing experience and/or training,
- lacking the necessary intellectual capacity,
- serious inefficiencies in the work performance,
- lack of proper supervision and competent leadership.
- And then there were additionally the more or less criminal aspects of:
- cadre deployment,

- nepotism and favoritism,
- various forms of corruption.

After 1994 the country had been parceled out into almost three hundred municipalities. Some of these were proper cities, the Metros, a few dozen were small towns, but the majority were country districts, often without a natural center, and usually without industrial or commercial taxpayers. The latter were therefore almost entirely dependent on government hand-outs for their survival. The situation was understandably worst in the smaller rural municipalities, which had neither the skills nor the resources available for doing properly their main job of service delivery.

The Councils of the vast majority of the urban and rural munici-palities were both unable and unwilling to adhere to the financial discipline prescribed by law. Unashamed, their members have ignored all rules, in the personal interest of the councilors or that of friends or party factions. And in many cases, they simply lacked the intellectual capacities required for their job.

Looking at the executives of these municipalities, the same sad picture was repeated. Their public servants were not selected based on competency, ethics or experience, but solely upon criteria such as party loyalty and personal connections. Accordingly, that is what their results looked like.

The same sad picture often appeared somewhere else in South Africa, for instance, when ESKOM was again and again unable to provide enough electricity needed by the country, or when the national soccer team had, again, missed an important game because somebody had goofed and omitted to make the necessary arrangements.

In this chapter I could easily have filled many more pages with further examples, but I do not like to stick the knife into a bleeding wound. Any objections to this latter statement may be left with the receptionist on the 327th floor of our cottage.

Cultural Differences

During one of my ambles through Johannesburg, shortly after our arrival in this country, I entered a shop which offered in their display window extremely expensive Italian hand-sewn shoes. To my question, who in this city could afford to buy shoes as expensive as these, the astonishing reply was: "Africans". The salesman explained that they were extremely fashion and status conscious and brand loyal, and that they were prepared to pay for their preferences. By the way, I felt rather humbled because I only had entered this shop to buy a pair of shoelaces!

Now, when some of the Africans had the means, ostentatious spending by them could be observed in many places. Most of these better-off Blacks were very well dressed and drove new BMW or Mercedes cars. A number of successful African businessmen had, for instance, a dozen or two dozen luxury cars in their garages. Such things usually only became public knowledge when the media or the police got interested in these people (often women), when another case of corruption had hit the fan.

This is not just my envy speaking. Such behavior attracts, or should attract, the attention of the detectives and the income tax inspectors. And thinking as a management consultant, the money would obviously have been better spent in their businesses or in profitable and legal productive investments in the economy.

Another typical example of different attitudes to the spending of money was demonstrated by African funerals. Africans often contribute for many years into burial insurance schemes. The large and profitable funeral insurance industry of this country apparently depends entirely on their African clients. Huge sums, very often probably ill-afforded, were being spent on these occasions. The costs must have been astronomical, and as an outsider one kept wondering how these people could afford this.

Often hundreds of mourners attended these functions, and we Non-Africans sometimes wondered, whether all of these mourners actually knew the deceased. But probably they did. After all, Africans were much more sociable inclined than the Europeans. In the townships and the camps of barracks and sheds, the 'informal settlements', everybody appeared to know everybody else. In any case, nobody could say which attitude was the better one.

This reminds me of another peculiarity. Despite the just-mentioned fact that they tended to know their neighbors very well, the police were usually faced with a wall of "I don't know" and "I have not seen or heard anything" when they were investigating crime in these surroundings.

It was not clear to me, whether this was due to the aftermath of the activities of the hated Apartheid police, or whether it was the solidarity of the poor with the criminal elements among them, also often seen in other countries. And this despite the fact, that the criminals in the townships and the shack camps most often prayed on their fellow poor Africans, harassed and robbed them and often raped and even killed their women and children.

Another aspect of further different social attitudes was the way that Africans usually ambled along a road or street. Whereas Europeans walked single or as couples, Africans could often be seen ambulating in groups of four or five abreast, involved in endless animated talking. And usually they were walking in the middle of the road or street, instead of on the verge or on the sidewalk, if there was one.

The situation was made worse by the fact that Africans had a tendency to move with the flow of traffic in the left lane of the road, in line with our driving on the left {ex British Empire!}, instead of walking against the traffic in the right-hand lane.

Walking with the flow of traffic and talking at full blast, if not wearing earplugs to listen to an MP3 player, made it impossible for them to see or hear traffic approaching from behind and, if necessary, to step aside in order to avoid being run over. This behavior could be observed even if it was dark and they were wearing dark clothing, and if it was raining, with the visibility down to almost nothing.

The danger of pedestrian road accidents was clearly not recognized, or it was ignored, even though it was well known that the majority of traffic fatalities in this country have always consisted of African pedestrians. To the best of my knowledge, neither the government nor the schools, and not anybody else, has ever made a meaningful effort to educate the African majority in this regard.

One of our daily observations were the dangerous road behavior of the learners of a nearby African school, marching along our narrow suburban roads in this fashion. We can only hope that nobody gets injured or killed.

The African propensity for talking instead of acting was one of the complaints often voiced in South Africa, even by many of the Africans themselves. But it seemed that the message was beginning to finally get through. Still, the Black politicians of all hues were most reluctant to change their established ways.

Every time a new law or similar change was introduced, this always caused an automatic tortured outcry by the leaders of many groups, complaining that they had neither been properly and timely informed, nor that they had been sufficiently consulted. Most of the time such claims were clearly unjustified, but that did not stop them from being made, in a kind of knee-jerk reaction.

One further subject to be mentioned here refers to the African attitude regarding cleanliness. In the long past Apartheid era, many

Whites had criticized them for their perceived lack of personal hygiene. This was completely unfair, by ignoring the realities of the dramatic difficulties they had in this regard: poverty and lack of, or vast distances to, access to clean water, amongst others.

The post-Apartheid era has clearly shown that this was a misconception by the Europeans. Obviously, only a minority of Africans has even today access to a daily shower and most, especially in the shack camps and the rural areas, still battle in this regard. Girls and women in many cases still have to walk long distances with a bucket of cloudy and sometimes polluted water on their heads.

Even poor Africans regularly buy their soap. It is therefore wrong to criticize here. There can be no doubt that they were definitely not personally deficient in this respect. I remember one of our African laborers in the concrete block yard, who after his shift always stripped down completely in our yard, even on cold days, and washed himself from head to toe.

Another tragic example in this regard, of the difficulties the African majority was facing to this day was the fact that most young rural girls still do not have access to sanitary towels, because their families cannot afford them, or because they are simply not available locally. Many of the girls are forced to miss school because of this. Some of our chain stores now invite customers to donate small amounts for the provision of these basic necessities.

Environment

This heading provides the opportunity to talk about the African attitude towards litter and rubbish, as well as its disposal. Here it has always been difficult to defend the prevailing situation. While the interiors of the African huts have always been spotlessly clean, their surrounds and the verges of the roads and the nearby bushes, and the environment generally, presented unfortunately a different story.

The average African appeared to think nothing of dropping on the spot, or wherever he was walking at that moment, the wrappings of whatever he had just unwrapped. If one would have suggested to him to pick up what he had just dropped, one would have earned an astonished questioning expression, if such was not interpreted by him as a racist affront, which could easily have turned into a life-threatening incident.

Accordingly, the African townships and informal settlements looked most often like rubbish dumps, because that was what they effectively were. Occasional cleansing activities were organized by some public-minded inhabitants with some volunteers, but shortly afterwards things were back to what they had been before.

As a matter of fact, the behavior of our Asian and Colored co-inhabitants was in this regard not much better than that of the Africans. The schools seemed, unfortunately, to do nothing in this respect. I suspect that the reason for this was that the attitudes of principals and teachers were no better than those of the parents of their pupils, because nobody had ever taught them about these things. But, as I remember, it also took decades in Europe, before attitudes in this regard eventually had changed there for the better.

To finalize this section, let us now look at the Environment, with a capital E, the pet subject nowadays of so many people all over the world. What was the African attitude towards global warming, contamination of the oceans with plastic debris, the decimation of plant and animal life, etc.? The subject simply did not exist in the minds of the majority of Africans. Until very recently, there has not been any thought about that at all. They were approximately in the same stage as the Europeans and Americans were before the last war, when such concerns had also not yet surfaced there.

Almost everywhere in the country could be found small dedicated groups of people caring about nature, and almost all of them were Europeans. They were recording and cataloguing the fauna and flora of South Africa, they were caring about endangered species of all of nature's members, they were pro-testing mismanaged rivers, wetlands and beaches and they were performing many more such vitally important tasks.

What was the interest and participation of Africans in these functions at the beginning of the post-Apartheid period? Zilch, nada, nitchewo! There were of course exceptions and a number of reasons for this lack of enthusiasm, but it has to be stated honestly that the feelings for and the awareness of the Environment were at this stage simply missing with the overwhelming majority of Africans. I think there is a very small improvement discernible, but I cannot be sure about that.

Crime/Violence

A further serious problem in South Africa has always been the propensity of many Africans to easily resort to violence, if a dispute developed or if there were differences of opinion. I am not qualified to even guess why this was so. It was unfortunately true that a large percentage of Africans all over the sub-Sahara African continent were ready, at the drop of a hat, to 'solve' any problems, particularly any political ones, with a gun or with a panga.

The perpetrators, egged-on by their leaders, were often the least educated members of their communities. But the other day a South African Deputy Minister was observed and videoed to have manhandled some lady friends in a nightclub. He first denied everything (SOP, Standing Operating Procedure), but he finally apologized to the country, so maybe, there still is some hope.

The numerous housing compounds for the itinerant single African laborers, which could be found in all the cities and at all the mines of South Africa, were hotbeds of political crimes and those against their inhabitants. Some hitmen specialists were available at fixed rates and could easily be found there, to travel anywhere in the country to commit murders 'on order', including the infamous farm killings. It was obviously difficult for the police to identify, to locate and to arrest these traveling criminals, because the Law and Order personnel usually received no assistance at all from the African population of these complexes.

Even before the end of Apartheid there were far too many guns in this country. A large percentage of private citizens and businesspeople possessed them. Only fools like me handed their weapons in at the nearest police station. Now there were clearly many thousands of illegal firearms in the hands of criminals. Large numbers had survived as a result of the aftermath of the Armed Struggle.

But they also had proliferated because of burglaries (often of police stations), and quite often they had been sold by soldiers or police officers. Over the years many thousands of guns have been reported missing from the army and the police, and things were apparently not much improving.

Further sources of firearms were illegal imports, smuggled or enabled by corrupt border and customs officers, as well as jerry-made guns, manufactured with primitive tools in some suburban or township workshop or in some rural huts. These handmade varieties were used primarily for tribal feuds and for settling personal and political differences in the expansive rural regions.

There was one other peculiarity to record here. This referred to our numerous gangsters. No, I'm not talking about Zuma and the Gupta family here, but about the US-style gangsters of the 'Organized Crime' variety. Certain parts of our cities were firmly in the hands of such gangs. For instance, easily identified ones of violent criminals, this time of Coloreds, could be found in the Cape Flats, the name of a large area near Cape Town.

One such neighborhood was the suburb of Mannenberg. Regularly, there were newspaper and television reports in South Africa about gang-related violence at this place, usually regarding bloody turf wars between the various gangs, or casualties suffered by bystanders in the crossfire at such occasions.

These were, for all practical purposes, no-go areas for the police, who in any case would never have received any co-operation from the inhabitants, if they were trying to solve one of the frequent murders and other crimes. What was always surprising to me was the fact that the police seemed to be powerless in dealing with these gangs. The claimed reason has always been the lack of cooperation by the victims.

That was obviously a valid point, in view of the feared violent repercussions by the gangs to any perceived cooperation with the police by the victims. On the other hand, there was never any doubt in my mind that the residents of these housing complexes knew every single member of every single one of these gangs.

The only other valid explanation I can think of, why they refused to assist the police, is the probability that there were gang members in virtually every single household, making it practically impossible for the inhabitants of these sub-economic housing complexes to hand their boys or husbands over to the police and the courts. These three-story apartment blocks, called "flats" in South Africa, were sociologically comparable to the high-rise "projects" in England, and of a similar odious reputation.

This reminded me of a relatively harmless incident, in comparison to the murders and rapes, which I had witnessed in the late 1960s in Port Elizabeth. A small group of African women was standing next to a shop entrance in the main business street.

An African man in his twenties or early thirties walked by and forcefully grabbed the breast of one of these women, who cried out loudly with pain. It was clear from what was said, they all spoke English or Afrikaans, that they did not know each other. Such gratuitous sexual violence was, unfortunately, rather common in this country.

Almost every day we read about crimes and the television showed scenes referring to rape or murder of babies and young girls and boys in the African townships, committed by African males who lived there and were known or suspected of such crimes. But often, they were also committed by relatives or neighbors.

This was a serious problem, where not much progress has been made over the last twenty years. As explained, the police were rather powerless to stop these crimes. The result was a sharp increase in lynch murders by the people. Some were, however, actually murders of witches, often male ones, or simply of hated individuals.

Two years ago, in a semi-rural industrial complex in KwaZulu-Natal, local Africans burned down a number of small factories, employing mostly unskilled African workers from this area. A few hundred laborers, supporting probably well over a thousand dependents, consequently lost their jobs. I forgot what reasons were reportedly given for such senseless behavior, because such unfortunate actions happened relatively often in South Africa.

The official crime statistics for a typical year in this country:

	Annually in thousands	Daily averages
Murder and attempted Murder	270	740
Robbery	174	477
Assault	348	953
Burglary, Theft	544	1 490
Common Theft	410	1 123
Shoplifting	69	189
Drunk Driving	76	208
Vehicle Hijacking	15	41
Arson	120	329
Illegal Firearms	15	41
Sex Offences	19	52
Sex Offences by Police	6	16
Drugs	259	715
Public Violence	n/a	n/a
Neglect of Children	n/a	n/a
Kidnapping	n/a	n/a
Crimen Injuria	n/a	n/a
False accusations	n/a	n/a

The 'not available' notes were to be taken with great circumspection. A number of incidences became known, where police station commanders had falsified the crime figures. They either did not want to report the full facts, in order to present a favorable picture of their efficiency in crime prevention. Or, very occasionally, they over-reported crimes, in the hope of obtaining additional resources.

It has always been clear to the South Africans that certain of these categories were drastically underreported, particularly those concerning children, women and sex offenses. There were no numbers at all quoted on rape, one of the more common crimes committed here on a daily basis, primarily of women and children in the remote rural areas.

Particularly disgusting were the crimes by Africans against the poorest of their own tribes, representing the vast majority of criminal acts in the black townships and the rural areas. A typical example: An ambulance was called for a very sick person and on arrival the driver was assaulted, the nurse was possibly raped, and their vehicle was in no time disassembled and the parts eventually sold on the Black Market. The same *modus operandi* was frequently used in the cases of repair teams of burst water pipes or broken-down power lines.

In addition to the problems caused by such breakdowns these criminals now had created another calamity; ambulance and maintenance teams refused to attend to their jobs in the townships and rural areas, because they were fearing for their lives.

Recently, a new criminal activity has become popular here; the dropping of rocks or blocks of concrete from bridges over the freeways. Sometimes just as a 'sport', which often ended in serious injuries or even in death, and therefore in murder. In other cases, the travelers were robbed after they had stopped to inspect the damages to their vehicles.

Two more recent criminal specialties in this country were the blowing open of ATMs and the armed hold-up of cash transporters, often quite violently and causing many deaths. Neither of these two specialties turned up in the above statistics. Even more 'productive' was the attack on a depot for these money trucks. In this case hundreds of millions of Rand were stolen and were never recovered, and nobody was ever convicted of this violent crime. An inside job? Apparently, but so what? That should be no excuse for never solving this major crime.

One of the most disturbing facts, in connection with all these crimes, was the often-seen utter senselessness of violent criminal acts. The burning down of schools, university buildings or libraries and places of work or worship were examples. And very seldom followed prosecutions and convictions of the perpetrators. When I approached the African officer in charge of our police station, he asked me: "Should we perhaps arrest all Africans?" I had the impression that the man was only half joking.

. . .

Xenophobia

This was a specific form of the widespread violence in this country, particularly amongst the Zulus. The male members of this tribe were proud to be seen, and they saw themselves, as fearless warriors and as men of substance, as owners of substantial cattle herds and as rulers over a large number of wives and children. Accordingly, the traditional Zulus looked down on traders, tradesmen and office workers, and generally speaking, on all those who were working in the economy.

Obviously, this idealized picture of the proud Zulu warrior would only be found occasionally; in reality, it would of course be the rare exception. One striking example for this macho thinking comes immediately to mind, that of our State President Zuma, with his harem and huge kraal.

A shebeen was originally an illegal Irish pub (Wikipedia), but in South Africa the term referred to a legal or illegal African pub in a township. Here the men could meet and spent a large part of their time discussing politics, sport, gossip, women and other pivotal subjects. It was well known that the majority of shebeens and township shops, in urban areas with a Zulu majority, were owned and operated not by Zulus, but by Somalis or Zimbabweans, or by members of some other tribes.

In 2008 the country saw some horrible xenophobic riots in townships of several large cities. Over the past few years South Africa had absorbed more than two hundred thousand refugees from various African countries in the north; some of these were several thousand kilometers away. Many of the newly arrived fugitives found employment, which was seen by the millions of unemployed South Africans as stealing of their job opportunities. An ideal incubator of xenophobia.

Every so often there was a new outbreak of xenophobia in the townships. Tensions were simmering and rumors were flying about the perceived misdeeds of the despised foreigners. Dark hints were dropped about the riches these 'deceiving' merchants had amassed on the back of the poor Zulus. For no justified reasons their shebeens and shops were plundered, and often enough, they were also burnt down.

If the owners and their families were unlucky, or too slow, they were likely to get killed. The displaced operators usually found refuge for a while in a church or a community hall, until emotions had simmered down again. Afterwards commerce carried on as before, credit was extended again, and everybody appeared to be happy. Till the next outbreak of violent xenophobia!

Tribalism/Tribal Violence

Some time ago more than twenty rural schools in Limpopo Province were vandalized and burnt down. Scarce textbooks, computers and furniture were destroyed or stolen, resulting in thousands of scholars being deprived of their education. It took many months, and sometimes years, until money was found, tenders were awarded (to ANC 'cadres', probably) and the schools were repaired or rebuilt.

In this specific case the vandalism was triggered by the planned administrative transfer of some villages from a Venda-speaking municipality to a Sotho-speaking one. The King of the Venda had fired-up the objections, but he had been careful to afterwards officially condemn the violence. They were all good politicians!

This kind of situation, a transfer of a district from one tribal area to one speaking a different language or dialect, usually meant unrest, and violence in turn. Assuming such an administrative transfer would have happened in America or Europe: would there have been more of a reaction than a few 'Letters to the Editor'?

Tribal conflicts were still very much alive today in South Africa, as well as in the rest of Black Africa. These tribal rivalries also accounted over the years for thousands of murders at the mines and in the municipal hostels which were housing thousands of single males away from their families.

One other aspect of tribalism was the question of polygamy. This system developed during the hunter - gatherer period of human development and was well justified at that time, because of the low survival chances of the men. Let us keep in mind that not all that long ago this era was still alive in Black Africa and generally ended only with the start of the colonial times. But remnants are still alive now, such as the San people in the Kalahari Desert, for instance.

Even in the following period of the itinerant herders of cattle, that of King Shaka and his violent and bellicose col-leagues, when huge numbers of African men were slaughtered, there was a substantial surplus of single women in this country. But nowadays, polygamy generally just served as a status symbol and/or was a relic of the tribal past and previous attitudes, as exercised so convincingly by a certain recent South African president.

Already during Apartheid, we had a handful of tribal Kings in this country, each with a couple of 'palaces' and a 'harem' of wives and dozens of children. The State has been paying for these "Monarchies within our Republic", without having received adequate rewards for these outlays. By this measure, such payments should have been considered by the Auditor General already a long time ago as wasteful expenditure.

In the "New South Africa" this carried on as before. The financial support for these monarchs required hundreds of millions of our tax money every year. They have neither been democratically elected by their respective tribes, nor have they been appointed as members of the public service, subject to the rules, regulations and controls of this body. They demanded to be paid by the State, without providing a clear-cut service to the benefit of either the State or their people.

Closely related to tribalism and the traditional leaders was the existence of tribal trust lands. These had been established many decades before our family came to South Africa. Therefore, I was not familiar with the details and the background of this arrangement. The basic thinking was clearly similar to that regarding the Amerindian Reservations in the USA.

These vast tracts of land in Zululand were under the control of the King of the Zulus and his *izinDuna*, appointed by him as his local officials. Mind you, the King of the Zulus, not the King of Zululand. There was a distinct difference between the two terms.

In the distant past the *izinDuna* were the commanders of the Zulu regiments, and generally served as the King's officers. They were the enforcers of his rules and orders. They could be loosely compared with the magistrates employed by the medieval rulers of Europe. The type of functions they performed for their King in modern times could best be described as a headman or as a go-between with his people.

A further important point, which should have been resolved a long time ago, was the question of the estimated two hundred thousand traditional healers or shamans in this country. There were two distinct groups of these:

- the herbalists or inyanga had valuable knowledge of indigenous medicinal plants and of traditional treatments, and they enjoyed the trust of the African population, particularly in the rural districts.
- with the diviners or sangomas there was a considerable

volume of witchcraft and charlatanry involved, which was used by them for bleeding their mostly poor clients financially dry, often without really helping them. To the best of my knowledge, they enjoyed similar support among the Africans, here again primarily in the rural districts.

The 'muti' which these sangomas used in practicing their trade may have been helpful in some cases, but when it was claimed by them that it would make the client invisible or immune to bullets, pangas or spears, then doubts must certainly be allowed. Even worse, reports have popped up again and again in the past of 'muti' murders and similar crimes, where Africans were killed to obtain certain body parts for the production of a potent special 'muti'.

Languages Policies

After the end of Apartheid, the new South Africa had decided to have eleven official languages, nine African ones in addition to English and Afrikaans, the two official languages during Apartheid. Obviously, in 1994 adequate provisions had to be made to deal with the language problems of the African majority at the courts, in government offices and in similar other situations.

But the aim should have been to arrive at a situation which was workable, efficient and economical. It should have been possible to find a more affordable solution to the language problem, without disadvantaging the various African tribes. The Whites, Indians and the Coloreds had no problem to start with, because they all more or less spoke either English or Afrikaans.

When our African politicians addressed their people and voters, they almost always used English, because this was the one generally understood language in the country. Even most of the Africans had a working understanding of this *lingua franca*. If one came across an African politician on television who used an African language, it was then immediately clear that he spoke exclusively to people of his own tribe, most likely in their tribal lands, where the knowledge of English was understandably rather limited.

Twenty years after the collapse of Apartheid an interesting and revealing observation could be made in this regard. Our African politicians overwhelmingly spoke a less than perfect English, with often very poor pronunciation. This was caused by their generally poor Bantu education and sometimes it appeared to be due to their advanced age.

On the other hand, a large number of young people of color spoke very good English. This was surprising, because many of the teachers who taught this language at school did not speak English much better than the politicians. The levels of their knowledge of English and their training as educators were generally insufficient for their jobs. I suspect the internet and the social media as the reasons why their pupils often spoke a better English than their teachers.

Gender Equality

This was after 1994 a real minefield of contradictory and inter-connected problems. Traditionally, the place of the African woman was, with some important exceptions, restricted to the family and her household. African males were generally very reluctant to accept a female as a superior. But this was now beginning to change, initially in the field of ANC party politics.

The ruling party was aiming for a fifty percent ratio of female MPs, the Members of Parliament, and for a respectable proportion of female ministers and important officials. This automatically meant that many male African politicians and public servants, even those in high positions, had now for the first time a female boss. In Africa this led initially to stress, but by now it has largely established itself as the norm.

A similar gender quota was also now demanded for the economy, but this has not been achieved yet. There it was naturally much more difficult to enforce such regulations.

Over the last fifty years one has observed similar parallel develop-ments in most developed countries, which are still ongoing, of raising the level of female participation in politics as well as in the economy. The infamous 'glass ceilings', particularly in the economy, are still prevalent, and not just in South Africa.

A secondary question has arisen in this connection, which to my knowledge has never been raised, at least not in public: were females on average as qualified as males in the fields of high positions in poli-tics and the public service? My impression was that this question has been confused with the one about equal rights and chances for them.

There can be no doubt that some of the ladies were definitely highly suitable, such as Mrs. Thatcher or Frau Merkel. But did this prove anything about the average (remember the 2.4 children of the Danish housewives)? We all know that the ladies are better than men on average when it comes to multi-tasking.

. . .

Labor Relations / Strikes / Unions

Some of the perennial violent conflicts were in the field of labor relations. Most union officials have still not come to grips with abandoning the socialist 'us and them' syndrome. The approach was still largely confrontational (and popular with the laborers), instead of seeking some form of constructive cooperation with the employers for the common good of all concerned.

It did not help that the original very sound COSATU concept of "one union for one industry" had collapsed, and that we now had rival unions in most industries, which were usually more concerned with stealing members from their rivals, than in establishing realistic working relationships with the respective employer organizations. Many such inter-union conflicts were nothing but personality clashes between union bosses.

Influenced by this rivalry, intimidation and even murder of union functionaries and members were often the result. Sometimes rather unrealistic wage demands were made, partially because of this rivalry. Let us take the platinum mining industry as an example of local labor relations. To start with, members of NUM, the National Union of Mineworkers, went on a wildcat strike which had not been authorized by their union.

These workers later left their union under protest for the lacking support, and they joined the newly created AMCU, the Association of Mineworkers and Construction Union, which then for six weeks waged a bitter legal strike against the mining company Lonmin, demanding the doubling of wages, despite the recent collapse in the global platinum price. Lonmin decided to break-off negotiations.

It was probably justified, for AMCU's President Joseph Mathunjwa to argue that the wages of the miners were too low. But the demand to double them had to hit a brick wall somewhere. The mines had no control over the price of the platinum ore they produced, which was being set by supply and demand in the overseas markets. This causality was either not understood, or it was willfully ignored as inconvenient by the bosses of the new union.

After the strike had ended successfully for the union, some mine shafts had to be closed by the company as a consequence of the doubled labor costs, and thousands of workers lost their jobs. The wage gains of the remaining miners were bought at tremendous costs all round. Including the devastating con-sequences for those who had lost their jobs, and even more so for their thousands of dependents.

The State also lost billions in tax revenue from the mining companies and was faced with thousands of additional unemployment claims and social grant payments. And the investors had also lost huge amounts of money due to the collapse of the share prices of the platinum mining companies. This had immediate repercussions on foreign investment sentiment, with a ripple effect on the local labor market and currency. In other words, there were losers on all sides.

A further complicating factor developed recently. It appeared that the ANC-affiliated labor (and political) union federation COSATU was breaking up. About half the member unions were trying to form a break-away new federation, which claimed to be apolitical, or at least not to be subservient to any political party. At the moment things are still very much in a state of flux.

The largest member union NUMSA, the National Union of Metalworkers of South Africa, broke away from COSATU already in 2013 and threatened to terminate its support of the ANC and the Communist Party in future elections, playing with the idea of forming yet another new party of their own.

As was usual in South Africa, personal rivalries were all-important in this respect. With all this infighting, political point-scoring and the lack of independence of COSATU, it was not too surprising that absolutely nobody paid any attention to the plight of the huge army of the unemployed. Yes, overseas labor unions were also not exactly known champions of the jobless. Their desperate situation was largely ignored by the labor movement. As soon as they had lost their job, I think that they ceased to be members and the union bosses largely lost interest in their fate.

Our labor laws were heavily biased in favor of the workers and their unions. The permission to strike and the protection of the strikers against dismissal was legally guaranteed, but the right of employers to lock out the strikers had been deleted from the law books.

This strengthening of the rights of the workforce looked naturally enough very good in the eyes of the laborers (and the vast majority of the voters!), but nobody had bothered to explain to them that the concomitant weakening of the national economy would hurt them eventually as well, and particularly in the employment field.

.   .   .

Skills Shortage/Training

One of the pet past-times of the political caste of South Africa has been the endless raking over the consequences of the Apartheid era, often serving as excuses for government short-comings. Naturally, there were also many valid claims made in this connection, particularly in regard to the infamous 'Bantu Education' of many generations of African learners, as described previously. This, and the Apartheid-enforced lack of professional work experience, were valid claims, as they accounted for many of the problems the country was still facing after twenty years of freedom.

Occasionally, some hesitant voices from some of the more enlightened Africans on all sides of the political spectrum could be heard, urging their fellow politicians to stop com-plaining so much, and to rather concentrate on solving the tremendous problems facing all of them.

The above situation was bad enough. But worse was the fact that twenty-five to forty percent of South Africans were unemployed, depending on which definition was used. These ratios reflected primarily the situation of the unskilled and under-educated Africans. The lack of education and training had resulted in a serious skills shortage in the country, simultaneously with the horrific unemployment scourge.

Secondary and Tertiary Education

This country has followed the Anglo-American system of trying to channel most of the pupils not only through the primary and secondary schools, but if possible at all, through the tertiary educational institutions as well.

Naturally, I am not qualified to judge the merits or demerits of this approach, but I can report what I personally have experienced in pre-war Germany, which was not exactly known as an educational desert. The next paragraph contains some guesswork of mine, and possibly may show some lapses of memory, but I believe that what I remember was generally pretty close to reality.

During my school years in Germany in the 1930s only approximately fifteen percent of the primary learners advanced to High School, and about seventy-five percent of these eventually obtained their *Abitur* (university pass). Of these, maybe eighty percent actually entered the tertiary level: the universities and special training colleges, such as teacher training or military colleges. And maybe eighty percent of those obtained their university diploma or a PhD.

The arithmetic of the above assumptions looked like this:

- 100% entered primary schools,
- 15% were admitted to High School,
- 11,25% obtained their university entry passes,
- 9,00% actually entered university,
- 7,20% managed a 'hard' university degree.

In my layman's opinion there exist 'hard' tertiary studies (e.g. mathematics, medicine, natural sciences, engineering, accounting), and there are 'soft' ones (e.g. social, arts, literature, sports). The boundaries between them are fluid, of course, but I would assume that for the first group of 'hard' studies higher minimum IQ scores are necessary to succeed, than are needed for the 'soft' courses.

The present-day modern states clearly required a higher percentage of university graduates than Germany needed in my time. But the IQ minimum requirements for the successful conclusion of any of the 'hard' study courses were presumably still the same.

If so, and if the average distribution of IQs in the population was unchanged, then the modern situation required for these disciplines to "advance" through the system also some less gifted students, namely those with IQs which would have been insufficient in the old days. This in turn would only be possible, if the bars to succeed would have been somewhat lowered.

I know that a lot of water has flown under the bridge in seventy years. And I have no clue about what the present situation in Germany is. But I suspect that our more liberal educational system in South Africa had something to do with some of our problems related to education. I have here just one pertinent question, because I have not been able to find this information anywhere: what percentage of the South African primary school starters (the 100%) end up with a 'hard' university degree (the 7,2% above)? A comparison of South Africa with the above historical German numbers would probably reflect a very different picture.

Naledi Pandor, the new Minister of Education, and one of the brightest spots in the present government, has just published a damning report about our university students. Less than a quarter of them finished their undergraduate studies in the allotted time (of usually three or four years), and about seventy percent needed seven years to achieve that. She raised the question, whether our school-leavers were really ready to commence and successfully complete a course in higher education when they enter university.

We all knew about the intentionally sub-standard primary and secondary Bantu education of the Apartheid era. But our present status in this field, twenty years later, was also nothing to write home about, meaning that vast numbers of scholars were simply not ready for university when they left High School.

Some of the reasons have been their often unqualified and/or unmotivated teachers, as well as a lack of teaching resources. But when applying cold logic, in my opinion the main reason was the repeated lowering of the standards, in order to be able to show fictitious improvements in the passing rates of 'matric'. In other words, by playing politics!

Another study has shown that a relatively large number of African university graduates were now unemployed. It took most of them several years to find a suitable job. This was, in addition to the country's pitiful economic situation, the result of what I call the 'Higher Education Cult', because most of the young people and their parents here felt entitled or compelled to seek an academic education.

The available job opportunities in a preferred academic field were often misunderstood, and the basics to successfully complete a university education were missing. Either the required IQ, the adequate secondary education, or the necessary self-discipline were absent, which were necessary to survive a long study period away from home, where students had to finance their extra-curricular life by part-time work, even if they had obtained the financing of their study fees, books and accommodation.

One of the side-effects of the bloated university population was the fact that the provision of student accommodation was also insufficient, which created its own additional serious problems; for the universities and for the students alike.

Considering that all parents wanted a better life for their children, this urge to enter tertiary institutions was fully understandable, but it was misguided. We must realize that the vast majority of these parents had, at best, only a hazy idea about the life at university, or even of the realities of life and work above the level of a laborer in the public service or the economy.

This ambitious attitude resulted in numerous failed students as well as many under-qualified academics, often without a realistic prospect for an elevated employment level. As a result, these failed or under-educated young persons suffered severe personality problems, such as depression and inferiority complexes, and society had wasted huge amounts of money and scarce educational resources.

This situation was exacerbated by the lack of a coordinated government approach to try and channel the educational and training aspirations of the people in the right directions. By far the most serious failure of the country was the fact that we had during the last twenty years produced millions of unskilled young people, instead of giving them a practical or technical basic training. Anybody with such skills would have had a reasonable chance of finding some kind of work, or even to start a small business.

These basic shortcomings were made worse by the lack of political will by government to direct the interest of parents and students away from the overcrowded universities to the much sounder prospects for most of them of entering technical colleges. Most would have been better off with a business or technical qualification. Occasionally, the politicians talked about this lower level of a more practical training, but not forcefully and consistently enough.

The South African job market obviously was in recession since the 2008 meltdown, and also unbalanced: relatively too many university graduates, insufficient numbers of technicians and qualified specialists, and practically no properly trained artisans. We were trying to hammer square pegs into round holes. Namely, to convert excessive numbers of unsuitable youngsters into academics. If everybody wants to become a lawyer or a doctor, then . . . .

Economy/Finance/Banks

The ANC government had inherited a largely bankrupt economy, due to the border wars, sanctions and boycotts. Initially, they had received plenty of international support and goodwill, but after a while these evaporated or, to be clearer, our inter-national friends were more and more disappointed by our performance, or lack thereof. Complicating the problems was, of course, the poor economic situation in South Africa during the last five years.

They could see that South Africa was intend to follow a socialist economic course, as had done the rest of Black Africa. The consequences became obvious very quickly: wrong priorities in the economy, wasteful expenditure, populism, nepotism, cadre deployment and, of course, corruption.

Being fixated on dealing with political subjects rather than with the economy, the ANC has never understood that in the long run the economy was much more important than any political doctrine. The fate of the Soviet Union, East Germany and Eastern Europe, Tanzania, Cuba, Venezuela, etc. should have brought home this basic fact by now, but no!

There were a number of things our post-Apartheid governments felt obliged to do, and ideally to do them right away after taking over. It was for the ANC of great psychological and political importance that African members of the ANC had to:

- Occupy the majority of the seats of Parliament, the provincial legislatures and the municipal councils.
- Get almost all cabinet positions.
- Be appointed as judges and prosecutors as widely as possible.
- Take up all senior public service positions of government, the provincial and the local government executive structures.
- Usurp all board seats and executive positions of the SOEs, and in as many companies in the economy as feasible.
- Fill all positions within the by now bloated ANC party.

Where this was politically unadvisable or impossible, a tame White, Indian or Colored ANC stand-in had to be found. All these aims were understandable, and to an extent justified and do-able, but not all of them simultaneously and at once! It was not too difficult to predict that this could never work satisfactorily in such a compressed timeframe. The required number of qualified and ethical Africans, ANC members or not, was patently not there.

The dire consequence was at all levels the deployment of unsuitable persons, lacking competence and, very soon, wide-spread corruption. Additionally, there were the problems caused by the absence of proper training, the missing experience with financial and economic problems, and the vulnerable ethics amongst politicians as well as public servants.

All these difficulties were aggravated by the miserable state of the South African economy. During the last two decades government had handled the situation poorly. They could not master the gumption to act decisively to establish the primate of the national economy over politics. They preferred political games over fixing the ailing economy.

Despite the clear negative demonstrations by their political idols, the ANC has still not learned that in the long run a capitalist free economy beats any political doctrine hands-down. Government had made the same mistakes as all the other socialist or communist countries, including the Soviet Union, but with the notable exception of China. They should have looked at this country, because it had found a workable solution of this problem.

This led in government circles to the inevitable conclusion that the Minister of Finance was required to be the provider of un-ending streams of cash. Luckily, our first few portfolio ministers kept the lid on government's wasteful spending, up to a point, despite lacking any experience in financial matters, but with obvious common sense.

They could, however, not prevent on their own all the political handouts based on populist demands by the ANC branches and politicians. The result was an ever-increasing debt burden, which ballooned our cost of borrowing, particularly from overseas, which in turn weakened the South African balance sheet and the currency. The inevitable result, after some initial improvements: a string of downgrades by the global rating agencies, which in turn raised the costs of further borrowing overseas.

An especially precarious position in our economy was occupied by the banks and the mines. The day Nelson Mandela was, after twenty-seven years, finally released from prison, he announced in an emotional speech that one of the first things the ANC government would have to undertake, was the nationalization of the country's banks and mines.

One had to keep in mind here that this man was for more than a quarter of a century cut off from the international way of thinking, which had always shown a tendency to perpetually keep changing. Plus, the fact that in prison he was surrounded by fellow socialists and communists. Luckily, he possessed a healthy portion of common sense!

His followers only saw the big money being handled by the banks and their consequent apparent position of power, ignoring the vital functions they performed in and for the economy. And they were mesmerized by the huge turnover at the mines and by their army of employees.

What they never grasped, however, was the fact that cadre deployment in nationalized companies would never be able to perpetuate their previous sound profit histories. And it would therefore not even create the previous streams of healthy taxation revenues for the State.

Instead, the virtually certain future huge losses of these firms would require repeated crippling bailouts by the state, which amounts could have been utilized more productively, for urgent social or developmental purposes. Even the employment numbers would most likely not have been sustained. There are hundreds of examples available from all over the world to support this gloomy picture of nationalized firms. The most striking ones, perhaps, turned up in South Africa after 2012, or so. Eskom alone will require more than forty billion US dollars to keep operating!

Positive Observations

After digesting dozens of pages in this chapter, most of them listing negative observations about the first twenty years of freedom, it is probably surprising to notice something positive mentioned about the New South Africa. To balance the books to a certain extent, there are indeed some positive aspects to record here.

This positive list is unfortunately very much shorter than the negative one. I plead forgiveness for this, because this is, after all, a report about my experiences, and not an African praise-singer's backside-licking effort.

Some of the positive points on the report card of the ANC and their government are, first of all, the overwhelmingly important fact that the Non-Whites have finally achieved their political freedom and the acknowledgement of their human rights and dignity. These were now guaranteed and embedded in the constitution and the life of all South Africans.

The handover of power did not result in violence against the minorities and was handled well by the ANC under the guidance of Nelson Mandela.

The vast majority of our judges of all race groups has upheld the law and defended the constitution against all sorts of shenanigans by some of the people in power, including the only recently disposed State President Zuma himself and his cronies, such as the Guptas.

Up to now, the subsequent ministers of finance have been allowed to conduct the fiscal and financial business of government in a relatively orderly fashion, resisting the worst calls by the politicians for reckless borrowing and spending. Such demands were not rare anywhere, but they were particularly dangerous for a developing country like South Africa, seeking a way out of an inherited financial quagmire.

Overseas investors have been buying back some of the assets they sold during the final Apartheid years, under pressure from their governments and the public opinion in their home countries.

One group of foreign-owned companies, which was doing quite well during the last twenty years, was the automotive industry, supported by favorable local legislation.

Another positive picture was provided by our banking industry. It had weathered the 2008 upsets very well. As a matter of fact, they fared much better than many other banks, in the USA, Great Britain and Germany, for instance.

The development of a healthy middle class of Africans was also very positive for the future of the country.

A further extremely positive factor was the performance of the recent Public Protector, a lady advocate who since 2009 had waged battle fearlessly and determined with all sorts of wrong-doers. This included President Zuma, whom she had accused to have enriched himself shamelessly by the so-called 'improvements' to his kraal in Zululand.

She had also been the first, as far as I know, to accuse publicly and officially the Gupta family of State Capture, aided and abetted by Zuma. She even disclosed shortcomings and mistakes committed by Parliament, effectively her boss.

There is another positive point, which looks minor and out of place here. Government had introduced legislation which made it illegal to buy or sell cell phones and SIM cards without proper registration of the buyers: name, address, ID number. In a developing country like South Africa such a measure was sensible, even though criminals would still be able to use stolen phones, but it would, at least, cramp their style somewhat.

The one positive factor which has impressed me personally most of all was the rather unexpected fact that the ANC remained true to their democratic roots, within the party and also when dealing with South Africa. They have proven that, when necessary, they were prepared to make sacrifices and swallow the bitter medicine, if that was required to preserve our democratic constitution. A huge improvement on what practically all the other newly established states in Black Africa have hitherto demonstrated.

What does all this add up to? Overall, to a dismal picture, indeed. Incessantly I have railed in these pages against socialists and communists. In both cases not in respect of their political theories in general, but exclusively with regard to their economic views and practices.

My target has been the economic conduct of the ANC governments since 1994. This combination of targets was no coincidence, because of the coalition with the Communist Party and the socialist leanings of the left wing of the ANC.

In many ways South Africa has presented to the world during these last two decades the picture of the typical 'Banana Republic' of Black Africa. Some of the shortcomings of the country were inherited and others had external causes, but we have to admit that in most cases we have shot ourselves in the foot! As mentioned above, we looked a bit better than most of the other sub-Sahara countries, but not by much. Anyway, that is the type of excuse which is only made by losers!

And what is the future going to be like? Naturally, I do not know, and I do not want to speculate. Let us hope for the best for the country and her people of all races and creeds!

To cap all the nonsense I have sprouted in these pages: in my opinion, Africans, after they have managed to escape their poverty trap, are not at all predestined to be socialists or communists, but they might rather develop in future into full-blooded capitalists!

PART VI

RIDING INTO THE SUNSET

16

EPILOGUE

2014 TO 2074 (WHEN I WILL CELEBRATE MY 150TH)

Well, well, I actually have made it to this round number '90', some-times somewhat against the odds. Should I therefore be entitled to pat myself on the back? Surely not, because reaching this milestone has not been achieved by myself, but primarily by various contributing factors; above all: luck, my wife and maybe genetics, with a little help from me.

Since I never was the sportive type, not even in my youth, I have tried during the last fifty years to keep my not exactly Olympic body in survival mode. Having stopped smoking at age thirty-nine, and not taking up mountain climbing and roller skating at eighty-five, probably has also helped some-what.

By staying away, as far as was possible and necessary, from excesses regarding food, drink, work and play (*nota bene* the delicate way of putting it), I have avoided the more obvious danger spots. During these many years I have learned to recognize my weaknesses as well as my strengths, and I have tried to live accordingly, but without being dogmatic about it.

In the meantime, I have become a strong believer in doing every-thing in moderation, but also with self-discipline, but obviously with the occasional lapses! And without becoming a fanatic about the subject. My wife, who is a well-organized woman, was extremely helpful in this regard.

One of the most important contributing factors for my still being around has been the fact that for the last fifty years I have been a very happy man.

But what about the genetics? Here I can only speculate: no siblings (except for the sister who died as a baby before I was born), the parents prematurely passed away due to the war, the paternal grandparents likewise, and the maternal ones probably as well.

Rather a sad genealogical picture, but what had happened was luckily neither conclusive nor hereditary. I simply had to learn, at a relatively early stage, to live with personal losses. Thus, the conclusion about the genetics must remain unresolved.

How well did I survive these ninety years? Generally speaking, I managed very well indeed. My vision is still adequate, apart from having to use reading glasses. Sometimes while reading, I worry about their diminishing effectiveness, until I realize five minutes later that I left them lying on the table.

My hearing is poor, particularly in one ear, which is probably the late result of my double middle-ear infection as a baby. Very expensive Swiss hearing aids do not help much and stay in their box most of the time. I hope the seller is not going to sue me, but I will defend my assessment.

Walking like a drunken sailor, without having to spend a fortune on expensive whisky, is age-connected, I have been told. Colliding with a door jamb or a piece of furniture, and often hitting the wrong computer key, all this has been diagnosed by my doctor as a loss of balance. Who would have thought of that? This aspect has definitely deteriorated badly, which is particularly noticeable early in the morning or if I have to get up at night. Then I stumble from wall to door post to another wall.

While typing this manuscript (an interesting linguistic contradiction in terms), my spellcheck is in over-drive. I make many more spelling mistakes than in earlier years. But I could still play chess at the same moderate level of competence at which I played fifty years ago.

Every morning during breakfast, we read two German and one French day calendars. I notice my unusual interest in the biographical notes of the VIPs, checking who is older and still alive. Morbid, but this is the only competition in which I can still participate.

As repeatedly stated earlier, my memory is good and bad at the same time. But this is no reason to complain, considering my slightly advanced age. As other people have discovered before me, our memories are selective, and generally too optimistic. The famous 'pink glasses' are a reality, just as our fallible memories are. We also tend to blank out certain unpleasant parts.

Very important for me, by 1994 I could still walk for reasonably long distances. At least once a week we walked nine kilometers on a round trip to the beach. Some years after this we had to reduce this to four kilometers, to our main retirement village and back. A pale shadow of what we used to do even three years ago.

On Mondays I used to walk four kilometers for my chess game, but this came recently to an end as well. Each morning I Walk another two kilometers to buy our newspaper. No big deal, but I am convinced that this exercise has contributed, at no cost, to my survival so far.

I have always been able to laugh at myself and I have never taken myself too seriously. This was possibly influenced by something my father taught me when I was ready to join the army: "if the Sergeant Major shouts at you, imagine him standing in front of the company in his long grubby underpants." During my short military life, I had more than once an opportunity to make use of this paternal advice.

Another thought which I never forgot: "always be yourself, because the people that matter don't mind, and the ones that mind don't matter." This wisdom did, however, not come from my father, but from a calendar leaf.

How far have I changed over this long period? The larceny, already started during the war, and later so pronounced during my Prisoner of War time, had completely disappeared by the time I had returned to Germany after the war. When I was later working in South Africa for our building company, as its sole director and the financial executive, I probably could have salted away the odd million dollars, but such a thought never occurred to me. Handling large sums of cash, which did not belong to me, never bothered me at all.

On the other hand, the rebellious disposition of my youth, possibly inherited from my maternal grandfather, never dis-appeared. I have always remained ready to challenge the established order and conventions, the 'Establishment', if they appeared wrong or illogical to me. In such situations I have never accepted "no" for an answer without a challenge.

This attitude was probably one of the underlying motivations for:

- My modest claim that the Universe is revolving, just like almost everything else in free movement in Nature.
- The challenge of a statement by Professor Stephen Hawkins, regarding the 'Big Bang', both of these made in my book "*Parallel Developments*" at www.amazon.com.
- My questioning the justification for the existence of a

major US Army installation in Europe, when I was merely ordered to survey their necessary staffing requirements.

- Tackling the South African Minister of Finance and the accounting profession bigwigs of the country, regarding an inconsistency in their Income Tax Act.
- My approaching the General in charge of the Detective Service of the South African police, in conjunction with the observed corruption at the state tender board.
- All the critical comments regarding the communist/socialist economic ideology of the new post-Apartheid South Africa in this book.

This leaves one crucial question: what, if anything, have I achieved in those ninety years? Not much, I'm afraid. I never became a General, neither in the German, nor in the British or the US Army. And I am still waiting for my well-deserved Nobel Prize citation. Furthermore, I did not even become a tiny little billionaire.

On the other hand, I managed to pass through the second half of my life as a most of the time happy chap. It pleases me that I have been able to avoid starvation for my wife and my family. And, very importantly, I believe I must have had something to do with fathering a perfectly good son, but details how this came about are lost in the depths of my memory.

All events, names and characters in this story, which is the continuation of my first book "*For All it Was Worth*", also at www.amazon.com, are of course fictitious, and any resemblance to actual persons, living or dead, and even geographic locations, are purely coincidental or were created by my fertile imagination.

You know: the usual story, the lawyers of any publisher anywhere always insist on including, to cover their client's back(side)!

PLEASE LEAVE A REVIEW

Thanks for reading *FOR BETTER OR FOR WORSE!* Your support makes it possible for this author to continue creating.

If you liked what you read, please **leave an honest review** wherever you bought this book. Your feedback is invaluable, and reviews help new readers discover my work.

To get in touch with me directly, please use one of the various contact methods listed by BIOCOMM PRESS at http://biocomm.eu/press

———

ABOUT THE AUTHOR

Bernhard R. Teicher was born in Dresden in 1924 – the year Hitler's "Mein Kampf" was published. Growing up during the pre-war Nazi years, he joined the Hitler Youth before he turned 9. Later in the army, following harsh basic training, he was sent to the Eastern front where he saw combat near Kursk. Captured by the Russians, he escaped and was transferred to the Italian campaign.

With his acquired knowledge of Italian, he volunteered for the special forces Division Brandenburg, where he was trained in sabotage and intelligence gathering. Operating with his comrades behind enemy lines, he wreaked havoc with the enemy's command, communication and logistical structures.

After the war, he returned to Germany where he worked in various management positions. In 1965, disillusioned by prospects in post-war Germany, he moved with his family to South Africa where he continued to work as a management consultant.

BOOKS BY BERNHARD R. TEICHER

For All It Was Worth: A Memoir of Hitler's Germany - Before, During and After WWII. AMAZON, 2017.

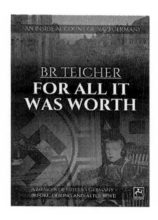

For Better Or For Worse: A Memoir of South Africa - During and After Apartheid. AMAZON, 2019.

Parallel Developments: A Geophysical / Paleontological Timeline from Big Bang to 3000BC. AMAZON, 2016.

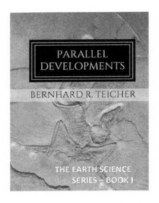

Rock Identification: A Compendium of Classifications. AMAZON, 2019.

Made in the USA
Middletown, DE
20 July 2020